The Mythmaker's Magic

The Mythmaker's Magic
Behind the Illusion of "Creation Science"

by

Delos B. McKown

Prometheus Books
Buffalo, New York

Published 1993 by Prometheus Books

The Mythmaker's Magic: Behind the Illusion of "Creation Science." Copyright © 1993 by Delos B. McKown. All rights reserved. No part of this publication may be reproduced, stored in a retrieval system, or transmitted in any form or by any means, electronic, mechanical, photocopying, recording, or otherwise, without prior written permission of the publisher, except in the case of brief quotations embodied in critical articles and reviews. Inquiries should be addressed to Prometheus Books, 59 John Glenn Drive, Buffalo, New York 14228-2197, 716-837-2475 / FAX: 716-835-6901.

97 96 95 94 93   5 4 3 2 1

Library of Congress Cataloging-in-Publication Data

McKown, Delos Banning.
 The mythmaker's magic : behind the illusion of "creation science" / by Delos B. McKown.
   p.   cm.
 Includes index.
 ISBN 978-0-87975-770-0
 1. Creationism—Controversial literature. 2. Religion and science—United States. I. Title.
BS651.M3976   1993
231.7'65—dc20   92-34549
                                                                              CIP

To Irene McKown and to the memory
of Laurel McKown for laying no straw
on their son's academic path

Contents

Acknowledgments	9
Introduction	11
1. Science, Pseudoscience, and Soteriology	21
2. What the "Scientific Creationists" Do Not Want You to Know and Hope You Are Too Foolish to Find Out	35
3. "Scientific Creationism": Axioms and Exegesis	67
4. The Fiction That Saves	81
5. Of Pandas and People: A Logical Analysis	93
6. Science, Creationism, and the Constitution	105
7. "Scientific Creationism" and Sour Prongs of Lemon	117
8. "Creation Science": Newspeak Before Its Time	133
9. How to Dose the "Scientific Creationists" with Their Own Medicine	141
10. What Now? What Next?	149
Index	169

Acknowledgments

I am especially indebted to two of my colleagues in the Philosophy Department at Auburn University. First, I would like to acknowledge the help of Professor Charles Brown, Ph.D., who read the entire manuscript and cast his extraordinarily logical eye on the whole of it. With his critical acumen at my disposal, I can rest assured that my arguments contain no illogicalities. Second, I would like to acknowledge the help of the one attorney among my colleagues, Professor Clifton Perry, Ph.D., J.D., L.L.M. He subjected to close scrutiny the two chapters most concerned with legal and constitutional matters and at one point helped me bring my argument into sharper focus than I had hitherto managed to do. He also supplied two very informative references, written especially for inclusion in this book. I am also indebted to two biologists, Professor John Frandsen, Ph.D., professor of Biology at Tuskegee University and Professor Kenneth Saladin, Ph.D., professor of Biology at Georgia College. They prompted me to simplify the writing, but not to change the content, in the one chapter having most to do with biological topics. Finally, I am indebted to Professor Peter Salpas, Ph.D., professor of Geology at Auburn, for sharing his expert knowledge of the age of moon rocks with me. The contributions of these five experts have been all (and only) to the good, no blame whatsoever accruing to them for any mistakes I may have made.

Introduction

There was once a wag who said that there are two kinds of people in the world: those who divide the people of the world into two kinds and those who do not. For the purposes of this book, I am going to help confirm the wag's witty view by dividing the world's people into two kinds: those who tend to base their beliefs on facts or who are willing to modify their beliefs to conform to facts, once these become known, and those who acquire their beliefs dogmatically or who alter or dismiss facts to fit their preexisting faith. Broadly speaking this book is *for* those who fit the first group but is *about* those who belong to the second group, or, more precisely, to a particular subdivision thereof.

Throughout this book I have aimed at the kind of intelligent, reasonably open-minded, public-spirited people who serve on the nation's school boards; also at the nation's science teachers, particularly in the public schools; and, last but not least, at scientists in general, whether engaged in education or not. Nobody, of course, is forbidden (by the author at least) to read this book, and others not envisioned as belonging to the targeted groups may find it valuable. The parents of school children come to mind as do all citizens who want high quality science instruction offered in the public schools.

This book is about those who are pleased to call themselves "Scientific Creationists." These people are but a species of the religious genus whose members I shall, henceforth, call Fundagelicals. This term is not meant to be funny (though chuckles need not be suppressed) but is, rather, intended as a shorthand way of referring to Fundamentalists, Evangelicals, and assorted religious rightists, including some very conservative Roman Catholics, Mormons, Orthodox Jews, and, any day now, Muslims. It is very tedious to have to enumerate all these groups (and others not named such as Southern Baptists and Lutherans) every time one wishes to refer to these birds of a religious feather. Hence the need for a term such as "fundagelical" and its derivatives. Whatever the doctrinal differences may be between Fundagelicals of various stripes (and these are numerous), they share a profound respect for the Bible, amounting in extreme cases to the conviction that it is without error (i.e., is inerrant or infallible).

This is certainly true of the "Scientific Creationists" who believe that the Bible is essentially and substantially truthful in all particulars, scientific, historical, and geographical, as well as metaphysical, moral, and spiritual, so to speak. Notions of inerrancy can, of course, come in watered down forms. *Religion Watch* (which is a monthly digest of trends and ideas in religion), vol. 1, no. 9 (July–August 1986), pp. 4–5, contains no fewer than seven degrees of inerrancy. In that which follows, 'inerrancy' will be taken to mean what it clearly indicates, the opposite of something having errors in it.

The contents of this book include, in one way or another, everything I have ever written on the subject of "Scientific Creationism," stretching over the past decade and a half. Most, if not all, of what I wrote on this subject at the beginning of these fifteen years remains as true today, I think, as it was when first set to paper. There have, of course, been some instances in which I have felt the need to expand upon or to update some of what I wrote earlier. Each of the following chapters begins with a short introduction revealing the circumstances of its writing. In some cases I have expanded upon topics in the text of the earlier writings, but for the most part the updating has occurred in the references appearing at the end of the affected chapters. Other chapters were written recently, expressly for this book. Still others were written midway between the oldest and the newest writings. In fact, during the past fifteen years there has been no time when I have not been actively engaged in thinking (if not in writing) about "Scientific Creationism" and the challenge it presents to our times.

Fundagelicals in general and "Scientific Creationists" in particular (together with many a theistic sympathizer) will, no doubt, accuse me of bias against their theology as this book unfolds and will attempt to reject it out of hand for perceiving it to say something that it never says. At no point herein nor in any of my published writings on any topic whatsoever have I ever declared unqualifiedly that the universe is not an artifact (or very like one) and that, therefore, it can have had no artificer, maker, creator, or contriver. The topic of theism as such, quite simply, does not come up in the pages that follow, nor does this book ever try to solve any metaphysical problems or to give any answers to any questions about the nature of the universe and how it came to be.

What may be perceived as bias is, in fact, something quite different. Let me explain. In the realm of intellect, the original sin is question begging. Question begging occurs whenever somebody declares a statement to be true or asserts an entity to exist, fails to confirm the truth of the statement or to demonstrate the existence of the alleged entity, and then proceeds in thought or discourse as though the confirmation had occurred or the demonstration had succeeded. For example, whenever a religious person begins with an article (or object) of faith and moves on to deal with that article (or object) of faith as though it were an acknowledged matter of fact without having supplied adequate evidence to justify the intellectual maneuver that has taken place, question begging has occurred. I do not intend to play this game. Question begging, however, is so common to human nature that I may on occasion commit this logical blunder myself— but never by intention. Were I to do so I would deserve the ensuing criticism, and this book could be justly faulted. The point I would like to reiterate is this: What may be perceived as bias against theology in the following pages is really my strenuous attempt at avoiding all question begging, or, put differently, at avoiding any reliance on questionable assumptions. Attempts at avoiding all question begging are not to be confused with bias against any particular belief, religious or otherwise.

In that which follows I, myself, shall never use the English word spelled with a capital 'G,' a lower case 'o,' and a lower case 'd' (in that order) as though I knew that it named any being, entity, or dimension of reality. Put in philosophical terms, I shall not assume that that common name (or referring term) has any referent. The reason is simple: I do not know that it does, and *my* faith in theism or lack thereof is not the topic of this book. Should the English word 'God' appear in the text in any of the following pages, it will be in a direct quotation or in a paraphrase of the stated belief(s) of some other person(s). The only exception to this is in chapter 9. The material there is satirical and is presented as though it were in a religious pamphlet or tract. So, in effect, the entire chapter might well be enclosed in quotation marks, except that that would break the illusion.

When referring to the object (or putative object) of the major article of faith of all Fundagelicals (including most especially the "Scientific Creationists") I shall use a term unique to me (as far as I know), that term being the 'Bible-god.' In this way, I hope to avoid begging the fundamental theological question and yet be able to write pointedly of the deity (presented for belief) in the Bible, a deity in which (or in whom) all Christian Fundagelicals lodge their faith. The referent, then, for my term, the 'Bible-god' will be of the character in the Bible variously called 'Yaweh' (YHWH in Hebrew), 'Jehovah' in English, or, more generically, 'the Lord.' Lest this approach to naming should seem to be excessively demeaning or unnecessarily restrictive, let me remind the reader that a character in literature may also be a historical person. In Robert Graves's famous novel, *I Claudius,* only experts in the Roman history of the time can be relied on to know the differences in the story between what the historical Claudius actually did, said, or thought and what Graves made up for him to do, say, or think. So, to say that the term 'Bible-god' refers to a character in the Bible is not to say that it can have no referent outside of scripture or outside of beliefs therein. Personally, I do not know that there is any such objective referent, but, then, this is not at issue and is in no way pertinent to what follows. This book is about the "Scientific Creationists," what *they* believe, and how good the reasons are for believing as they do and for acting thereon. Since I am writing about the "Scientific Creationists," and not about my own world view, judgments as to how well I have carried out my intentions should be limited to how accurately I have exposed their position for inspection and criticism and how adequately I have explained it.

Just as I have chosen to call the deity-character of the Old and New Testaments the Bible-god, so, too, I have elected to call the evil one (or type of one) variously called 'Lucifer,' 'Satan,' or 'Beelzebub' the 'Bible-devil.' Moreover, I shall treat the names 'Noah,' the 'Noachian flood,' and 'Noah's ark' in the same way, as a character, an event, and an object, respectively, named in the Bible to be sure, but not confirmed to have existed or ever to have happened by any independent source. This does not constitute denial, merely uncertainty and suspension of belief. To continue I shall take such terms as 'divine,' 'miracle,' 'spirit,' 'soul,' 'salvation,' 'redemption,' and 'everlasting life' to mean only what they appear to mean in the Bible and will not assume that they name any referents outside of its pages or beyond the beliefs of those religious people who lodge their faith in its contents. Finally, I shall mention the terms 'heaven' and 'hell' in the same way, making no assumptions whatsoever as to any places, conditions, or states of being that are named with these words. These biblical terms have all been uttered or written by so many millions of people on so many millions of occasions during the past two thousand years or more in Western culture that they seem to name the most substantial of realities, places, or states of being, but none of this is known to be so. These are terms that appear properly in declarations of faith, not in statements of established fact, and they should always be treated as such, with the need for the appropriate verbal distinctions ever in mind. This I have tried to do in all that follows so as to avoid question begging.

While still on the subject of words, names, or referring terms, I shall hereafter put double quotes (as follows) around the capitalized words, "Scientific Creationism," "Scientific Creationist(s)," and "Creation Science." In each case these double quotes shall mean so-called—nothing more, nothing less—just so-called. It is for the "Scientific Creationists" to prove that these terms have intelligible referents; it is not for us to assume it for them, as they would like us to do. Let them demonstrate to us that these are not vacuous terms but that they really do name something objective outside the heads of those who are pleased to employ them. I have not felt it desirable to capitalize 'fundagelical,' and I have not used 'fundagelically.' I shall use single quotes (as immediately above) in the standard way, i.e., shall merely be calling attention to the word, term, or phrase at issue itself, rather than to any other referent it may have.

The terms "bible scholar(s)" or "biblical sholar(s)" are not very well understood by the average person. Either term could refer (1) to any untrained person able, nevertheless, to recite Bible verses glibly or to look up biblical passages adeptly, (2) to the sort of person who could and would teach in highly dogmatic bible schools (such as Jerry Falwell's Liberty University) where orthodox creedal affirmations are a necessary condition for employment, (3) to the kind of Old and New Testament scholars who could be found in the better sort of theological seminaries training college graduates for the pastoral ministry, or (4) to experts of various sorts in biblical scholarship doing research and teaching graduate students in the leading universities of the Western world. A variant of category 4 includes experts, similarly trained, who teach undergraduates in any academically respectable college. When I refer to biblical scholars in the pages to follow, I shall have in mind preeminently those who fit category 4 above and to a lesser extent category 3. I shall never take account of what passes for thought among those who fit the first two categories. The reasons for this are simple and straightforward. The members of categories 3 and 4 can be depended on generally to put respect for truth above the demands of religious faith, whereas those in category 2 can be depended on to put the demands of faith far above any dispassionate search for truth (or who will simply christen whatever they believe about the Bible as the truth). Those in category 1 are completely inconsequential for our purposes and can safely be ignored.

It should be noted in passing that I have used the King James version of the Bible throughout, not because it is the most accurate translation, but because it is the favorite version of English-speaking Fundagelicals. I have not wanted at any time to become vulnerable to attack for using newer versions that might be open to the charge of being the product of modern, liberal scholarship, so-called. Such scholarship, no matter how accurate, is in Fundagelical opinion suspect at best, tainted at worst. On a few occasions I have referred to another version(s), but only to enhance the King James.

Respecting the biblical text itself, I have tried on all occasions to approach it in a straightforward, literalistic way. My only concern with biblical exegesis (i.e., interpretation) is to grasp what the original author(s) intended the original recipient(s) to understand by the message(s) being sent. There are, of course, passages in the Bible that were never intended to be taken literally (for example, see John 7:38-39), but such passages play little or no part in the challenge to modern education mounted by the "Scientific Creationists." Since theirs is a literalistic approach whenever it suits their purposes, I am content to use the same literalistic approach, even when it does not suit *their* purposes.

The major problem scientists and science educators have had in responding effectively to "Scientific Creationism" results in large part from the low level of sophistication in science that the average American exhibits. Not knowing the nature of genuinely significant hypotheses and not knowing what counts as confirmation of (or as disconfirmation of) whatever hypothesis is at issue, ordinary Americans can only fall back on the word of those they take to be authorities. So, for every genuine authority figure in science who steps forward to say something negative about "Creation Science," the "Scientific Creationists" try to roll out a rival authority who, using the appropriate scientific jargon, attacks the critic and confuses the public simultaneously. This leaves ordinary Americans to pay their money, so to speak, and take their choice on the basis of what they like the sound of best. This is a very poor way to judge what is and what is not good science. For the most part, no such problem will arise in the pages that follow, because I have not fallen back on science to refute "Scientific Creationism," except in the most general way. Nor have I relied on my readers' understanding of science to judge for themselves issues that they may really not be able to judge accurately for themselves. On the contrary, I will proceed to refute "Scientific Creationism" on its own terms as nearly as possible. This requires patience but no great amount of sophistication on the part of either the author or the reader. In any case, we will not have to pick our way through the mine fields of science and pseudoscience, enveloped all the while in the din of unintelligible jargon. Mathematical sophistication will not be required either. Common sense and ordinary understanding informed by a few relevant facts should suffice.

No introduction to a book such as this could be complete without a description of secular humanism. Next to the Bible-devil, hard-line Communists, and religious liberals (i.e., apostates to the "Scientific Creationists"), there are no people toward whom these Fundagelicals feel greater animosity than secular humanists. The term 'secular' in 'secular humanism' is to be understood as opposite in meaning to 'sacred.' Secular humanism refrains from dividing the world's contents into two types: the sacred (or holy) on the one hand and the secular (or the profane) on the other. In short, secular humanists are either very dubious about the existence of the sacred as an objective property of things or they deny it altogether.

The term 'humanism' is more difficult to manage because over the centuries it has become bloated with meanings. Those who are very humane toward other people, in contrast to the savage or merciless (such as the Hitlers of the world) can be called humanists or humanistic. Moreover, during the Renaissance such people as Erasmus and Sir Thomas More came to be known as humanists, but theirs was largely a *literary* humanism. They began to study and prize the strictly human works known as the Roman and Greek classics, as well as biblical literature, and to read pagan philosophy appreciatively along with "sacred" theology. This kind of humanism did not, however, cause its practicioners to renounce or otherwise attack their religious faith. In a related way, we often categorize as humanists nowadays those who are professionally involved in the humanities. People who teach philosophy, the classics, foreign languages, English literature, world (or comparative) literatures, history, and even religion (academically treated) find themselves lumped together in humanities faculties in American colleges and universities. Few experiences are more incongruous than encountering a rock-ribbed Fundagelical who is called a humanist, because he/she teaches in the English department of some school or other. I have attempted (so far in vain) to eliminate such confusion and cognitive dissonance by introducing the word *'humanitist'* to name all who have to do with the humanities, leaving the word 'humanist' to name the philosophical position presented below.

Secular humanists are what philosophers call naturalists, by which is meant all who are dubious of, dismiss as irrelevant, or otherwise deny what is commonly understood by the term 'supernatural.' So, a philosophical naturalist is one who disagrees with supernaturalists, not one who disagrees with philosophical artificialists, there being no such philosophical position. To continue, as secular humanists see it, morality is not handed down in an absolute fashion by any supernatural being but emerges, rather, from the sociobiological conditions of human life. Put differently, humanity is the source, center, and end of ethics. It should be noted that this sharp focus on humanity does not necessarily exclude moral concern for animal welfare. Respecting right human relations in decision making, secular humanists are democratic, not autocratic, dictatorial, or totalitarian.

Respecting knowledge, secular humanists are scientific in outlook. Since they worship nothing, they can hardly worship science as they have sometimes been falsely accused of doing. Nor do they regard science as perfect or able to answer all questions. It is no more perfect than the people who utilize its methods of inquiry. It is just that over the past five hundred years the various sciences have developed the most rigorous means of testing hypotheses and of confirming or of disconfirming theories yet developed by human ingenuity. If something better lies ahead, secular humanists will, no doubt, espouse it. In the meantime they rely on science to tell them *about* the world rather than on "revelation," "divination," prayer, meditation, untested intuition, tradition, or authority of any kind.

Some humanists, including such famous figures as Julian Huxley and John Dewey, together with numerous lesser lights, have tried to be religious about their world view or life stance, so to speak, and have taken themselves to be "religious humanists." The "Scientific Creationists" pounce on this term and try to herd all secular humanists into this corral. They then point to belief in evolution as the unifying "religious doctrine" (their term, not mine) of all humanists (excluding the professional humanitists mentioned above). Once the facts are known, however, this ploy fails. Secular humanists are not at all religious as the world ordinarily understands religion. They do not believe in the Bible-god or in any other scripture-god, nor in any deity philosophically conceived (i.e., in any philoso-god); do not worship any such alleged entity as sacred or holy; do not pray to him, her, it (or any of the above); do not seek moral guidance or any kind of revelation therefrom; and do not expect postmortem rewards or punishments based on their beliefs or lack thereof. Put as bluntly as possible, secular humanists are either agnostics or atheists. They do, of course, have a world view, are concerned with morality, and associate with one another on occasion, but none of this constitutes religion, unless by some fantastic sleight-of-hand 'irreligion' has come to mean 'religion.'

Parenthetically, the "Scientific Creationists" have trouble, it would seem, getting straight on what might be thought of as the garden variety of secularism. Its relation to secular humanism is the same as that of dog to hound. All secular humanists are secularists, but not all secularists are thoroughgoing naturalists, philosophically speaking, and are not, therefore, secular humanists. By the garden variety of secularist, I mean anybody who, even if religious, wants to keep religion out of government in general and out of the public schools in particular. Since such people are not likely to be fundagelical in outlook, it pleases the "Scientific Creationists" to lump them together with secular humanists.

At this point a curious fact about religion needs to be noted. Suppose, for example, that a questionnaire were developed to see what people who are not experts believe about the following statement: The planet Jupiter has no solid surface (or crust) but is gaseous. There are three obvious answers: (1) I believe that this is a true statement, (2) I do not know that it is true and hence have no belief in the matter, and (3) I believe that it is false. Compare this with what looks to be a parallel assertion: The Bible-god is the true deity and actually exists. Once again there are three possibilities: (1) I believe that this is a true statement (Judeo-Christian theism), (2) I do not know that it is true and hence have no belief in the matter (agnosticism), and (3) I believe that it is false (atheism). Most people will not become excited enough about the nature of Jupiter to feel threatened by those who believe something different than they, and if persuasion were to become an issue, the parties to the controversy could be persuaded to change their minds justifiably only by an appeal to such data as astronomers or space probes could supply. In no case could mere confidence in a given answer carry the day.

How different it is in religion. Fundagelicals in general and "Scientific Creationists" in particular will feel threatened by agnostics and atheists and will likely act vigorously against unbelief. They may also feel deep animosity toward individual agnostics and atheists. The attitude of the Ayatollah Khomeini (and of his fellow Iranian Shi'ites) toward Salman Rushdie for his book *Satanic Verses* illustrates the point vividly. If Western culture today were still at the level now reached by Iranian culture, and if Charles Darwin had only recently published his *The Origin of Species*, it is not hard to imagine that Dr. Henry M. Morris, the grand old guru of "Scientific Creationism," and his rhetorically gifted associate, Dr. Duane T. Gish, would rise up (with their many followers) to smite the infidel. Unlike the dispute over the nature of Jupiter, there is no way questions involving theism can be resolved by any known fact(s). Whenever agnosticism or atheism are put down, it is through the power of faith, and faith alone, together with repressive actions based thereon.

Given that most of the following pages deal directly with the same subject matter and that fully half of these pages were written without this book in mind, it is to be expected that some repetition and redundancy will occur. Some I have edited out. The repetitions and redundancies I have retained serve three purposes: (1) to underscore the crucial points that make this book different from other books on "Scientific Creationism," (2) to fix these points firmly in my readers' minds, and (3) to keep my readers from having to do too much page flipping, forward and back, to see what I had said about a given topic elsewhere. One and the same point is often approached differently in a given chapter than is the same point in some other chapter(s). At numerous points in the text I have called attention to other passages elsewhere in the text and in the references at the end of the various chapters. With respect to references mentioning Supreme Court decisions, I have often given the full citation rather than referring the reader to a note at the end of some other chapter that also gives the full citation. On other occasions it has seemed to me enough simply to name particular cases, especially the ones that are well known. I hope that such repetitions and redundancies as there are will be helpful rather than annoying.

1

Science, Pseudoscience, and Soteriology

Introduction

Acts 19:11–16 says that the seven sons of a Jewish high priest, named Sceva, went about as vagabond exorcists pronouncing the name of Jesus (as preached by St. Paul) over those possessed by evil spirits. On one such occasion, the evil spirit being cast out said, "Jesus I know, and Paul I know; but who are ye?" Even now I can hear my readers mutter, "Science we know, and pseudoscience we know; but what on earth is soteriology?" The answer will come to the patient within the first few pages that follow. The impatient, of course, may consult their dictionaries at once. No matter how this theological term becomes familiar to the reader, it is crucial to an understanding of the current conflict between Fundagelicals in general and secular educators in the public schools.

Sometime in 1991 I was invited to prepare a paper for delivery at a meeting of the Iowa Committee of Correspondence. This group, associated with the National Center for Science Education of Berkeley, California, has carried on a long battle with the "Scientific Creationists" over the subject of biological evolution in public education. I finished the paper rather quickly but did not deliver it until March 21, 1992. In the meantime I approached my publisher about putting together in a slim volume the various essays I had written on "Scientific Creationism." Upon having my proposal accepted, I began to reflect on how might best be organized that which I had written. It was not long before it dawned on me that the paper recently prepared for the Iowa Committee could serve very well as the first chapter of this book. Here, then, it appears for the first time in print.

In addition to taking up the topic of soteriology, which is as easy to grasp as it is necessary for understanding the present conflict, I am also able (with this chapter) to put the fray into historical perspective and even to hazard a prediction as to where we shall go from here. In this regard, the past is, indeed, a prologue to the future.

* * *

We live in an age that was prophesied—prophesied neither by some antique seer or other nor by a latter-day Nostradamus, but by a Nobel Laureate in physiology and medicine for 1965. The prophet in question was Jacques Monod. Two paragraphs from his book, *Chance and Necessity*, should be imprinted on the brains and impressed on the emotions of scientists and science educators everywhere. He wrote:

> In the course of three centuries science, founded upon the postulate of objectivity, has conquered its place in society—in men's practice, but not in their hearts. Modern societies are built upon science. They owe it their wealth, their power, and the certitude that tomorrow far greater wealth and power still will be ours if we so wish. But there is this too: just as an initial "choice" in the biological evolution of a species can be binding upon its entire future, so the choice of scientific *practice*, an unconscious choice in the beginning, has launched the evolution of culture on a one-way path; onto a track which nineteenth-century scientism saw leading infallibly upward to an empyrean noon hour for mankind, whereas what we see opening before us today is an abyss of darkness.
>
> Modern societies accepted the treasures and the power that science laid in their laps. But they have not accepted—they have scarcely even heard—its profounder message: the defining of a new and unique source of truth, and the demand for a thorough revision of ethical premises, for a total break with the animist tradition, the definitive abandonment of the "old covenant," the necessity of forging a new one. Armed with all the powers, enjoying all the riches they owe to science, our societies are still trying to live by and to teach systems of values already blasted at the root by science itself.
>
> No society before ours was ever rent by contradictions so agonizing.[1]

Parenthetically, the "Scientific Creationists" are the uniquely American contribution to the unfolding here of Monod's dire prophecy. One fears that they may not be the only pseudoscientists to become active in this apocalypse.

The psycho-social engine of what Monod calls the "animist tradition" operating under its "old covenant" needs to be recognized unflinchingly for what it is and encountered head-on, especially by scientists and science educators, and school board members. The eminent British mathematician/American philosopher, Alfred North Whitehead, provided a useful start for achieving these goals when he wrote:

> But as between religion and arithmetic, other things are not equal. You *use* arithmetic, but you *are* religious. Arithmetic of course enters into your nature, so far as nature involves a multiplicity of things. No one is invariably "justified" by his faith in the multiplication table. But in some sense or other, justification is the basis of all religion. Your character is developed according to your faith. This is the primary religious truth from which no one can escape. Religion is a force of belief cleansing the inward parts.[2]

So far so good, but Whitehead's views on religion need expanding. To arithmetic (and mathematics in general) he should have added science, for we also *use* science and nobody is invariably "justified" by it, if ever. Science does not cleanse one's "inward parts" any more than does the multiplication table.

Jacob Bronowski once observed insightfully that the human animal is a "social solitary," in vital need of the human group yet very independent of it in certain ways.[3] We are, in short, a social primate and do very badly when abandoned or neglected by the nuclear family, biological or adoptive; when shunned by the extended family of neighbors or distant relatives; or when expelled from the clan or tribe. Few of us aspire to be hermits, dooming ourselves to lives of social isolation. Nevertheless, in various ways and at various times individual humans in striving to do and be what they crave to do and be individually may turn in frustration and anger on kith and kin; may reject home and hearth; may deprive their fellows of life, limb, liberty, or property; and may even assault their own culture, flouting, ridiculing, or subverting it. To prevent such ravages, the social group acts at once to clone itself in each new arrival. In addition to the carrot and the stick, the chief mechanism for accomplishing this is the development of conscience. In order to enjoy a sense of belonging, acceptance, self-esteem, and love, thus winning assistance in survival, each normal child must and does become sensitive to social demands for conformity. One result of the failure to conform sufficiently is, of course, the bad conscience, the painful conscience, the demeaning conscience, which in varying degrees all lead to the feeling of "inward parts" that are filthy, and that must be cleansed through forgiveness.

The process of socialization leaves scars, physical in many cases, psychological in virtually all. Often, if not invariably, the wounds inflicted in curbing our behavior so as to make us safe for our society fester with embarrassment, guilt, and shame in varying degrees during much if not the whole of our lives. Like other religions, Judaism and Christianity morally reinforced the societies from which they arose by providing supernatural sanctions for what those societies deemed good and bad, right and wrong, tolerated and tabooed—the process continuing to this day. Thus, to the need for forgiveness from those we have wronged, and for taboos broken, we also find ourselves with a compelling need for forgiveness from the presumed deity upholding the sanctions at issue. Christianity, as we all know, leaves the situation fraught with even greater peril for the individual through its doctrines of original sin and total depravity, making all individuals guilty before its deity for *their very being*, not simply for their antisocial actions. Thus does a bad conscience lead to a thoroughly dirty self, a self depraved by its very nature, a self that not only *is* not forgiven satisfactorily by other people but that *cannot* be forgiven by them, but only by a supernatural savior. The most sensitive people, of course, suffer most under this theological scheme of things and crave most longingly for release from their guilt, for final forgiveness, and for that cleansing of the "inward parts" tantamount to justification. Moreover, those who fancy that they will live after death need absolute assurance that their sins will not pursue them beyond the grave to a tribunal presided over by a judge beyond whom there is no court of appeals. In short, such people feel extreme need not simply for justification here and now but for mercy and salvation hereafter. Legions of Christian clergy (of all types and times) testify to these facts as have millions upon millions of visits to the Catholic confessional, the psychologist's office, and the psychiatrist's couch.

While orthodox Christianity was adding the threat of an angry deity to the normal fears and frustrations of socialization and to the pains and punishments of ordinary living, it was also painting another, far rosier, picture. The deity, according to the gospel, is long-suffering even toward fallen humanity. A descendant of the deity came to live among us, taking our sins upon himself through a self-sacrificial death and in the process justifying all who have faith in him or who receive the grace to acquire such faith. Thus are the "inward parts" of the Christian cleansed according to orthodox doctrine, and thus is the believer saved unto everlasting life. The Greek word for savior is *soter*; for salvation, *soteria*, hence the English world 'soteriology,' which names that branch of Christian theology dealing specifically with redemption. The pertinent question for us is this: What does soteriology have to do with science and pseudoscience in contemporary America?

* * *

Except for hard drugs and for falling hopelessly in love with absolutely the worst kind of person, nothing so scrambles the human brain as does religion. From this confusion have come more than fifty definitions attempting to encapsulate its essence. If we could only ascertain once and for all *what* it is, then we could ask whether or not it conflicts with science, and, if so, whether by nature or merely incidentally.[4] William Provine, a biologist and historian of science at Cornell, has written that if you go to church, you have to check your brains at the door. Says he, "The implications of modern science . . . are clearly inconsistent with most religious traditions."[5] At the opposite extreme is Duane T. Gish who holds a doctorate in biochemistry. Says Gish, "After many years of intense study of the problem of origins from both the scientific and Biblical viewpoints, I am convinced that the facts of science and Biblical truths combine to declare, 'In the beginning God created. . . .' "[6] For the scriptural inerrantist, such as Gish, there is and can be no conflict between science and religion. The Gishes of the world will simply emasculate science as needed, thus rendering it docile and compliant with whatever their theology requires. Into this fray jumped no less a scientist than Stephen J. Gould who in 1982 announced that there is no conflict between "true science and religion."[7] This is an astonishing statement from one so learned, and is patently false, certainly at the theological level. Even if Gould meant to say (as seems likely) that there is no conflict between science and true religion, a problem remains (also see chapter 6). Upon analysis, true religion can only consist of the following: The deity believed in (1) cannot have a self-contradictory nature, (2) cannot be contrary to any fact (for example, cannot have hated hydrogen and forbidden it to exist, since the universe is full of it), and (3) cannot be inimical to anything human beings discover about the universe. This position is nothing but a very spare form of latter-day deism and is, according to Provine, tantamount to atheism. Intellectually only a few people believe in so minimal a deity disemboweled by Gould in order to create concord between science and "true religion." Gould's "true religion" has little or no appeal for most people, because it is devoid of soteriology. In short, those who might believe in it gain nothing for their belief, making it pointless.

Much closer to the fundamentalist, i.e., inerrantist, position than many would find comfortable is *The Dialogue Between Theology and Science,* a position paper adopted by the 122nd General Assembly of the Presbyterian Church in the United States. This, it must be remembered, is a mainline denomination with a long tradition of learning and scholarship. "Theology," says the *Dialogue,* "is the discipline that guides our thinking about God, ourselves, and the world, life here and hereafter in relationship to God." It goes on saying, "Natural science is our ordered thought about creation or, more particularly, 'nature.'" There can, therefore, be no genuine conflict between theology and science, because their subject matters are different. We are also told that "science is a prime means by which we may faithfully glorify God here and now."[8] This position does not emasculate science as does "Scientific Creationism," but it does tame it by putting it on a tether. Common to each of the foregoing views is an exclusive focus on the *cognitive* aspect of religion, in short, on theology. Religion, however, is more than theology.[9] It is also a sanctifier of morality, a celebrant of tradition, and a repository of ritual. When these other aspects or roles of religion are added to its cognitive aspects, it finally becomes possible to speak sensibly about it. With minor modifications here is what I wrote of it in 1978:

> Insofar as science and religion carry out different, noncompetitive functions, meeting different needs, they do not conflict. For example, the art of a metallurgist in producing a scalpel in no way conflicts with the function of a rabbi in relieving a Jewish boy of his foreskin; the activities of a hydraulic engineer in helping to supply municipal water to the churches of a city in no way conflicts with a Baptist preacher's function in submerging converts in that water; the secular work of a chemist in producing embalming fluid for the mortuary trade in no way conflicts with the sacred work of a priest as he intones the consoling words of eternal life while performing the last rites for the dead. Many religious needs, motivations, and ministrations take place in contexts remote to the secular goals of everyday life and the commonplace scientific-technological means thereto. But this is not the whole story.
>
> Any well-developed, historical religion contains an intellectual component. In the religions one does not favor, this is called mythology. In the religion one does favor it is called theology and is perceived to be a bona fide branch of knowledge. Whatever the various religious thought systems may be called, they will contain assertions, proclaimed as true, about cosmology, cosmogony, and causality. None of these assertions will have been based on logical or scientific inquiry but will, rather, have been predicated on incorrigible revelations, or intuitions, or both. Herein the seeds of conflict are sown.
>
> Powerful religious establishments have often arbitrarily claimed the right to speak definitively not only in matters of faith and morals but also in the areas of natural philosophy, i.e., in cosmology, cosmogony, and causality—to say nothing of anthropology and psychology. Scientists might have thought that such concerns should fall exclusively within the province of science, rather than in religion, but not so.
>
> In any case, the mythologies and theologies that cloak religions intellectually and in which believers snuggle up as if in a cocoon are vulnerable to scientific presuppositions concerning the intelligibility of the universal system, to logical methods of inquiry, and to techniques of testing and validation.[10]

So, to summarize, science and religion do not conflict where they cannot conflict but often conflict where conflict is possible. The problem is to acquire the wit to discern the one from the other.

* * *

Western soteriology, that great and hoary system of beliefs and practices that cleanses the "inward parts" of Western humanity, reduces anxiety in the valley of the shadow of death, and gives hope of a happy hereafter is much more profoundly anti-intellectual than most people realize or care to admit. In Genesis 11 we come upon the builders of Babel, people who have brick for stone and bitumen for mortar. These ambitious folk propose to build a city featuring a skyscraper. Upon hearing of this, the Bible-god comes down to have a look and makes two pronouncements, one true, one false. First, "[T]his is only the beginning of what they will do," says he. How true! We have come a long way since Babel's builders, and with no end in sight. Second, "[N]othing," says he, "that they propose to do will now be impossible for them." This is an incredible error, particularly in a deity progressing toward omniscience. It is not in the cards that human beings shall be able to do just anything or everything that they desire or can imagine. Hence, the Bible-god need not have felt so threatened. Nevertheless, acting on his anxiety over human technological mastery, he dispersed Babel's builders, confused their language, and, thereby, tried to prevent cooperation in any future schemes that might rival his power.

The same theme is to be found in the so-called wisdom literature of the Old Testament. Proverbs 1:7 announces that the "fear of the Lord is the beginning of knowledge." Psalm 111:10 reiterates this but changes knowledge to wisdom. Job 5:13 declares that the Lord "takes the wise in their own craftiness," and that "the schemes of the wily are brought to a quick end." At first sight the New Testament may seem to offer relief on this head. Who in Western culture has not heard the words attributed to Jesus in John 8:32, "[Y]ou shall know the truth, and the truth shall make you free"? It is staggering to consider how many universities have misappropriated this saying as the epitome of their endeavors. A quick perusal of the context will show that the truth at issue is *soteriological* truth, that what John is attributing to Jesus implies the need for a kind of Gnosticism on the part of his disciples as the route to salvation.[11] What we today call scientific knowledge, i.e., beliefs warranted by logical empiricism, is completely outside the Gnostic pale and would have been rejected out of hand not only by St. John but by Jesus as well.

The Bible's worst offender against human intelligence, broadly conceived, is St. Paul. The naked truth of his anti-intellectualism stands for all to read in 1 Corinthians 1:18–31 and 3:18–20. This most anxious of sinners, possessing what to him was a dysfunctional religion (though he did not call it that), found release and redemption in his unique (but mysterious) relationship to Jesus.[12] To explain his deliverance and recommend himself to the early church, justifiably apprehensive of him, Paul developed a theology distressing both to Jewish Christians and to Jews in general. Undaunted, he strove to convert them all based on nothing more than his own soteriological experiences and on certain passages in the Old Testament allegedly prophetic of Jesus. Nevertheless, most Jews rejected Paul, finding the execution of Jesus, the reputed Messiah (or King), a hopeless stumbling-block.

It was Paul's encounter with Greek intellectuals, however, that provoked his assault on literacy, learning, and logic (1 Cor. 1:20). Admitting to the Greeks (i.e., to philosophers) that his message was not rational but was, rather, moronic (*moros* in Greek), he rejoiced, nonetheless, in its power to save; the Bible-god's foolishness, according to him, being wiser than man's wisdom (1 Cor 1:25). To cap it off he claimed that those who would be truly wise should become fools (1 Cor. 3:18). For intellectuals, then, the road to salvation, à la Paul, lies through self-stultification. In this most convenient of ways, he also exempted himself and his message from all kinds of criticism coming from literate, learned, or logical circles. Taking its cue from the Apostle to the Gentiles, the Church has always fallen back on Pauline anti-intellectualism whenever knowledge of any kind has become uncomfortable to be around or too threatening to bear.

Thus, Tertullian could say of the resurrection of Jesus, "It is certain, because it is impossible." Luther could announce, "Reason is the greatest enemy that faith has," and execrate it as the "Devil's Whore." Kierkegaard could rejoice in pious paradox in book after book and accept on faith alone the ultimate paradox, the doctrine of the incarnation, Bible-god become man, the eternal become temporal, the infinite, finite, and the ever-living deity, dead on the cross. In our time Karl Barth, commonly believed to have been the greatest Protestant theologian of the twentieth century, could say serenely (as I once heard him say) that whereas philosophers merely deal with ideas, Christian theologians deal with the "facts of God," just as scientists deal with the facts of nature. Moreover, Christian "faith means knowledge," he announced. Finally, "Christianity is neither subrational, irrational, nor suprarational, but rational in the proper sense" of the term. As such no mere human epistemology (he assured me gravely) can ever encompass the truths of God.[13]

Nor science, we might add in the same vein, ever encompass all the truths of the Bible-god's world. Claiming that there is no theory of human knowledge that can encompass the truths of the Bible-god, which presumably are beyond rational criticism, accomplishes exactly what St. Paul accomplished through his notion of the redemptive foolishness of the Bible-god: foolishness wiser than the wisdom of the most intelligent, educated people. In each case Christian truths are exempted from having to measure up to the normal standards expected of statements claiming to be true.

However easy it may be to claim such exemptions in theory, it is much more difficult for theologians to establish these in the real world. Prior to Copernicus, for example, it was part and parcel of the Christian world view to accept the geocentric theory of the universe. Scarcely any Christian in the technically advanced world believes it today. Also, prior to Darwin it was common belief that the Bible-god had created all living things, essentially as they are today, by fiat and in rapid succession. Scarcely any educated Christian believes this today except those who think that their salvation requires it.[14] Prior to Freud scarcely any Christian could have been found who would have welcomed his theory of human nature. Subsequent to his life's work, however, many Christians, including psychologists and psychotherapists (both Catholic and Protestant), have absorbed his conceptions and begun to think with these as though no serious contradictions existed between Freudian and Christian concepts of human nature. So, in fact, that which is alleged to be beyond criticism appears occasionally, at least, to be modified by it (or by rationality) and that which is beyond normal standards of evidence appears from time to time to accept criticism and change its ways.

It is now possible to enunciate three general principles: First, no known religion (of historical significance) is quick to incorporate new scientific discoveries into its body of beliefs—unless these reinforce its soteriology; second, if new scientific discoveries call into question its soteriological claims, any religion can be expected to resist these strenuously; and third, no ecclesiastical structure is eager to accept new scientific discoveries if these weaken its authority by calling into question what it has been teaching. The problem for religion in seeking the truth is simply this: Those who seek the truth may find it and in finding it be horrified—or, more likely, horrify others.

* * *

One result of the collision between the still young, powerful, and burgeoning tradition of Western science and the much older and far more powerful tradition of Western soteriology is the creation of pseudoscience. This, of course, is not the only source of pseudoscience: Wishful thinking, magical thinking, fraud, and plain madness can also produce pseudoscience. Nevertheless, in America in this generation the collision of science with soteriology has spawned the preeminent pseudoscience, the one called "Scientific Creationism." Consider the "Scientific Creationists": Situated as they are in technically advanced societies, living at a time when the scientific model of knowledge is dominant, not having widespread ecclesiastical control over education (as did the medieval church), and believing that their eternal life in bliss demands a literal reading of the Bible, it was all but inevitable that they should develop a pseudoscience of human origins, allegedly alternative to the real article presented by modern science. Every scientist in the country who is not committed to some distorting ideology or other can show what is wrong with "Creation Science," why its assumptions are suspect, why it has no methodology worthy of the name, and why it cannot specify conditions that would falsify (and hence test) its conclusions. What is far less obvious to many scientists and science educators is the motivation behind it.

Wendell R. Bird, a leading legal light for the "Scientific Creationists," made it crystal clear when he wrote:

> The origin of the world, life, and man is a vital subject to Christians. If Adam did not literally fall into sin, Christ did not need to shed His blood on the cross, and men do not need to be saved from anything (Rom. 5:12, 18; 1 Cor. 15:45, 49–50). If the inspired writings of Moses are disbelieved, the gospel words of Jesus Christ will be disbelieved also (John 5:46–47). Jesus Christ taught that God created Adam and Eve, and that God sent a worldwide flood to judge man (Mark 10:6; Luke 17:27). And scripture prophesies that liberal scoffers in these last days will deny the divine creation and the worldwide flood (2 Peter 3:3, 5–6). Creation is fundamental to Christianity. . . .[15]

Even though the Bible does not require literal belief in itself for salvation (see chapter 4), the "Scientific Creationists," being scriptural literalists, believe that it does.[16] Believing this they must also believe what they take to be essential in the Bible, no matter how foolish, in order to feel assured of everlasting bliss, while simultaneously being delivered from the threats of perpetual torment in a postmortem existence. To save themselves, their children, and all for whom they care from anything un- or antibiblical, they must reject evolution as being a mere theory that, moreover, is as religious as any religion and must claim that "Scientific Creationism" is as scientific as any science.[17] Their biblical cosmogony (the Bible scarcely contains any cosmology worthy of the name) must be defended at all costs, for their salvation depends on it. Thus does soteriology give birth to pseudoscience in a scientific age. Nor will this situation improve anytime in the foreseeable future. Here is what I once wrote about this unhappy prospect:

By the mid-1800s, the reality of evolution had not only been discerned by Darwin and Wallace, but each had independently supplied fruitful theories for understanding how it happens. Yet 130 years later "Scientific Creationists" aggrieve American public education, beleaguer legislators, and clog courts with their antique idea of "special creation." It is not that such folk can accept no new ideas (thus avoiding all future shock) but that they can jettison none, no matter how naive, that they believe conduces to salvation. On behalf of traditional wisdom dogmatized, the "Scientific Creationists" and their ideological ilk are willing to fight and blight anything, including science, that threatens the safety afforded by their world view. The ominous question is this: What is happening in science today (or happened yesteryear) that will convulse pious idealogues in the twenty-first century similarly? Whatever it is, it will conscript those of us who can reconcile ourselves to the results of advancing intellect to contend with those who cannot. We will be to them and they to us as acrimonious aliens, sharing the same planet but not the same world.

Several candidates threatening to be to the twenty-first century what the evolution controversy has been to the twentieth leap to mind. Consider the following. No matter the approach to modern cosmology, it augurs ill for adherents of the god of Abraham, Moses, Isaiah, Jesus, Paul, and Muhammad. Indeed, how odd the god the Jews do choose—and the Christians and the Muslims. Moreover, the more we understand our brains by "chemicalizing" their functions, the more the person is "biologised," and the greater our success in mapping the human genome, with its myriad markers of predilection and vulnerability, the more difficult it will be to see human beings as a little lower than the angels. A little higher than the animals, but of *their* kind, is more like it! Furthermore, some studies in neurophysiology indicate that our brains select among alternatives before delivering to consciousness intutions of choice. If so, what of the vaunted "free will" upon which so much of Western religion, morality, and jurisprudence is based? With notions of deity held hostage to cosmology, with the alleged spark of divinity in us deeply doubted, and with free will at risk, what stock can be placed on intimations of immortality? Precious little, if any, it would seem.

The "Scientific Creationists" are symptomatic of a culture at war with itself over the acquisition of knowledge it does not want and can scarcely absorb with equanimity, if at all. The twenty-first century will likely witness, as never before, the battle of science with soteriology, of free inquiry with religious dogma desperately held and tenaciously maintained.[18]

Notes

1. Jacques Monod, *Chance and Necessity* (New York: Alfred A. Knopf, 1971): 170–71.
2. Alfred North Whitehead, *Religion in the Making* (New York: Macmillan Co., 1927): 13–18.

32 THE MYTHMAKER'S MAGIC

3. Jacob Bronowski, *The Ascent of Man* (Boston: Little, Brown and Company, 1973): 411.
4. See James Leuba, *A Psychological Study of Religion* (New York: AMS Press, 1969), see Appendix: 339–61. New attempts at encapsulating the essence of religion have, of course, been added since his compilation of forty-eight definitions. One thinks, for example, of Paul Tillich's well-known definition of religion as ultimate concern.
5. "Scientists, Face It! Science and Religion are Incompatible," *The Scientist* (September 5, 1988): 10.
6. *Evolution: The Fossils Say NO!* (San Diego: Creation-Life Publishers, 1972): 10.
7. "Creationism: Genesis vs. Geology," *Atlantic* (September 1982): 14.
8. Copyrighted in 1982 by the Stated Clerk of the General Assembly, Presbyterian Church in the U.S., lines 168–81.
9. Andrew D. White was keenly aware of this when he wrote his classic work, *History of the Warfare of Science with Theology in Christendom* (New York: George Brasillier, 1955). White, the first president of Cornell University and an Episcopalian, made it very clear that the warfare was not between science and the Christian religion but between science and the theology produced by those Christians who focus primarily on the intellectual content of their religion.
10. "Close Encounters of an Ominous Kind: Science and Religion in Contemporary America," *The Register* (Phi Lambda Upsilon) 63, no. 2 (Fall 1978): 39–40; also reprinted in *The Humanist* 39, no. 1 (January–February 1979): 6; and reprinted as "Contemporary Religion vs. Science," in *Chemtech* (June 1981): 338.
11. The English word 'Gnosticism' comes from the Greek *gnosis*, which means knowledge. Historically, Gnosticism refers to a family of soteriological systems whose adherents believed that salvation came through *knowledge* of a special type, which human beings, properly prepared, could acquire.
12. For a radical reappraisal of Paul, see Hyam Maccoby, *The Mythmaker: Paul and the Invention of Christianity* (London: Weidenfeld and Nicolson, 1986).
13. Appeared in slightly altered form in my "The 'Escape Goat' of Christianity," *Free Inquiry* 7, no. 2 (Spring 1987): 34. See the entry on Tertullian in *The Columbia Encyclopedia*. For Luther on reason as the enemy of faith, see the entry on him in John Bartlett, *Familiar Quotations* (Boston: Little, Brown and Company, 1966), p. 180, taken from Luther's *Table Talk*. For the remark about the Devil's Whore, see the entry on Luther in *The Encyclopedia of Philosophy*. Also see Kierkegaard's *Concluding Unscientific Postscript* (Princeton University Press, 1941), pp. 513 ff. See Karl Barth, *Dogmatics in Outline* (New York: Philosophical Library, 1949): 22–23. My encounter with Barth occurred while I was a student at the Graduate School of Ecumenical Studies of the World Council of Churches in Switzerland, in 1956. To claim that Christian faith is rational in the *proper* sense of the word has the same effect as St. Paul's claim that his gospel, though foolish in the eyes of the wise of this world, is the wisdom of the Bible-god unto salvation. The object in each case is to prevent the normal standards for truth from being applied to Christian dogmas.
14. Liberal Protestants in the mainline denominations have, in varying numbers, accepted Darwinism throughout the twentieth century. Moreover, Pope Pius XII wrote in his encyclical, *Humani generis*, in 1950: "The Teaching of the Church leaves the doctrine of Evolution an open question, as long as it confines its speculations to the development, from other living matter already in existence, of the human body." (That souls are immediately created by God is a view which the Catholic faith imposes on us.) Thus, the Roman Catholic Church has officially made its peace with evolution and stands on the sidelines in all that follows having to do with the "Scientific Creationist" attitude toward evolution and Darwinism. This is not true, however, with respect to individual believers. There exist several small Catholic creationists groups, and individual Catholics have been prominent in lobbying for "Creation Science." See *Religion Watch* 3, no. 9 (July–August 1988): 3–4. It is also important to know

that the Mormon Church has taken no official position on evolution. See National Center for Science Education *Reports* 10, no. 1 (January-February 1990): 21.

15. "Evolution in Public Schools and Creation in Students' Homes: What Creationists Can Do," in Institute for Creation Research, *Impact Series*, no. 69 (March 1979).

16. See my "Humanism, Disbelief, and Bibliolatry," *The Humanist* (May/June 1990): 7-8.

17. This is a common theme of such leading creationists as Henry Morris, former president of the Creation Research Society and now director of the Institute for Creation Research. See the work he edited called *Scientific Creationism* (Public School Edition) (San Diego: Creation-Life Publishers, 1974): 196 and 3 ff.

18. From my article, "Unwanted Knowledge," *Free Inquiry* 8, no. 3 (Summer 1988): 22. See also "Does Science Leave Room For Soul?" *Nature* 356 (April 30, 1992): 729. In this article one learns that according to the new book *Understanding the Present* by Bryan Appleyard, "science is inimical to the human spirit and its needs."

2

What the "Scientific Creationists" Do Not Want You to Know and Hope You Are Too Foolish to Find Out

Introduction

On the back wall of the First Unitarian Church of Omaha, Nebraska, there is a plaque which reads as follows:

> Newton Mann
> 1836–1926
> Minister of this Church
> 1889 . . . 1910
> Poet Scientist Scholar
> First American Preacher to
> Accept and Proclaim the
> Philosophy of Evolution

The year of this acceptance and proclamation of evolution was 1859, the very year of Charles Darwin's *The Origin of Species;* the place was Cincinnati, Ohio; the event was extraordinary!

In 1989, First Unitarian began a year-long celebration of the arrival of this remarkable man in Omaha one hundred years earlier. It was a signal honor for me to be invited to give the inaugural lecture. Mine was but one of more than a dozen presentations to follow. These were published as *On Perceiving the Truth of Things*, the subtitle being *The Legacy of the Reverend Newton Mann*. The Reverend Ronald Knapp, current minister of First Unitarian, edited the various contributions which were then published by First Unitarian (1990), partially funded by the Unitarian Universalist Denominational Grants Panel. The contents of this book are not copyrighted.

In writing "What the 'Scientific Creationists' Do Not Want You to Know and Hope You Are Too Foolish to Find Out," I targeted the same kind of audience as I expect my readers to be. With this in mind I wrote as though I were preparing a kind of manual or guide book to be used by beginners in understanding and at the same time in exposing "Scientific Creationism." This chapter is by far the longest, because it is the most comprehensive single statement on the subject I have ever written. The material in it has been slightly edited and updated, especially in the references, and has been expanded at one point. Other chapters will refer to this chapter as the core of the book.

"Scientific Creationism": A Hardy Perennial

Believers in biblical inerrancy in general and those who are pleased to call themselves "Scientific Creationists" in particular lost a big battle June 19, 1987. On that day the Supreme Court ruled in *Edwards* v. *Aguillard* that public schools are not required to give equal (or any) time to "Creation Science" if and when evolution and theories explaining it are taught.[1] The "Scientific Creationists," however, recognize the loss for what it was: a lost battle, not a lost war, and even less a lost cause. Nor should anyone else confuse these. It is very clear that the war will go on.

Religion Watch (a newsletter monitoring trends in contemporary religion around the world) carried the following story several months after the decision above:

> The *New York Times* (August 2) reports that the Louisiana defeat didn't stop the thriving creationist textbook publishing business. One such publisher says that the 30,000 creationist texts in use are being distributed among Orthodox Jewish and public schools as well as in Christian schools. Many creationists are not too convinced that their cause in public schools has even been weakened by the Louisiana ruling. The fundamentalist *Biblical Evangelist* quips, "Go ahead, teachers, teach creation science in your classes to your heart's content—with the blessings of the United States Supreme Court!' The paper quotes creationist leader Duane Gish that the court "ruled that no state can force teachers to teach creation science, but it did say teachers could teach creationism if they wanted to." The *Bible Science Newsletter* (August) claims that the Supreme Court

gave a "gift to creationists" in ruling that a valid secular purpose exists in presenting evidence for creation. "[E]ducators have been placed on notice that the law may not support censorship of information on creation...." (*World,* P.O. Box 2330, Ashville, NC 28802; *Biblical Evangelist,* P.O. Drawer 940, Ingleside, TX 78362-0940; *Bible-Science Newsletter,* 2911 E. 42nd St., Minneapolis, MN 55406)

Religion Watch also quotes the evangelical newsweekly, *World* (of July 6) saying that the *Aguillard* ruling is "better for Christianity" for the following reason:

To ask unconvinced teachers to tell the marvelously dramatic story of God's making all things . . . may be worse than letting them tell a falsehood. . . . [E]ven if the Supreme Court had allowed the Louisiana law, it would have been the classic case of way too little and way too late. Far better to let everyone know that the cupboard is bare than to trick kids with junk food.[2]

In short, if the "Scientific Creationists" are defeated in the courts and blocked on the national level, they will seek different, nonjudicial routes to gain their ends and will content themselves with working less obviously, but not necessarily less effectively, on the local level. They and their sympathizers will find their way onto school boards and textbook selection committees and into administrative offices and classrooms (see also chapter 10). Aside from alert, active, well-intentioned citizens who believe in the separation of church and state, appreciate scientific rigor, and do not want matters of fact confused with articles of faith in the schools, what is needed is a kind of manual that treats "Scientific Creationism" accurately and thoroughly but which also refutes it on its own terms as nearly as possible rather than on scientifically sophisticated terms, and, in so doing, shows clearly why it should have no place in the public schools curriculum. At all times a manual of the kind suggested should be clear and pointed, free from jargon and scholarly pretension, and ever aware of readers who are intelligent and open-minded but who are not highly trained in the scientific areas with which the "Scientific Creationists" have axes to grind. People who are scientifically trained can, of course, respond on their own terms, but even they may find this manual useful for other reasons.

Getting Straight on Science and Creation

The words 'scientific' and 'creationism' can obviously be spoken or written together in this order, over and again, but when put together in this way their joint meaning bears watching. Respecting 'scientific' it is clear that by training and/or profession some people are scientists and others are not. Granted that there is some blurring of lines between pure and applied science, i.e., between scientific investigation for its own sake and the technical applications thereof as in the difference between medical research, for example, and clinical practice. It is probably good enough to say that what is scientific is what astronomers, physicists, chemists, geologists, biologists, and other people who investigate nature do when they are on the job.

'Creationism' names the position upheld by people who take the universe to be an artifact, i.e., who believe that it was brought into being, put together, or otherwise fabricated by an agency (or artificer) external and superior to it. This agency is typically described as being supernatural or transcendent and in the usage of religious people as "divine." In English the word 'God,' of course, most commonly names this alleged creative agency. Obviously, people who do not take the universe to be an artifact (or like one) do not support creationism in the sense at issue. Two loose uses of 'creation' should be avoided. First, 'the whole of creation' used as a synonym for 'the entire universe' begs the question whenever 'creation' calls up the meanings of creationism as described above. Second, it is also question begging to superimpose theological implications on the term 'moment of creation' which may mean no more than the *sudden* appearance of the universe as physicists now view it. For example, many cosmologists refer to what happened during the first few trillionths of a second after the Big Bang as creation but do not mean thereby to suggest that the cosmos is an artifact.

We are left with the following four classifications of people: (1) Those who are not scientists and who do not believe the universe to be an artifact, (2) those who are not scientists and who do believe the universe to be an artifact, (3) those who are scientists and who do not believe the universe to be an artifact, and (4) those who are scientists and who do believe the universe to be an artifact. Only the two categories above containing 'scientists' (i.e., 3 and 4) are of further interest. Though we seldom, if ever, hear scientists call themselves 'scientific noncreationists,' this term is more acceptable logically than the (by now) very familiar term "Scientific Creationists." The reasons for this are fairly obvious when pointed out. Scientists investigate the nature of what is available to human brains through experience. Experience, as used here, is not limited to what the naked eye, for example, can see but also includes what such extensions of the eye as the most advanced electron microscope or the most sophisticated telescope can also "see" and make available to us indirectly. If there are data in the universe that are not available to any of our human senses (or to the various extensions thereof) or if this information systematically baffles our human reasoning capabilities, then such information (or data) is transcendent to brains like ours and remains not only unknown but unknowable. The point is that scientific knowledge is knowledge of nature, not of supernature. It is knowledge of our cosmos, not of some supercosmos, of which ours might be an inferior spinoff. In short, though we humans may not wish to investigate everything investigatable, we *can only* investigate what our brains find investigateable.

Science proceeds according to the law of parsimony which says that the simplest adequate explanation is to be preferred to more complicated but adequate explanations. Scientists might, for example, approach nature (a) as though it were simply the Given, something to be accepted on its own terms, however mysterious, and explained without reference to anything else, or (b) as though it were an artifact, the effect of prior causality, perhaps even of causality that is conscious and intentional, having purposes. In point of fact, no law of nature, as formulated, makes reference to approach (b), no scientific theory now being devised for testing (or undergoing testing) makes reference to or utilizes (b), no scientific report or article in any reputable journal anywhere in the world even hints at (b), and no work-a-day scientist, while on the job, ever uses (b). In each case, approach (a) is enough to get on with the business of science and is clearly more parsimonious.

Since scientists conduct their business without taking, or needing to take, the universe to be an artifact, since they, having only natural means at their disposal, cannot confront any (supernatural or extranatural [sic]) artificer of the (natural) universe, and since none of their explanations of the mechanisms of nature are or can be linked to anything that might properly be called divine purpose, there is a strong *prima facie* case for their being *scientific noncreationists*. Those creationists who call themselves scientific will point out at once that the absence of evidence (for an artificer) is not evidence of absence. Perhaps not, but the absence of evidence is not evidence of presence either. At the risk of immodesty, the author reveals McKown's Maxim, to wit: The invisible and the nonexistent look very much alike.

Anybody, whether scientifically trained or not, who believes the universe to be an artifact does so on nonscientific grounds—on grounds of untested intuition, hope, trust, or whatever. Theologically speaking, "Scientific Creationism" is based on faith and faith alone. Since the term is not really descriptive of any position, one has to look elsewhere to explain its use. Scientific knowledge has become the dominant mode of knowledge in all technically advanced societies. Accordingly, it is not a mark of honor in our time and place to be labeled unscientific. Quite the contrary! It thus becomes important to partisans of various ideologies to christen their positions scientific or to claim that they are *as* scientific as are any of their rivals.[3] Among many it is sufficient nowadays to say in defending creationism: The Bible teaches it, I believe it, and that is all there is to it. It is much more persuasive to say: I believe it, because it is scientific, and that is all there is to it. Put in simplest terms, the 'scientific' stuck onto the front of 'creationism' is a propaganda ploy.[4]

This ploy is disconcertingly successful. There are at least five reasons, or clusters thereof, that help explain this. First, "Scientific Creationists" often possess excellent skills of communication in general and are good debaters in particular. Knowing well what the average American intuits or wants to hear, they deliver just that—to the consternation of scientists and educators.[5] Second, many religious people not caring to distinguish too clearly between matters of fact and articles of faith want as much secular support for the latter as possible, i.e., they want the public schools, for example, to reinforce what children learn in Sunday schools and at home. Third, our public schools have not produced even a moderate level of scientific sophistication in the general public and have left many with little or no interest in understanding nature through scientific methods. Fourth, our culture either gives the Bible precedence over all other books or grants it nothing less than parity with the very best of these. Multitudes of people are content to believe in what the Bible says (or is perceived to say) without feeling any need to read it critically. Fifth, the American sense of fairness, admirable in social and political life, runs amok in science and science education. Copernicus, for example, was not right as to whether the earth moves around the sun or vice versa because a *majority* of his contemporaries agreed with him. They emphatically did not, but he was still right about the issue. Nor should the geocentric theory of the heavens, which he overcame on good scientific grounds, continue to be taught *as science* side by side with the heliocentric theory of the solar system which he established. The very idea that it is only fair to continue giving equal time to both sides in such disputes is absurd, as will be shown later in graphic detail. Scientific hypotheses are confirmed by observational or experimental results, not by referenda or appeals to fairness. Theories that are disconfirmed or superseded drop by the wayside, victims of their own error, not of unfairness.

"Scientific Creationism" and the Trappings of Science

There is more to being a "Scientific Creationist" than merely believing the universe to be a divine artifact, a belief which is shared with theists in general. The "Scientific Creationists" also believe in a very young universe, probably not more than ten thousand years old at most to hear them tell it. From the standpoint of modern radiometric dating techniques, this date is as arbitrary as it is mistaken. From the standpoint of commitment to the doctrine of biblical inerrancy, however, it is neither arbitrary nor mistaken but conforms roughly to the history and genealogies of the Old Testament. Furthermore, the "Scientific Creationists" deny the possibility of evolution not because science indicates that it is impossible but because the Bible teaches a contrary doctrine. With so much religion showing through their position the "Scientific Creationists" feel the urgency of dressing up their doctrine in the trappings of science.

Many of the leading "Scientific Creationists" belong to an organization, the Creation Research Society, which poses as a scientific organization. This group publishes a journal, *Creation Research Society Quarterly*, which continues the make-believe but at the same time puts the lie to it. Emblazoned across the front cover of each issue of this journal is the creedal affirmation: "For in six days the Lord made heaven and earth, the sea, and all that in them is, and rested on the seventh—Exodus 20:11." No journal that is recognized by the international scientific community as scientific carries a creedal affirmation. Whether or not this creed is true, belief in it is a matter of religious faith, and of faith alone, not of scientific investigation.

Inside each issue of this journal (on the second page of text in recent issues) one learns that a condition for membership is the commitment "to full belief in the Biblical record of creation and early history, and thus to the concept of dynamic special creation (as opposed to evolution) both of the universe and the earth with its complexity of living forms. . . ." No genuinely scientific organization requires such a condition for membership, and none is opposed to evolution—which would be much like being opposed to gravitation or to magnetism. The commitment above is purely and thoroughly religious. No one of the parts of this qualifying condition is based on science but, rather, on faith and faith alone.

On the second page of text of each recent issue of the journal one learns that all members subscribe to the following dogmas:

1. The Bible in the Written Word of God, and because it is inspired throughout, all its assertions are historically and scientifically true in all the original autographs.[6] To the student of nature this means that the account of origins in Genesis is a factual presentation of simple historical truths.
2. All basic types of living things, including man, were made by direct creative acts of God during the Creation Week described in Genesis. Whatever biological changes have occurred since Creation Week have accomplished only changes within the original created kinds.

3. The Great Flood described in Genesis, commonly referred to as the Noachian Flood, was an historical event worldwide in its extent and effect.
4. We are an organization of Christian men and women of science who accept Jesus Christ as our Lord and Saviour. The account of the special creation of Adam and Eve as one man and woman and their subsequent fall into sin is the basis for our belief in the necessity of a Saviour for all mankind. Therefore, salvation can come only through accepting Jesus Christ as our Saviour.

These are, one and all, the dogmas of Christian biblical inerrantists, i.e., of people who claim divine authorship for the Bible and assert that if any mistakes appear in it they are the result of the human transmission of the text from the so-called but unseen "divine autographs," not mistakes of the author. (Jewish biblical inerrantists could accept the first three points above.) Each of these dogmas is purely and thoroughly religious, and none is scientific in any sense.

So, the names of the parent organization (Creation Research Society) and its journal (*Creation Research Society Quarterly*) are misleading and amount to not very well disguised propaganda. It would be more accurate to call the society the Creation Rationalization Society or, perhaps, the Creation Justification Society. Either of these names would add moral integrity to the enterprise by identifying what it is really all about.

Only *Two* Theories of Origins? Surely Not!

The "Scientific Creationists" continue their less than candid ways when they try to make it seem that there are only two scientific approaches to understanding the origin of the universe. One is the approach normally taken to be scientific. This approach is naturalistic (i.e., nonsupernaturalistic), an approach that does not treat the universe as an artifact nor attempt by human means to get beyond it to an alleged artificer. This approach takes the universe to have begun (or this phase of it to have begun) 12 to 20 billion years ago. It accepts the evolution of stars as a fact, views the sun as being in a later generation of stellar bodies than the first, and holds the earth to be about 4.5 billion years old. It also maintains that the evolution of life (including human life) is a fact even though the origin of life remains mysterious as do some of the mechanisms of evolution. Despite the fact than many scientists are religious and believe their approach to nature to be compatible with their religion, the "Scientific Creationists" claim that the naturalistic approach is inherently godless, is based on faith alone, and is nothing more than the philosophy of secular humanism.[7] In this way the "Scientific Creationists" try to cut modern science down to their size, degrading it to the level of a mere philosophy or secular religion, if the latter makes any sense. In trying to reduce science to the level of faith, the "Scientific Creationists" attempt to put it on a par with their own faith—leaving *two rival faiths* fighting it out for the hearts and minds of human beings. This, at least, is what their propaganda aims to do.

The only other "scientific" approach to nature that the "Scientific Creationists" recognize is their own approach. It is based on the Bible (but not on the *whole* Bible as will be seen later), is an approach based on faith alone, but is presented to the public as though it were scientific or were at least *as* scientific as any other approach. Simultaneously with degrading modern science to the level of faith or mere philosophy, the "Scientific Creationists" try to uplift their own faith to the level of fact, thus establishing what looks like (but is not) parity between the two positions. For this sleight-of-hand to work most effectively, the onlookers must be kept in the dark about other approaches to explaining the universe, as scientific as anything the "Scientific Creationists" have to offer.

Are we really being asked to believe that in the whole of Western intellectual history there are only *two* theories of origins worthy of attention, the biblical (presented as science) and the Darwinian or evolutionary (demoted to dogma)? Yes, but, of course, this is false. There is another ancient and honorable tradition whose theories are more philosophical than religious and more concerned with explanation for its own sake than for cultic purposes. It is the tradition that stems from Plato, but who would dream of asking for equal time for it in public education? Scarcely anybody, and this is just where the "Scientific Creationists" want the matter to rest. They should not be accommodated in this desire.

Equal Time for Plato and Emanationism

In Plato's *Protagoras* (Steph. 320c–323a) there is an account of human origins as delightful as it is insightful.[8] The gods it seems made the frames of all mortal creatures, as it were, but left the outfitting of each kind of animal and man to the brothers Prometheus (foresight) and Epimetheus (hindsight). Epimetheus begged Prometheus to let him do the outfitting, subject to the latter's final inspection. Why Prometheus belied his name and agreed to this proposition beggars the imagination, but he did, and away he went. Such is myth, whether biblical, Platonic, or what have you. Anyway, Epimetheus, having at hand a great supply of faculties (powers), characteristics, traits, and the like set to work following a principle of compensation that would insure survival for each species. To the large and strong he gave lumbering locomotion, to the small and defenseless he gave speed. To some he gave armaments, to others skill in avoiding danger. Some received wings for flying, others claws for burrowing. To some he gave hard skins to ward off the elements, to others hair and downy hide, these not only for protection but to act as built-in bedclothes. Hard hooves went to those that walked on sharp stones, softer toes to those that crept upon sand, and paddle-like feet, one may suppose, to swamp dwellers.

All seemed to be going splendidly when there came down the assembly line a chassis that Epimetheus had apparently not expected or had, more likely, forgotten. Having exhausted the entire inventory of traits useful for survival, Epimetheus could only stand and dither at the sorry fate of man, "naked, unshod, unbedded, and unarmed" as the poor creature was. But, in the nick of time, Prometheus returned, took one look, and sped away to steal fire from Hephaestus and skill in the arts from Athena. And, so, human beings, akin to the gods thereby, took to technology as the proverbial duck to water. Moreover, by virtue of the arts they now possessed, "men soon discovered articulate speech and names, and invented houses and clothes and shoes and bedding and got food from the earth."

From high Olympus, Zeus, however, recognized that all was still not well. When humans were widely scattered, for example, they were not adept at protecting themselves from wild animals, and when bunched together in fortified cities, they fell to fighting among themselves for want of political skills. So Zeus supplemented the thefts of Prometheus with gifts of his own—respect for others and a sense of justice. Thus outfitted, the general run of human beings possess fire, arts and crafts, piety, language, fellow-feeling, and civic virtue. As etiological myths go (i.e., myths of origin), this is a masterpiece. It recognizes our singular nakedness among land mammals and our general nonspecialization biologically speaking, notes that we alone are religious, takes account of the importance of fire to technology, relates the development of language to technology, and seeks to explain how and why life in large aggregations (or cities) is possible among us. Compared to this myth, the Bible's stories of human origins are impoverished. Three cheers for Plato! Equal time for Plato in the classrooms whenever the question of human origins arises.

Upon first hearing of it, equal time for Plato would stun the "Scientific Creationists," then they would heap scorn upon the idea, and finally, more crafty heads among them prevailing, they would dismiss it as unscientific. Remembering, a bit later, that good science yields predictive power, they would cite Genesis 3:17b, ". . . cursed is the ground for thy sake," in reference to the alleged original sin of Adam and Eve. If that were the case, then one ought to be able to predict something such as entropy. With that rhetorical flourish, they could point triumphantly to the second law of thermodynamics (of which more later) and say, See, the universe is running down, cursed as it has been by the Bible-god. Platonic enthusiasts, however, could easily play the same game responding in kind by contending that if Epimetheus had been left to outfit the animals and man, he would have done something foolish such as leaving man undone, and, assuredly, nature produced in us a "naked ape," so Epimetheus must have botched the job. Each of these arguments is identical in form, invalid, and unscientific.

Sensing that all is not going well, the "Scientific Creationists" might wish to claim that their position involves far more than just a theory of human origins. It also addresses cosmic origins. Well and good, but here the scope, imaginativeness, and critical acumen of Plato far exceed anything in the Bible. Moreover, his theorizing in this difficult area (too complex to go into here) led to a new theory of how things came to be, the theory of emanation, developed by Plotinus (A.D. 205-270), a latter-day disciple, as an alternative to creationism, biblical or otherwise. Emanationism maintains that the single, superabundant, divine unity (called "the One") overflowed, as it were, into all lesser gradations of being. The closest analogy in current scientific theorizing would be the freezing out of matter from an original prematerial, super-hot singularity containing all potentialities of subsequent physical actualization. If the "Scientific Creationists" were really serious about a theory of origins, at once religious and reasonably compatible with current scientific cosmology, they would be supporting Plotinus, not the author(s) of Genesis. But, of course, they do not want equal time for any kind of Platonism. Furthermore, they hope that Americans will not find out about it, for then there would be more than just the two models of origins that they are pleased to recognize.

Not only would the "Scientific Creationists" like us to believe that there are just two theories (or models) of cosmic-human origins worthy of note, they would also like us to believe naively that their theory is based squarely on science and is neither religiously inspired nor biblically motivated. Moreover, they would have us believe that the astonishing conformity (nay, identity) between the teachings of "Scientific Creationism" and the doctrines of biblical literalism are just a happy coincidence! Fortunately, there is an acid test for this claim. One has only to submit the creation accounts in the Bible to a *prima facie* reading and critical analysis. Whenever this happens in their presence, the "Scientific Creationists" lose their feigned objectivity, drop their alleged science, and leap into battle with anybody applying this test. Upon reading the following pages, which show how to apply it, the reader is urged to apply the test at issue at the earliest opportunity and as often thereafter as is appropriate.

The Big Wash of Genesis, Chapter One

Unlike modern scientific cosmology that begins with a Big Bang, the Bible begins with a Big Wash. There is water everywhere, over head and under foot, wall to wall water, so to speak. Moreover, the Bible-god is never said (in any of the five creation accounts that follow) to have made all this water. It is simply present, just a given. The Bible notices nothing peculiar about this surprising primal element nor bothers to explain it (the Bible-god does not make water in the scriptures until Psalm 95:5 where it appears as an afterthought). Anyway, having come upon all this water, the Bible-god makes an air bubble (the firmament, or sky, or the heavens) in the middle of it (Gen. 1:6). At the bottom of this bubble lies the earth, more or less flat and stretched out over the waters beneath it (Ps. 136:6). This curious air bubble, hemispheric in shape, separates the waters above it (and all around it) from those below it (Ps. 148:4). The Bible-god opens the windows of heaven (Gen. 7:11) when he wants rain to pour down on the earth and closes these when he wants to stop the rain (Gen. 8:2). Meanwhile the foundations of the great deep (the water under the earth) are opened (Gen. 7:11), and water gushes up. These quit gushing when the fountains are plugged (Gen. 8:2).

High up in the bubble, but below the waters over it, the Bible-god positions the sun, moon, and stars. These are not in *outer* space as currently understood, but in *inner* space, i.e., in the same sky as the one the birds fly through (Gen. 1:20). In mysterious ways these "sky-lights" move up, pass overhead, and then go down and around (i.e., underneath) the flat earth before coming up again. Their task is to give light by day or by night and to establish Jewish holy days or other fixed points in the calendar (Gen. 1:14). There is no doubt that these sky-lights move around the earth, not vice versa, because on one occasion Joshua commanded the sun to stand still, and it obeyed, or at least so says Joshua 10:12–13. The Bible's profound ignorance of astronomy and celestial mechanics is made evident in the prophecy that the time will come when the stars will fall from heaven (Mark 13:25). Imagine even a diminutive star *falling onto* Planet Earth! Mere sky-lights overhead, however, could fall from heaven to earth without incongruity or even, perhaps, without much damage, but certainly not stars as we now comprehend these to exist.

How the Moon Puts the Lie to "Scientific Creationism"

The "Scientific Creationists" make much of Noah's flood, an alleged catastrophe that is supposed to have happened within about the last ten thousand years. So wrenching was this worldwide event, according to them, that rock strata were dislocated, rearranged, demagnetized, and utterly undone in terms of radioactive decay with the result that radiometric dating techniques are suspect at best and useless for anything older than the Bible takes the earth to be. Hence the earth cannot be four or more billion years old as the radiometric data indicate, or so goes the argument. The Noachian flood was supposed to have covered the highest mountains so that when the waters receded sufficiently, Noah and his floating menagerie (which some now believe to have included the dinosaurs!) settled down on the highest land mass known to the Bible, the mountains of Ararat (Gen. 8:4).[9] This does not mean that the Himalayas (the highest mountain range) were lower than the mountains of Ararat in Bible times but that the Bible stories were quite simply ignorant of all distant geography in general and of the earth's topography in particular, including mountain ranges higher than Ararat.

The antique scenario described above confronts the "Scientific Creationists" with an insoluble problem, one which cannot be solved by their theory of catastrophism. The Bible never suggests that the flood's waters rose to the height of the moon but merely rose above the mountains of Ararat (slightly less than 17,000 feet). Additionally, Genesis 1:13-14 announces that the moon is one day younger than the earth. Since the moon's rocks, strata, etc. could not have suffered a watery catastrophe, i.e., been disordered by Noah's flood as the earth's were supposed to have been, and since the moon is a day younger than the earth, what does one make of radiometric data indicating that the moon is between 4.35 and 4.47 billion years old?[10] The "Scientific Creationists" can never resolve this problem convincingly. Those who would live by myth must be prepared to die by it.

The Other Creation Story in Genesis: The Big Drought Theory

Insofar as they reveal their theological agenda, the "Scientific Creationists" want people to ignore the obvious differences between the two creation stories in Genesis (1:1-2:4a and 2:4b-25) and believe, or continue believing, that these stories are essentially the same, thus helping to preserve the erroneous idea that there are no contradictions, falsehoods, or inconsistencies in the Bible. They hope to persuade the public that the obvious differences between the two creation stories at issue are the result of different methods of exposition, i.e., that Genesis 1:1-2:4a is arranged chronologically whereas Genesis 2:4b-25 is arranged topically, or logged differently, but like so much else that they say, this too is false.

Genesis 2:4b–25 is even more earthbound in outlook than Genesis 1:1–2:4b. Whereas the latter is interested in the creation of the sun, moon, and stars as lights up in the air circling around the earth, the former focuses quickly upon the earth and retains that focus. In keeping with the Big Bang theory of modern cosmology and the Big Wash theory of Genesis 1:1–2:4a, we might call the version beginning with Genesis 2:4b the Big Drought theory, because the earth is protrayed as dry, no rain yet having fallen. But then in Genesis 2:6 a mist rose up (from mysterious and unexplained sources) and watered the whole face of the ground. Thus was moistened the dust of the earth from which Adam was to be formed (Gen. 2:7) as a kind of animated mud ball, as the biblical scholar Gerald Larue has put it.[11] Then the Bible-god planted a garden eastward in Eden (Gen. 2:8) and soon put Adam there to cultivate it (Gen. 2:15). But, alas, the poor man was alone and needed a helper suited to him and his gardening. So the Bible-god animated many more mud balls (i.e., the animals) and brought them to Adam to see what he would call them (Gen. 2:19).

Following the text literally, the "Scientific Creationists" know in their hearts that language cannot have taken long ages to develop, for Adam on his natal day named every animal in the world. Such precocity in thinking up names is matched only by his blinding speed, for before that one day was done, Adam had named every beast of the field and fowl of the air. The problem was that none sufficed at gardening (Gen. 2:20). Why the Bible-god should have engaged in such false starts as these is never explained. Only as an afterthought, and perhaps in some desperation, was the human female created (Gen. 2:22) from one of Adam's ribs in the hope that she would meet the need.

Unless one has already been beguiled into believing that the Bible is without error, it is clear to a common-sense reading that the two creation stories in Genesis, though distantly related, are largely independent and from different sources. The first creation story to appear in Genesis, as we now have the text, mentions six days of creation (i.e., a Hebrew work week), whereas the second version mentions but a single day (Gen. 1:31 vs. 2:4b). The first story places the creation of dry land on the third day, whereas it appears at the very beginning in the second story (Gen. 1:9 vs. 2:5). The first story puts the creation of vegetation on the third day, three days prior to the appearance of man and woman, whereas the second places the creation of man prior to the appearance of vegetation (Gen. 1:11–12 vs. 2:7). The first story announces the creation of birds and aquatic animals on the fifth day, whereas the second version places man first, then botanical species, then animals (Gen. 1:20–21 vs. 2:7–8, 19). The first story puts the creation of land-dwelling animals and man and woman on the sixth day, whereas the second places man first before any other living thing and woman last, toward the end of the creation day one must suppose (Gen. 1:26–27 vs. 2:21–23). Taken literally, these stories are contraries, i.e., if one were true, the other would have to be false at the points detailed above, but both could be false simultaneously, and that is precisely the case. The first story, which knows next to nothing of the real nature of the solar system, is as false as the second, which, in claiming that the first woman was made from a rib of the first man, knows nothing about biology. Moreover, the first story knows nothing of galaxies flying from each other, and the second has no idea of how impossibly many animals Adam would have had to name on his natal day. Finally, to give but one more example, neither knows of the primates, the closest relatives to human beings. The two stories of origins in Genesis are simply ignorant of monkeys and apes.

As if these were not problems enough for biblical literalists, the Bible contains three more creation stories. The "Scientific Creationists" are not quick to call these to attention, for to do so would simply compound their problems with biblical inerrancy. Nevertheless, in keeping with their creed, they must assent to them all, despite the numerous contrary claims that result.

The Big Wisdom Theory Versus the Big Sea Monster Theory of Origins

In Proverbs 8:22–31, the Bible offers us yet another creation tale, not so much the creation of the cosmos (and therefore not a cosmology as currently understood) but the creation of the earth (and therefore a cosmogony). Maintaining parallelism, this one could be called the Big Wisdom theory. In this portrayal a separate being (or so it is made to seem) called Wisdom and identified as feminine was the first entity to be formed by the Bible-god, was indeed "set up from everlasting, from the beginning, or ever the earth was" (Prov. 8:23). Remember, the first act of creation in Genesis 1:3 is light; in Genesis 2:4b the heavens and the earth are mentioned, then the focus turns quickly to fabricating the first human male. The relation, if any, of Wisdom to the primal water(s) of Genesis 1:2 is not specified, but she clearly precedes what the Bible here calls "the depths" (Prov. 8:24), the mountains (Prov. 8:25), the earth (Prov. 8:26), the heavens (Prov. 8:27), the clouds (Prov. 8:28), the sea and the foundations of the earth (Prov. 8:29). Liberal scholars, at least, would like it to seem that Wisdom is not so much a separate entity as a personified aspect of the Bible-god.[12] Wisdom, however, is portrayed here as the Bible-god's first creation, as distinct from him, and as active in creation, working gladly on his behalf.

The most dramatic version of cosmogony afforded by the Bible is nowhere collected into a single extended passage but is strewn about, especially in Job, Psalms, and Isaiah. The gist of it is that our world is the product of (or is at least associated with) a battle between the Bible-god and a great dragon-like sea monster, variously called Leviathan or Rahab. Job 26:12-13 (in the Revised Standard Version) says that the Bible-god smote Rahab and that his hand pierced the fleeing snake. Psalm 74:13-14 makes it plural and says that the Bible-god broke the heads of sea monsters, of Leviathans. Psalm 89:10-11 goes further and reports that the Bible-god broke Rahab in pieces. What, one wonders, happened to the pieces? Isaiah 51:9-10 puts Rahab's dismemberment into a cosmogonic context as do Job 26 and Psalms 74 and 89. Perhaps the earth (or portions thereof) was made out of these pieces. The Big Sea Monster theory of creation shows parallels with other ancient Near Eastern creation myths, but it need not detain us further.[13] It is enough to notice that it is yet another biblical theory of creation, one which the "Scientific Creationists" do not refer to much, if at all, unless prodded to do so. Perhaps they would tell, scientifically of course, how the great but mysterious sea monster came to be and how the earth came to be from this monster or monsters.

Not One World to Explain, But Two

Last but by no means least is the New Testament's version of creation which is found in 2 Peter 3:5-13. It begins as does Genesis 1:2 with wall to wall water. Here the heavens and the earth were formed by divine command out of (with or using) water, but the world so created, the world that *then* [italics mine] came into being (out of primal water) was annihilated by that same water (2 Pet. 3:6). One must assume that this refers to Noah's flood, but the text does not say so explicitly. Elsewhere in the Bible, it is assumed that the earth recovered from the flood, but here the meaning of the Greek *apoleto* is annihilation, not mere destruction. This must be inferred, because 2 Peter 3:7 then mentions the heavens and the earth that *now* [italics mine] are. So there is not just one world to account for, but two! Second Peter 3:10 then turns to focus on the fate of the second heaven and the second earth. Unlike the first annihilation that came about by water, the next time it will be by fire, a kind of cosmic meltdown (2 Pet. 3:12). Despite Hebrews 11:3, which is often cited to claim that the world was created by the Bible-god out of nothingness, the primal waters of Genesis 1:2 and 2 Peter 3:6 are never accounted for satisfactorily in any biblical theory of origins. Perhaps the "Scientific Creationists," who appear to be not so scientific after all, could clarify this issue, but, alas, they completely ignore the problem posed here by the two worlds created, to all appearances, sequentially.[14]

Why the Bible's Five Creation Stories Are Unscientific

It should be obvious by now that none of the biblical stories of origins is scientific in any sense of the word. These are but fanciful tales, far more akin to *Beowulf* than to Big Bang theorizing. No biblical theory of origins is based on open-minded, systematic, critical observation. None includes an empirically testable theory, i.e., none specifies what evidence, if any, would support a given story of origins and none indicates what data, if any, would undercut it. None has proved fruitful in leading to further lines of scientific inquiry. None can be expressed mathematically as Einstein, for example, expressed the relationship of energy to mass in his famous equation, $e = mc^2$. In modern scientific cosmology, any successful TOE (Theory Of Everything) will, on the contrary, be mathematically expressible. The "Scientific Creationists" are able to press their case that "Creation Science" is really scientific (in more than name) only because the average American is either too poorly informed to know any better or wants to believe too much to care about what is and what is not science.

Academic Freedom: A Red Herring

Unable to make good on their claim that "Creation Science" is genuinely scientific, but having at their disposal legions of Americans who are eager to be misled (on the nature of science at least), the "Scientific Creationists" have resorted to a variety of ploys—political, legal, and academic—to gain their ends. One of their complaints (in the courts) is that the public schools in refusing to give equal time to "Creation Science" inhibit free speech and deny academic freedom to teachers who are merely trying to introduce "Creation Science" as a viable alternative to evolution whenever the topic of human origins comes up. A closely related complaint is that students have an academic right to instruction in "Creation Science" so that balance can be attained whenever evolution comes up in an otherwise secular curriculum (also see chapters 7 and 10). Each of these complaints deserves scrutiny.

Academic freedom (guaranteed through tenure, professional memberships, or administrative policies, etc.) has traditionally meant that a teacher is to be protected from undue pressure, interference, or intrusion when teaching the *subject matter* in which the teacher has been trained and for the teaching of which he/she has been hired. Even though the American Association of University Professors does not focus its concern on primary and secondary school teachers in the public schools, it is instructive to see what it has had to say about academic freedom. Here in part is its position: "The teacher is entitled to freedom in the classroom in discussing his [her] subject, but he [she] should be careful not to introduce into his [her] teaching controversial matter which has no relation to his [her] subject."[15] In short, what individual citizens are free to say in any public forum without fear of error or of suppression they are not free to say as teachers in the public schools when circumscribed by the requirements of a given discipline whose contents they have been hired to teach.

A case in point occurred in Illinois in 1987. There a certain Ray Webster, teaching social studies in a junior high school, persisted in introducing "Creation Science." Ordered to cease and desist, he filed suit claiming that he was being censored in violation of his First Amendment rights to free speech.[16] However, the Federal District Court in his area dismissed the case. Upon appeal he suffered another setback, for the Seventh Circuit Court upheld the District Court's dismissal saying that "there is a compelling state interest in the choice and adherence to a suitable curriculum" for both students and society and that it "cannot be left to the individual teachers to teach what they please."[17] Ruling as it did the Circuit Court relied on the case of *Hazelwood School District* v. *Kuhlmeir* in which the Supreme Court held that school officials do not violate the First Amendment ". . . so long as their actions are reasonably related to legitimate pedagogical concerns."[18] In conclusion, academic freedom is to be understood as a bulwark against unwarranted intrusions into a teacher's freedom to speak within the framework of his/her area(s) of expertise; it is not carte blanche to introduce fictions as facts or superstitions as science.

Given that public school teachers do not have a First Amendment right to introduce "Creation Science" into a curriculum that has been designed by a state to achieve certain agreed-upon pedagogical goals, what about the legal right, if any, of students to be offered instruction in "Creation Science" in the public schools? Again, it is a matter of time, place, and situation. Students as persons are at complete liberty to seek instruction in "Creation Science" or in any other aspect of religion on their own time outside the formal offerings of the public school.[19] Academic freedom does not refer to any legal or constitutional right of students to hear (or be taught) whatever they want to hear or be taught (or whatever their parents what them to hear or be taught) in the public schools. Once academic freedom is understood as the courts understand it and not as the "Scientific Creationists" want it understood, its use over and again as a complaint can be seen for what it is—a red herring.[20]

The "Scientific Creationists," of course, want people to believe that "Creation Science" *is* relevant to the topic of human origins, that it *is* an appropriate alternative to evolution, that "intelligent design" (see chapter 5) names the same kind of scientific theorizing as does Darwin's theory of evolution which maintains descent with difference due to natural selection. On the surface, to be sure, there is some small commonality in subject matter, but then too there is some small commonality between astronomy and astrology, namely, each refers to stars and planets. There the similarity ceases. Current speculation as to whether or not one or more solar systems (in addition to ours) have been detected is a matter for astronomers and astrophysicists, not for astrologers, to determine. In exactly parallel fashion, whether or not Darwin's theory of descent with difference due to natural selection tells the whole story of human origins or must be corrected or supplanted by another, better theory is a matter for paleontologists and biologists, not for "Scientific Creationists" to determine. The attempt at comparing astronomers and astrologers, and a similar attempt at comparing evolutionary biologists and "Scientific Creationists" is not at all like trying to compare oranges and apples. On the contrary, it is more like trying to compare oranges with orange crates, things that clearly belong in different kingdoms. In short, "Scientific Creationism" bears only the most superficial relationship to evolutionary biology. Thus, when teachers, who are supposed to be teaching a unit of biology touching on human evolution, introduce "Creation Science," they are clearly outside the field of expertise for which they were hired and are not at liberty to say just anything they please, under the presumed protection of academic freedom.

Equal Time for the Stork in Obstetrics

To give equal time to "Creation Science" whenever cosmology, geology, or biology are at issue in public school classes would be identical to giving equal time to the stork whenever obstetrics is taught in medical schools, or giving equal time to Mother Goose and her goslings whenever the origin of snow is at issue in meteorology classes, or to giving equal time to Jack Frost when the death of tree leaves in the fall is at issue in botany departments, or giving equal time to magical practices in colleges of engineering. Americans are at liberty to believe in any kind of humbug they like, including that which masquerades as science, but, surely, the public schools are not required in the name of academic freedom to aid and abet all kinds of humbug by giving equal time to anything and everything children believe or would like to study.

Americans can, of course, adopt and speak openly about any explanatory fiction whatsoever, but they have no right not to be laughed at or to be hooted out of laboratories and classrooms if they espouse explanatory fictions that are laughable. It is not a violation of students' First Amendment rights for a school to avoid instruction in pseudoscience or to try to avoid wasting class time talking about it. For example, whatever may be the rights and sensibilities of young astrologers, it is not incumbent on astronomy teachers to give them equal time to prattle on about horoscopes. Precisely the same is true of creation pseudoscience.

Whatever their religious, artistic, or other values may be, the five biblical stories of origins, retold above, are fanciful and speculative in the extreme. When taken literally, they are false and contrary to each other in numerous ways; when made to seem to be consistent with science or based thereon, they are preposterous. Yet the "Scientific Creationists" must believe them all, because these people take the Bible (on faith and faith alone) to be divinely inspired and, therefore, without significant errors either in fact or logic. Gaining equal time for "Creation Science" in public education would be to a sensible curriculum what the camel's nose under the proverbial tent would be to occupants thereof. Potentially, the whole beast would crawl into the public schools as it has already crawled into private fundagelical schools.

How "Scientific Creationism" Wins in America

Despite the fact that there are more than just two theories of origins that might compete for attention in the public schools, and despite the fact that the "Scientific Creationists" can point to nothing scientific to support their favorite theory of origins, they are, more than likely, winning against the combined power of American science and science education in the public schools. They have much assisting them all the way from their own never-say-die determination to the unfortunate ignorance shown by the American people of what is and what is not science and of how each is determined. But there is more: They can absolutely depend on the average American's fear of criticizing religion in general and Christianity in particular.

Moreover, there are thousands upon thousands of scientists ranging all the way from researchers at major research institutions, including leading universities, down to well-educated nonspecialists who simply cannot believe that significant numbers of people could take "Creation Science" seriously. To this one can only say that there were many who did not take the Ayatollah Khomeini seriously either until he had taken over and turned Iran into a theocracy. There was, however, nothing in his Shi'ite Islam more primitive than creation pseudoscience. Furthermore, the "Scientific Creationists" are just as much scriptural literalists and inerrantists as was Khomeini. It is just that different scriptures are at issue, the Koran in his case, the Bible in theirs. One must also recognize in the American cultural mix the well-known lethargy-factor which holds that bad news will go away if left to itself or that enough people are already attending to it. "Let George do it," is the slogan of such people. The result of all this is that the "Scientific Creationists" have a remarkably clear field on which to run their ball.

They have already made the United States the laughingstock of scientifically sophisticated people everywhere. They have helped to worsen an already disgraceful situation in public science education and have weakened us in scientific competition with other advanced nations that do not have to carry such ideological baggage.[21] Nor will they stop with what they have accomplished so far. Next, if not already, they will take a bead on community colleges, then on the weaker four-year colleges and universities, and finally on the major research institutions of the country. Already they are appearing on doctoral examining committees in science and engineering.[22] Their handiwork in the primary and secondary schools, whether public or church-related, will, if not already, confront professors of science with students who are so benighted scientifically that science instruction will become remedial for the first two years of college at least. Furthermore, the "Scientific Creationists" will not only continue to insinuate themselves into textbook selection committees and school boards, they will also try to find their way onto the boards of public as well as private groups whose task is to evaluate research proposals and to fund scientific projects. Imagine what will happen to proposals in areas of potential conflict with "Creation Science"! Meanwhile the "Scientific Creationists" will pressure politicians constantly to do their bidding.

Let us not deceive ourselves about the devotees of "Creation Science." The bad news they represent will not go away, nor are enough people already dealing with them effectively. At best, they are unyielding dogmatists, at worst, fanatics. To them the very idea of evolution, whether Darwinian or otherwise, is abhorrent, because it is unbiblical or even satanically inspired in their view. These "true believers" are certain that the Bible-god not only created heaven and earth but also did it just yesterday, so to speak, because the Bible indicates it. They are positive of this, because their faith (or credulity) maintains that the Bible is literally the Bible-god's inerrant word, and the Bible-god, like the ancient Hebrews, never seems to have heard of evolution, cosmic, stellar, planetary, or biological. For the "Scientific Creationists" there can be no compromise between the Bible-god's infallible word and the Bible-devil's lying ways (i.e., every position in religion different from theirs). This is not a matter for negotiation, not an issue to be ironed out in some calm and reasonable way, not something about which gentle folk can reach accord amicably. No, this is war! Moreover, to the "Scientific Creationists" the enemy is not merely composed of a corporal's guard of secular humanists and Jews and a gaggle of professional evolutionists. It is also composed of millions of liberal Christians and Jews, indeed, of everyone, including the nonreligious, who does not definitely side with the unsupportable religious position of the "Scientific Creationists."

What Makes the "Scientific Creationists" Tick

Having been made the enemy of their particular brand of highly dogmatic, partisan religion, whether we want to be or not, what can we do but fight their pernicious influence? And fight we should, using every honorable weapon available to us including patriotism and politics, education and enlightenment, science and satire. As in many, if not most, struggles, it probably helps to know the enemy well. The key to understanding the "Scientific Creationists" lies in soteriology—in the religious doctrine of redemption or salvation—as pointed out in the preceding chapter. The "Scientific Creationists" say as much with one of the doctrines to which they openly subscribe:

> We are an organization of Christian men and women of science who accept Jesus Christ as our Lord and Saviour. The account of the special creation of Adam and Eve as one man and woman and their subsequent fall into sin is the basis for our belief in the necessity of a Saviour for all mankind. Therefore, salvation can come only through accepting Jesus Christ as our Saviour.[23]

It is one thing to believe that the universe is an artifact and that it must, therefore, have had (or still have) a maker. In other words, it is one thing to be a deist, broadly speaking; it is quite different to believe additionally that all human beings are doomed to offend this artificer (through original sin and total depravity) and to stand in immortal peril of his endless displeasure and punishments. It is also quite a different matter to believe that there *must* be a savior to preserve the saved unto everlasting life in bliss. There is no clear, logical connection between the first belief above, which is common to theists in general, and the second and third beliefs above, which are common to Christianity and to some extent to Islam. Whether or not we humans have offended the maker of heaven and earth (assuming there to be one), why should we not be after death precisely what we were before conception, namely, nothing at all? What *necessitates* that once we are born we must all remain permanent fixtures of the universe here and hereafter? Compared to other living beings known to us, we humans have, no doubt, some reasons for species-pride, but compared with other, as yet unknown, beings that may populate the universe, how can we be so cock-sure that we are the apple of any cosmic artificer's eye? The answer lies *within* us, not outside us. It lies in human egoism, in self-regard. In short, one can argue that we think much too highly of ourselves, value our lives far too much for any deity we can imagine to ignore our deepest wishes. This conviction is not at all inconsistent with the notions of original sin and total depravity and the consequent need multitudes feel for a "cleansing of the inward parts" for redemption.

Psychologically, one must approach the situation from two different directions. On the one hand are (a) the common desire to avoid death and the unwillingness of many to entertain the possibility of personal extinction, (b) extreme reluctance in accepting the permanent loss of loved ones, and (c) the dread of long-lasting, if not everlasting, punishment after death. On the other hand are (x) deeply felt needs for forgiveness and at least occasional experiences of being forgiven, (y) the feeling in religious conversion of being forgiven for one's very being, of being cleansed of one's past sins, even though one continues to err morally, and (z) the hope (amounting to absolute assurance) that come what may in this life, all will be well in an endless life to come.

Thus, repelled by hell and propelled by heaven, as it were, the "Scientific Creationists" will believe anything (no matter how absurd) that guarantees (in their view) escape from the former and success in gaining the latter. To be more specific, if believing in the existence of an infallible book the literal acceptance of whose contents contributes to the effect of making one feel cleansed of all fault and of providing one with the conviction of safe passage through this life and through any life to come, then one will believe in the infallibility of whatever book it may be, Bible, Koran, Adi (Holy) Granth, or whatever. In the case of the "Scientific Creationists" the book at issue, of course, is the Bible, but anyone who reads it in the normal way of reading books will recognize that it is probably right about some things and certainly wrong about others. That it may sometimes be accurate historically or geographically is clearly no guarantee that it is ever right scientifically or theologically.

Take, for example, the error the Bible makes in the value of pi. In 1 Kings 7:23 we learn of a round vessel ten cubits in diameter and thirty cubits in circumference. To the secular reader, this is simply a mistake, an indication that the biblical Hebrews were not as straight on geometry as they might have been. To the religious liberal, Christian or Jew, this is, indeed, a mistake but in an area of no consequence to moral or religious truths. Such people will contend that factual errors of this kind and other kinds in no way detract from spiritual areas in which the Bible is (to them) authoritative. "Scientific Creationists," however, must approach 1 Kings 7:23 in one of three radically different ways. First, they may mortify their intellects, as they often and willingly do, and believe that pi = 3.0 rather than 3.14159 (because they are already committed to belief in inerrant scripture). Second, they may rationalize as follows: the Bible-god got pi just right in the original autographs he wrote (or had written), but, alas, we no longer have these but are stuck with a version in which humans either made mistakes in textual transmission, or in which the Bible-devil has been at play, mischievously altering the text. Third, they may contend that these relationships are just right provided that the thirty cubits are a result of measuring the circumference on the outside of the rim and that the ten cubits are the result of measuring the diameter from inside rim to inside rim. Then it is just a matter of making the bowl the proper thickness to confirm what the Bible says about the measurements.[24] Why an omnipotent deity should reveal his will to humankind in so slack a way defies description. The second and third choices above, of course, amount to special pleading and are transparent dodges. The "Scientific Creationists," however, are willing to believe anything that they take to be crucial to their salvation, no price in credulity being too high.

Arguments, controversies, and disputes with dogmatists are different than arguments, controversies, and disputes with nondogmatists, even when the latter become aroused and engage in heated exchanges. An opinionated but utterly uninformed sectarian who doggedly maintains that the earth is flat and round like a plate (rather than a ball) may frustrate, anger, and provoke shouting on the part of people who know better. Those who have conclusive evidence for the truth of their views do not become dogmatic merely because they may sometimes shout at the ignorant. Moreover, an even-tempered person may be extremely dogmatic without ever raising his/her voice. For example, it is hard to imagine Cardinal Ratzinger ever shouting, yet he is very nearly at the pinnacle of Roman Catholic dogmatists, being at present the guardian of Catholic orthodoxy. Logically, dogmatism has little or nothing to do with whether one has a vehement personality or a placid disposition. It is, rather, something about the assertions the dogmatist makes that make these dogmatic. *Webster's New Collegiate Dictionary* gives as one definition of dogma the following: "a point of view or tenet put forth as authoritative without adequate grounds," and the *Random House Dictionary* defines dogmatism as any "unfounded positiveness in matters of opinion." In religion, a dogma is that which is asserted on faith in some religious authority or other, such as the scriptures, the teachings of the Church Fathers, the pronouncements of the pope, or the mouthings of a charismatic leader, and so forth.

Scientific Versus Pseudoscientific Disputes

Genuine scientific disputes are not the same as purely dogmatic disputes, even though they may appear to be similar, becoming heated or even rancorous. For the past several years there has been a sometimes nasty dispute as to whether the dinosaurs perished over a relatively short period ending about sixty-five million years ago and, if so, whether or not their extinction was due to the atmospheric conditions resulting from a comet's impact upon some part of the earth's landmass.[25] One side contends that such an impact would have so befouled the atmosphere with particles that the sun's rays would have been deflected, leading to a massive disruption in the food chain upon which the dinosaurs depended. The other side looks more to vulcanism and rising temperatures at the time which disrupted dinosaurian reproduction. Still others contend that the dinosaurs did not disappear abruptly anyway. Name calling and alleged attempts at ruining scientific careers have resulted. How like a squabble over heresy in some religious sect or other! But only at first blush.

Two fundamentally different features separate the conflict from any purely religious dispute. First, no matter how religious the quarrel may sound, no party on either side of the dinosaur demise debate has threatened the opposition with hell if they persist in their mistaken beliefs, and none has offered salvation for believing in the truth, wherever it may lie. In short, scientific disputes, unlike theological ones, have no soteriological dimension. Scientific knowledge is not saving knowledge in the religious sense. Second, the preponderance of evidence will eventually silence one side, or the other, or both if the facts of nature demand a new and as yet unconceived theory of the dinosaur's departure. In science, it is not scientists but nature that has both the first and the last word. She has the first word in that it is what nature presents to observation (i.e., leaves lying about) that stimulates theorizing or puzzling over why or how it came to be that what is lying about is what is lying about and not something else. Nature has the last word in that every theory, to survive, must be successfully tested against nature, passing every test, failing none. It is only in areas of little or no conclusive evidence that rancorous scientific theorizing can occur or persist for long—among rational people at least. Anyone who has read much in the history of the development of Christian doctrines, for example, will know how different disputes are among theologians.

Grasping at the Straw Called Entropy

The seeming science of the "Scientific Creationists" is nowhere more transparently desperate than in their attempt at making it seem that the Bible (in Gen. 3:17b) is aware of entropy, i.e., of the second law of thermodynamics. By associating themselves with a basic idea of science they would deceive the unwary into thinking that their position, therefore, is truly scientific. Alas, this pretension is scuttled by being biblically unsound, logically fallacious, and quite simply false.

The second law of thermodynamics tells us that in any system involving the use (or flow) of energy some of it is lost in the form of heat that is unrecoverable and unusable. Since the universe can be understood to be a closed system (receiving no energy input from outside itself) and since it contains processes that result in heat loss, there is increasing entropy. The point to note is that this is a universal principle, i.e., it is applicable to the universe as a whole.

Genesis 3:17b, on the contrary, is specifically earthbound, refers to ground (or soil) that can be used for garden plots, and has no applicability as a universal principle as does the second law. The Bible verse in question says "[C]ursed is the ground because of you; in toil you shall eat of it all the days of your life." This is supposed to be part of the Bible-god's punishment for the original sin committed first by Eve and then by Adam. Because they ate disobediently of the fruit of the tree of the knowledge of good and evil (a species of tree we no longer appear to have), the Bible-god cursed the ground in that thorns and thistles were to spring from it, in that humans were doomed to have to work the soil rather than being able to pluck food effortlessly from lush forests, for example, and in that the work was to be toilsome indeed, bespangling human brows with sweat. Entropy has nothing to do with the ease with which undesirable plants (i.e., weeds) grow where desirable ones are preferred. Nor does the second law have anything to do with whether or not one can sustain oneself by a walk in the woods each day plucking nuts and berries as one goes along or whether one has to engage in hardscrabble farming to survive. Finally, since our bodies radiate heat whether we work or not, the penalty of hard work has to do with human discomfort, not with increasing entropy. Unfortunately, scriptural inerrantists such as the "Scientific Creationists" are not always true to their holy book, especially when it serves their purposes not to be. Nobody can successfully read the second law of thermodynamics into Genesis 3:17b.

The "Scientific Creationists" want to make it seem that since the Bible-god cursed the ground (i.e., made entropy increase) there has never been and is not now enough energy available for evolution to occur, for higher and more complex organisms to emerge, over time, from lower and less complex ones. Not only does this article of faith and faith alone lead to bad biblical interpretation, it also commits a common fallacy in thought, to the fallacy of Division. In essence this fallacy consists of attributing to the parts of a system what is true of the system as a whole. For example, though it may be true of the universe as a whole that it is vast beyond comprehension, it does not follow that the tiny moons of Mars, which are parts of the universe, are also, therefore, vast beyond comprehension. By the same token, though the universe itself may gain no energy from outside itself, it does not follow that parts of it, such as the moons of Mars, gain no energy from outside themselves. The moons of Mars, in fact, receive some solar energy and thus acquire an energy input from outside themselves. So much for the logical blunder the "Scientific Creationists" make.

The earth, of course, being much larger than these moons and thirty-five or more million miles closer to the sun, receives enormously more radiant energy than they. Isaac Asimov noted that the sun currently radiates energy at the rate of 4.2 million tons of solar mass per second.[26] Even though it has been expending itself prodigiously for the past six billion years, it is still composed of enough fuel to shine for billions of years to come. The earth, as all unbiased physicists know, receives its fair share of this great outpouring of energy. Thus, it is simply false to claim as the "Scientific Creationists" do that there never has been and is not now enough energy to power evolution.

The Fiction that Saves, the Facts that Damn

Perhaps we should feel sorry for the "Scientific Creationists"; perhaps like the bird in the gilded cage, they are more to be pitied than censured. They have made up and laid on themselves a requirement for salvation, it would seem, that the New Testament does not require (also see especially chapter 4). Nowhere does it say that those who are to be saved must believe in the Old Testament literally. It did not exist in Jesus' time as the unified collection of writings we now possess and to which we give that name. The various books of Mosaic law (such as Exodus and Leviticus), the prophetic writings (such as Isaiah and Jeremiah), the historical books (such as 1 and 2 Kings), and the wisdom literature (such as Job and Proverbs) were not gathered together and pronounced authoritative for Jewish faith until A.D. 90, about sixty years after the traditional date of Jesus' death. What would have been accepted as binding in his day, if anything, were the books that contained the Mosaic law, but Jesus is portrayed as altering this material at will, at least according to one gospel writer.

In Matthew 5:21-22, Jesus is recorded as saying, "Ye have heard that it was said of old time, Thou shalt not kill, and whosoever shall kill shall be in danger of judgment. But I say unto you, That whosoever is angry with his brother without a cause shall be in danger of the judgment: and whosoever shall say to his brother, Raca [an insulting term] shall be in danger of the council: but whosoever shall say, Thou fool, shall be in danger of hell fire." Here Jesus not only modifies the law, he also adds the punishment of hell fire, something that the Mosaic law does not do. To continue in this vein, Matthew 5:31-39 says:

> It hath been said, Whosoever shall put away his wife, let him give her a writing of divorcement: But I say unto you, That whosoever shall put away his wife, saving for the cause of fornication, causeth her to commit adultery: and whosoever shall marry her that is divorced committeth adultery. Again, ye have heard that it hath been said of them of old time, Thou shalt not forswear thyself, but shalt perform unto the Lord thine oaths: But I say unto you, Swear not at all; neither by heaven; for it is God's throne: nor by the earth, for it is his footstool: neither by Jerusalem; for it is the city of the Great King. Neither shalt thou swear by thy head, because thou canst not make one hair white or black. But let your communication be, Yea, yea; Nay, nay: for whatsoever is more than these cometh of evil. Ye have heard that it hath been said, An eye for an eye, and a tooth for a tooth: But I say unto you, That ye resist not evil: but whosoever shall smite thee on thy right cheek, turn to him the other also.

The changes Jesus makes here are sweeping. In keeping with his willingness to change the law, Jesus is also reported (in Mark 2:27) to have said that the sabbath was made for man, not man for the sabbath. Put in theological terms Jesus is pictured in the verses above as being antinomian, as being to a considerable degree outside the Mosaic law, if not against it.

Moreover, St. Paul was willing to contradict or to ignore certain parts of the Old Testament. For example, in 1 Corinthians 7:29 he says, "But this I say brethren, the time is short: it remaineth; that . . . they that have wives be as though they had none." In other words Paul is saying here that Christians should henceforth live celibately. This is in direct contradiction to Genesis 1:28 that says, "Be fruitful and multiply, and replenish the earth." This is the first commandment to appear in the Bible, as we now have its books arranged, and it is given without qualification. At the very least, St. Paul had a qualification in mind that he thought should justify ignoring this commandment. Another example of his disregard concerns circumcision. Genesis 17:10-12 says:

This is my covenant, which ye shall keep, between me and you and thy seed after thee; Every man child among you shall be circumcised. And ye shall circumcise the flesh of your foreskin; and it shall be a token of the covenant betwixt me and you. And he that is eight days old shall be circumcised among you, every man child in your generations, he that is born in the house, or bought with money of any stranger, which is not of thy seed.

To this St. Paul says in Galatians 5:2–6:

Behold, I Paul say unto you, that if ye be circumcised, Christ shall profit you nothing. For I testify again to every man that is circumcised, that he is a debtor to the whole law. Christ is become of no effect unto you, whosoever of you are justified by the law; ye are fallen from grace. For we through the Spirit wait for the hope of righteousness by faith. For in Jesus Christ neither circumcision availeth any thing, nor uncircumcision; but faith which worketh by love.

We should also remember that the New Testament's version of creation (in 2 Peter 3:5–12), which was described earlier, does not simply repeat the creation story in Genesis 1:1–2:4a but goes on to talk about the creation of a second heaven and a second earth. If Jesus, St. Paul, and the author of 2 Peter can disregard, expand upon, or alter the Old Testament at points, why do the "Scientific Creationists" imagine that they must accept the whole Bible as being inerrant? The answer is simple: Without giving the slightest evidence that human beings live on after death, the "Scientific Creationists" are willing to grasp at any straw—even a fictitious one—in the hope that *they* will get to go to heaven when they die or will get to go to the place that they call heaven.

Whether or not this is a particularly noble motive, what the "Scientific Creationists" are doing can be seen as grotesquely absurd when approached as follows. It is curious, is it not, that the Bible-god makes the same mistakes in fact as the Bible's authors make and is presented as knowing nothing that they did not know about the world of everyday experience. They mistook the value of pi; he mistook the value of pi. They thought Mt. Ararat to be the highest mountain (rather than Everest which is two miles higher); he thought Ararat to be the highest mountain. They thought that the Sun, Moon, and stars circled the Earth in the firmament *below* the source of rain; he thought the same. They know nothing of marsupials; he knew nothing of marsupials. The Bible's authors knew nothing of Neanderthal man; he knew nothing of Neanderthal man. They knew nothing of galaxies hurtling apart from one another, of the great age of the solar system, of organic evolution, or of molecular genetics; he knew nothing of any of these either. The Archaic Hebrews are not to be blamed for not knowing what they could not have known nor for having the extremely limited knowledge of other archaic peoples, but the "Scientific Creationists" are to be blamed for taking the limited science and the pseudoscience of the Bible's day and making it into *the* science for all time. All this just so *they* can get to live in everlasting bliss when they die!

Even though the Bible supports the idea of a flat earth, no informed person nowadays pays heed to flat-earthers. The evidence against this idea is so overwhelming that even most inerrantists have given up on that one. Yes, even the religious right has been able to live with a globular planet. The same fate awaits the "Scientific Creationists" as overtook the flat-earthers. New fossil discoveries supporting the fact of organic evolution occur with what must be frightening regularity for the believers in Bible-science. The understanding of tectonic plate movements (which cause chunks of continents to break off and float away across the oceans) shows why animals in newly isolated places, such as Australia, begin to develop in different and novel ways from those left behind. The relatively recent discovery that pygmy chimpanzees (or bonobos) and humans share about 98 percent of the same genetic material, and other advances in molecular genetics spell eventual doom for the "Scientific Creationists." They will, one day, be perceived as the same kind of cranks as those who make up the Flat Earth society today. But when? That is the question, and how much damage will they do in the meantime? For the foreseeable future, however, they will continue to convulse science education in public education and hold school children hostage to their fanciful and frantic attempts at being able to live on after death in pleasant surroundings. Imagine how pathetic it must be to try to maintain a faith that says that accepting nonbiblical facts about the world (but facts nevertheless) will damn one's soul to everlasting torment or cause one to risk such a fate. Surely children in the public schools should not be afflicted by such a self-induced and unnecessary delusion.

Notes

1. The full title is *Edwards, Governor of Louisiana, et al.* v. *Aguillard et al.* 482 U.S. 578 (1987). The *Aguillard* decision constitutes the most crushing blow of a constitutional nature yet suffered by the "Scientific Creationists."

2. *Religion Watch* 2, no. 10 (September 1987): 2. For a summary of current goings-on, see chapter 10.

3. See n. 17 in the preceding chapter.

4. This is not the first time this ploy, or one very like it, has been used. In the nineteenth century, Mary Baker Eddy called her completely religious metaphysics Christian *Science* (italics mine) and entitled her most famous book *Science and Health* (1875). The by now familiar words *Key to the Scriptures* were added to the original title later (in 1883).

5. *U.S. News & World Report* of December 23, 1991, carried the results of a recent Gallup Poll showing that 47 percent of Americans believe that the Bible-god created human beings as the "Scientific Creationists" maintain. Another 40 percent believe that the Bible-god created human beings but did so in conjunction with evolutionary processes. Only 9 percent took an exclusively naturalistic, evolutionary view involving no deity. *Free Inquiry* 12, no. 1 (Winter 1991–92), p. 61, carried the results of a poll by MTV and Yankelovich Clancy Shulman showing that 90 percent of young people in America believe in the Bible-god and that 76 percent believe in hell. *The Secular Humanist Bulletin* of *Free Inquiry* 7, no. 2 (September 1991), p. 2, carried a recent Gallup Poll indicating that of all Americans, 78 percent believe in a place of eternal reward, 60 percent believe in a place of eternal punishment, 55 percent believe in the Bible-devil, and 49 percent believe in satanic possession.

6. The terms 'original autographs' and 'divine autographs' would never be used in serious conversation or writing by the kind of biblical scholars who could teach at the leading colleges, universities, and academically respectable seminaries here or abroad. The terms in question presuppose (on faith alone) that there was a "God-breathed" text (of each biblical writing or book) at the beginning of the Bible-god's revelation (or self-disclosure) to the Hebrew or Christian recipient(s) thereof. These so-called God-breathed texts (or autographs) are supposed to have been absolutely accurate in every way, being without error of any kind. The exact mechanism whereby these were presumably delivered is not important. What is important is that we no longer have the original autographs but only copies of copies of copies. Why the originals have been taken from us is never made clear. In any case, the "Scientific Creationists" admit that errors have crept into the transmission process whereby the copies of the copies of the copies of scripture have reached us. Part of this is due to human fallibility, and part of it is due to the Bible-devil who, presumably, has busied himself trying to pervert the text and mislead readers, thus jeopardizing their chances to live in eternal bliss after death. This is not a convincing line of argumentation to any except those who find this kind of rationalization appealing, nor does it give any genuine support to the idea that the "original autographs" were correct in every detail, scientific, historical, and spiritual, whatever spiritual may be understood to mean.

7. 'Godless secular humanism' was a term often heard during the late 1970s to the mid-1980s but much less following the *Aguillard* decision, probably because the attempt to make secular humanism into a religion failed to serve the purposes the "Scientific Creationists" had hoped for it. If the charge that it was a religion could be made to stick, then they could claim that its presence in the public schools was a violation of the Establishment Clause of the First Amendment. Placing 'godless' in front of 'secular humanism' is on the one hand redundant; on the other hand is a means of inflaming the passions of theists, especially of the fundagelical variety. See "The Right's New Bogeyman," *Newsweek* (July 6, 1981): 48ff. Herein is included a picture of the Rev. Tim LaHaye, a prominent Fundagelical, with the subscript, "Making humanism a dirty word."

8. *The Collected Dialogues of Plato*, ed. by Edith Hamilton and Huntington Cairns (New York: Random House, Pantheon Books, 1963).

9. Not everyone thinks that representatives of the dinosaurs made it onto Noah's ark and that this explains their absence in historical times. See *The Secular Humanist Bulletin* (produced by *Free Inquiry*) 6, no. 2 (May 1990): 4. However, Dr. Henry Morris, the "foremost Scientific Creationist," is reported to have said that "Noah had dinosaurs on the ark, because the book of Isaiah [mentions] Behemoth and Leviathan which he believes are a dinosaur and plesiosaur" respectively. See Jim Cherry, M.D., "Creationist Henry Morris 'Reviewed'," National Center for Science Education *Reports* 11, no. 2 (Summer 1991): 7.

10. The calculated age of moon rocks ranges from about 4.35 billion years in N. Nakamura, M. Tatsumoto, P. D. Nunes, D. M. Unruh, A. P. Schwab, and T. R. Wildman, "4.4 b.y.-old clast in Boulder 7, Apollo 17: A Comprehensive Chronological Study by U-pb, Rb-Sr and Sm-Nd Methods," *Proceedings of the Seventh Lunar Science Conference* (1976),

pp. 2309-33 to 4.47 billion in E. K. Jessberger, J. C. Huneke, F. A. Podosek, and G. J. Wasserburg, "High-resolution Argon Analysis of Neutron-irradiated Apollo 16 Rocks and Separated Minerals," *Proceedings of the Fifth Lunar Science Conference* (1974): 1419–49.

11. Gerald Larue, Professor Emeritus of Biblical Archaeology at the University of Southern California, used this marvelously descriptive term in an address at the annual meeting of the American Humanist Association, Winter Park, Florida (1978). It was my good fortune to be in attendance.

12. See the *Interpreter's Dictionary of the Bible* (Nashville: Abingdon Press, 1962): 860.

13. E. O. James, *The Ancient Gods* (New York: G. P. Putnam's Sons, 1960), chap. 7, esp. pp. 215–24. Any modern introduction to the Old Testament of scholarly repute will make reference to the topic at issue.

14. See chapter 9. Also see my novel, *With Faith and Fury* (Buffalo, N.Y.: Prometheus Books, 1985). This tragicomic novel had as one of its major goals the satirizing of "Scientific Creationism," with something like it but more bizarre.

15. *Academic Freedom and Tenure: A Handbook of the American Association of University Professors*, ed. by Louis Joughin (Madison: University of Wisconsin Press, 1967): 35–36.

16. *Webster* v. *New Lenox School Dist.* No. 122, 917 F.2d 1004, 1005 [63 Ed.Law Rep. (749)] (7th Cir. 1990).

17. Ibid., at 1007, citing *Palmer* v. *Board of Education*, 603 F.2d 1271, 1274 (7th Cir. 1979).

18. Ibid., at 1008, citing *Hazelwood School District* v. *Kuhlmeir*, 484 U.S. 260, 108 S.Ct. 562, 571, 98 L.Ed.2d 592 [43 Ed.Law Rep. (515)] (1988).

19. In connection with *Webster*, a student named Matthew Dunne sued claiming that he had a First Amendment right to receive information about "Creation Science." The court dismissed this on the ground that the school board's compelling interest in avoiding Establishment Clause violations and in protecting the First Amendment rights of other students outweighed his desire to obtain instruction in "Creation Science." Ibid., at 1007, n. 2.

20. In 1991 John Peloza, a California high school teacher who had been teaching "Creation Science," was told to cease and desist. Like Webster he sued in Federal District Court claiming that his freedom of speech was being infringed upon. The case was dismissed, Judge David W. Williams likening Peloza to a "loose cannon." See the National Center for Science Education *Reports* 11, no. 2 (Summer 1991): 1, 6 and vol. 11, no. 4 (Winter 1991): 1, 17.

21. In the early 1980s, George Packard, dean of Advanced International Studies at Johns Hopkins University, observed as follows: "One of Japan's distinct advantages in the next century will be precisely its lack of ideological or religious baggage." The "Scientific Creationists" illustrate appallingly well just how much religious baggage we Americans carry, courtesy of our soteriological tradition.

22. This has already occurred at Auburn University where the author teaches philosophy.

23. See any issue of *Creation Research Society Quarterly* for its creedal position.

24. See "Creationist Mathematics" in National Center for Science Education *Reports* (July-August 1989): 20.

25. Malcolm Brown, "Debate Over Dinosaur Extinction Takes an Unusually Rancorous Turn," *The New York Times* (January 19, 1988).

26. Isaac Asimov, *Asimov's Guide to Science* (New York: Basic Books, Inc., Publishers, 1965): 46.

3
"Scientific Creationism": Axioms and Exegesis

Introduction

Axioms, as everybody knows, are propositions so basic to a system of thought that they cannot be derived from anything else, certainly not from anything more fundamental than they. On the contrary, axioms serve to explain that which is implicit in or derivable from themselves. Here one can profitably think of the theorems of plane geometry that are derived from the axioms Euclid laid down. The term 'exegesis' is commonly used in biblical studies wherein it means the most accurate possible interpretation of scriptural texts. It is the opposite of 'eisegesis,' which is committed when one reads one's own meanings into a text, whether they were intended or not.

This chapter consists of the first systematic piece I ever wrote about "Scientific Creationism." It appeared in *Free Inquiry*, vol. 1, no. 3 (Summer 1981). I wrote it in alarm at the rapid progress of "Creation Science" in the public schools and among Americans in general. I thought at the time, and still think, that the most highly educated people in our society do not really believe that anybody could take "Creation Science" seriously. How wrong they are! In any case, I decided to axiomatize the system (perhaps for the first time ever) by stating what the "Scientific Creationists" take to be *self-evident truths* and then by drawing out certain corollaries. The task here is not to be judgmental but to give the best exegesis (i.e., the most exact interpretation possible) of those axioms.

Although it is now dated, I have retained the introductory material that originally led up to the axioms and their corollaries. This material is still valuable, I think, for its general thrust. With some supplementation in the references, it can be made current as I have tried to do. What is of greatest importance is to get scientists, science educators, school board members, and concerned citizens to take the "Scientific Creationists" as seriously as they take themselves.

* * *

Like many an old favorite "Brand So-and-So" in TV commercials, biblical creationism is put out these days in a new improved version, or at least the package is new. It is not called biblical (or divine) creationism anymore. Now it is called "Scientific Creationism," and it is selling very well in the United States. Given the enduring appetite that many people have for the product and the vigor with which it is being promoted, the reader should not wonder at its successes.

Consider the following (and shudder at it) if you will: Currently, there are more than fifty creationist (anti-evolutionist) associations in the country.[1] The leading groups are the Creation Research Society (CRS), founded in 1963, of Ann Arbor, Michigan; the Institute for Creation Research (ICR), founded in 1970, of the Christian Heritage College (under the jurisdiction of the Scott Memorial Baptist Church) of San Diego, California; and the Creation Science Research Center (CSRC), also of San Diego. Furthermore, San Diego is the home of the Creation-Life Publishers, a private corporation that produces and distributes ICR books, pamphlets, didactic cartoon strips, and audiovisual materials in abundance, and at low cost. Among these is a text called *A Two-Model Approach to Origins.* Like the ICR, the CRS (in addition to publishing its *Quarterly*) also has sponsored a text, *Biology: A Search for Order in Complexity* (plus a teacher's manual), published by the Zondervan publishing house in Grand Rapids, Michigan. Professor John Newton Moore, Ed.D., coeditor of this text, has taught a course in "creation science" for college credit at Michigan State University.[2] Similar content is (or has been) taught in the University of North Carolina system and at the University of West Virginia where there is also a course in how to instruct teachers to teach "creation science" in elementary and secondary schools (after all it *does* demand a special cast of mind). Moreover, a petition to teach "Scientific Creationism" has been circulated at Auburn University (in Alabama) where a professor of aerospace engineering has expressed hope that an interdisciplinary course in "creation science" may be taught in the foreseeable future.[3] In some fifteen states, bills have been introduced that would require equal time for the so-called creation model in any public school that teaches the general theory of evolution, and in the twenty-seven states having statewide text adoptions, creationist pressure is being applied. Furthermore, numerous lawsuits have been filed against individual school systems alleging that where the general theory of evolution is being taught the godless religion of secular humanism is also being taught and that this is being done with the blessings of state and federal governments, thus establishing a religion in defiance of the First Amendment (see the general introductory chapter to this book).[4]

None of the above is meant to suggest that "Scientific Creationism" is about to achieve parity with the general theory of evolution in public education, nor to suggest that the various creationist groups (with their vigorous promotional ploys involving media techniques, workshops, conferences, conventions, form-letter suggestions for writing to papers and politicians, etc.) are about to brainwash an entire nation. Temporarily, at least, the "Scientific Creationists" have been balked in Georgia and Iowa. Meanwhile, however, South Carolina has acted to permit local option in the matter. Since "Scientific Creationists" do not give up easily, if at all, other successes of this sort must be expected (these occurred most prominently in Arkansas and Louisiana).[5]

More worrisome, to me at least, than the activities catalogued above is the legal position mapped out for the "Scientific Creationists" by Wendell R. Bird (a theistic evolutionist in his benighted youth, since reformed) in his article "Freedom of Religion and Science Instruction in Public Schools" in the *Yale Law Journal* (January 1978, pp. 515–70).[6] In sketching the constitutional situation, attorney Bird reminds us that the Establishment Clause of the First Amendment demands substantial but not absolute separation of church and state. It does not, for example, prohibit all recognition of our theistic heritage in public education, nor reference to a creator or maker of heaven and earth, nor discussion of teleology on a cosmic scale.

So saying, attorney Bird argues (1) that public school instruction in the general theory of evolution abridges the believing student's right to the free exercise of religion if it is taught exclusively (thus elevated to fact), undermines religious conviction, violates religious practices, and compels unconscionable declarations of beliefs (answers on examinations one must suppose); (2) that public school instruction is coercive through prescribed courses, conditioned beliefs, teacher influence, and peer pressure; (3) that the state has no compelling interest in presenting information concerning human origins or in presenting the general theory of evolution exclusively; and (4) that the state could find less burdensome, yet sufficient, means of teaching the theory.

To Bird, the constitutional (or, perhaps, the casuistic) remedy consists in giving equal time to "Scientific Creationism" with its alternative model of origins. Whereas biblical creationism is admittedly a religious position that would violate the First Amendment, "Scientific Creationism," according to him, is a scientific position (here one perceives a new package for "Brand So-and-So") that benefits no religion as such (for religion, read "denomination"). Lest the reader fear that "Scientific Creationism," as an alternative to the general theory of evolution, might open the floodgates to many alternative religious theories, Bird notes that the courts have already held it unreasonable to give equal time to all religious theories of origins. Thus, the public schools would be left with only two models, the evolutionary model of godless secular humanism (in reality a disguised religious position) and the model of "Scientific Creationism" (which just happens to conform with literalist readings of Genesis but is not religious, being scientific instead).

Attorney Bird concludes with a caveat: Since the Constitution does not require the individual states to provide public schools, and since states have the authority to remove instruction in an academic discipline, a state could eliminate troublesome material from the curriculum—if it should become too litigious, for example. Thus, the biological sciences or aspects thereof might simply disappear from the public schools in one or more states.[7]

It may come as a surprise to many scientists and as a rude shock even to multitudes of theistic evolutionists (those who, whether scientist or not, have reconciled divine creation with evolutionary mechanisms), to learn that the general theory of evolution is a dogma of the godless religion of secular humanism and, *ipso facto,* religious.[8] Even more taxing on one's credulity is the contention that the Bible-god's miraculous creation of the earth and the universe (about ten thousand years ago), his equally miraculous creation of each species of living thing by fiat, and the Noachian flood (also miraculous one must suppose) are all and equally constituents of a *scientifically* respectable model of origins.

In these (latter?) days of naturalism and relativism, much emphasis has been placed on the transience and tenuousness of scientific models, attention being focused on the notion that such models (or paradigms) do not so much conflict with one another directly as they first eclipse and then replace one another. Although the "Scientific Creationists" pose today as the aggrieved allies of elemental fairness and simple justice (in their plea that their paradigm be given equal time with the general theory of evolution), who is so naive as to disbelieve that they hope one day to eclipse that "dogma of secular humanism"? But, what precisely, is the scientific paradigm with which they would eclipse and then replace the godless, but religious, model of evolution? To make their paradigm complete and explicit, perhaps for the first time in print, I have axiomatized it and drawn four pertinent corollaries. Here, then, are the sixteen axioms of "Scientific Creationism":

The Axioms of "Scientific Creationism"

1. There are souls.
2. Human beings are, or have, souls.
3. Human souls survive the death of their bodies in a state of everlasting bliss or damnation.
4. There is knowledge.
5. Functionally, knowledge is of three types: Saving knowledge (of the Bible-god), which conduces to eternal bliss; damning knowledge (any heretical or false belief), which leads to eternal torment; and natural knowledge (i.e., knowledge of this world), which leads to neither.
6. The Bible-god exists and has acted, acts now, and will act as the Bible specifies.
7. Among the modes of self-disclosure to human beings that the Bible-god employs are the "divine autographs" known as the Holy Bible.
8. Barring minor human errors in textual transmission, the Bible is inerrant and self-consistent, even if sometimes paradoxical or beyond human comprehension.
9. Any biblical text that might seem to be false or inconsistent (or that exceeds the believer's credulity) can be accepted confidently as true and consistent even though it may need to be allegorized, parabolized, or otherwise piously altered to conform to the standards of inerrancy already posited.
10. Any information, belief, knowledge, theory, or discovery inconsistent with saving knowledge is not merely false but potentially or actually damning, even demonic in origin.
11. A soul's eternal felicity is best served by saving knowledge but not at all by damning knowledge or neutral knowledge.
12. Neutral knowledge may jeopardize the soul of anyone who becomes boastful in the acquisition or possession thereof.
13. Exclusive and thoroughgoing reliance on natural modes of human inquiry is vainglorious, seriously jeopardizing the soul that will not humble its natural powers and seek divine guidance and correction.
14. Genesis 3:17b asserts increasing entropy (from the time specified forward) and renders evolution after the creation impossible, the two being contradictory.
15. The flood, recorded in Genesis 7:11ff., was a planetary catastrophe that has invalidated all uniformitarian assumptions relative to ante-Noachian times and conditions and has rendered unreliable all scientific techniques or data relative thereto.
16. There are and can be no data that actually contradict the preceding axioms singly, severally, or in toto.

From these axioms four corollaries can be drawn that help clarify the worldview of the "Scientific Creationists."

The Axioms' Corollaries

1. Since the Bible-god has done what the Bible says of him (axioms 6–8), having created the world in six ordinary days (Gen. 1:5–13), having created each type of living thing by fiat, and having bidden each to bring forth after its own kind (Gen. 1:12, 21, 24), the origin of species cannot have been evolutionary, whether conceived theistically or atheistically.
2. Since no species evolved into another species prior to the institution of entropy (corollary 1) and since none could have done so thereafter (axiom 14), no transitional forms between species have been found in the fossil record or elsewhere, nor can any be found, there being none.
3. Despite putative scientific evidence to the contrary, the age of the earth cannot be calculated apart from the genealogical and historical information internal to the Bible (axioms 8, 15).
4. Since the Bible-god created the earth (Gen. 1:9–10) before the sun, moon, and stars (Gen. 1:14–19), it follows that they are younger, if only by one day, than the planet, despite any scientific conjectures or contentions to the contrary (axiom 16).

Clear though the axioms are (to all who are conversant with Judeo-Christian theology) and rigorously drawn though the corollaries are, the paradigm of "Scientific Creationism" may still bemuse the reader. Thus, some may find the following exegesis (i.e., the accurate reading out of the meaning) helpful in rounding out the system and seeing it whole.

The Exegesis of the Axioms and their Corollaries

At first blush, axioms 1, 2, and 3 may seem superfluous, yet without these axioms "Scientific Creationism" would lose all vitality, its paradigm being no more than an intellectual curiosity, like the creation myth of the Akkadians, for example. It is in the alleged fact that postmortem weal and woe await the human soul (whatever a soul is and however a human being is or possesses one) that counts. "Scientific Creationists," believing that they will live on after they die, dread eternal hell as greatly as they yearn for everlasting bliss.

Axiom 4 is meant to say less than it might seem to some to say. It is not intended to settle ancient and obdurate epistemological puzzles by announcement or superciliously to demote such assertions as, "There is faith" and "There is belief." It merely says that there is information available to human beings the consequences of which are made explicit in axiom 5.

Concerning axiom 5, it should be noted that neither the deity of the *Koran* (Allah) nor the principal deity of the *Bhagavad-Gita* (Krishna), to take but two examples, will do. Allegedly, saving knowledge issues only from the Bible-god. Nor will natural piety, probity, sobriety, and the like suffice; neither will good works of a merely secular sort. Heretical or false are any beliefs, religious or otherwise, incompatible with those accepted by biblical literalists, that is, by Christian Fundagelicals. So-called liberal Christians, or Modernists, may be liberal, or modernistic, or both, but are not truly Christian. Neutral knowledge consists of any kind of secular information—historical, scientific, literary, or practical—that is not inconsistent with saving knowledge and does not, therefore, imperil the soul.

Axiom 6 could hardly be plainer, nor is axiom 7 anything but pellucid. Thus it is not their contents that need explicating but, rather, the way they function together, each contributing half to the circle of faith and each certifying the truth of the other. To say that Jack really did steal the giant's gold because it is written that he climbed the beanstalk is but a pale reflection of this redoubt of religion, the Holy Book certifying the deity who in turn certifies the Holy Book!

Axiom 8 necessitates that all apparent inconsistencies in the Bible are just that—apparent. This, however, points up various curiosities in the two accounts of creation in the first two chapters of Genesis. In the first chapter, a primeval watery chaos (v. 2) antedates the creation of light (v. 3), sky (v. 6), and earth (v. 9). Thereafter, the Bible-god created the first living things, seed-bearing grasses, herbs, and fruit trees (v. 11). Next came the sun, moon, and stars (vv. 14–16). Then came fish and fowl (v. 20). On the final day of creation, cattle and creeping things came forth (v. 24), and, last of all, humankind, male and female (v. 27).

But, not so, according to the second chapter of Genesis. Gone is the primeval watery chaos, replaced instead by a parched earth containing as yet no living thing (v. 5). Then a mist arose watering the whole face of the ground (v. 6), and the Bible-god made man of moistened earth (v. 7). Next, this deity planted a garden in Eden and placed the man therein (v. 8). In due time, every tree pleasant to see and good for food came forth, including the tree of the knowledge of good and evil (v. 9), a specimen of a species we no longer appear to possess. Having put the man in the garden to tend it, the Bible-god announced that it was not good for the man to be alone and resolved to make a suitable helper for him (v. 18).

Thereupon the Bible-god formed every beast of the field and brought them to Adam to see what he would call them (v. 19), as though that exercise in nomenclature would help determine which would be the most suitable helper. (Adam does not appear to have named the fishes, but, then, no fish would have made the grade as a gardener.) Perceiving that none of the creatures named was altogether suitable for gardening (or whatever), the Bible-god made woman from one of the man's ribs (v. 22) and, thus, prefigured cloning (see chapter 2 for a fuller account).

To the profane eye, the two creation stories in Genesis contain numerous inconsistencies, but these are only *apparent* according to the biblical literalist. If you, incredulous reader, should still demur and maintain that (when taken together as inerrant) the two stories are hopelessly incomprehensible or paradoxical, you will likely be told that though it may seem so to finite minds, to the Bible-god's infinite mind the two are true and consistent throughout. Moreover, it may be suggested, warningly, that there are some things unsafe for finite minds to try to fathom.

Although the secular reader's credulity may, long since, have been exceeded, the true believer's credulity has not, all of which introduces axiom 9, which contains the prescription for treating that condition should the need arise. Fortunately (for pedagogical purposes), the first chapter of Genesis contains information that far exceeds the credulity of many, if not all, believers and forces them to use axiom 9's prescription. The information at issue is that from horizon to horizon and all across the top of the sky there is a vast body of water (v. 7). Moreover, some of the rain, at least, that falls to earth comes not from clouds but from beyond the orbit of the moon and the station of the sun, to say nothing of the stars, for they are all *in* the sky (v. 14), whereas the waters in question are *above* it. Nor is this an unsupported inference: Genesis 7:11 and 8:2 affirm it (see chapter 2 for a fuller account). To date, the author has encountered no believer who gladly subscribes to this view, yet inerrant scripture demands it. Such, then, is the motivation for allegorizing, parabolizing, or otherwise piously altering the text(s) so that the believer's credulity may not be stretched beyond its limits, limits which have been created by life in the modern world.

Scientists are not innocent of controversy, nor are they strangers to intellectual combat. To illustrate, consider three cosmologies of our time: (a) the Big-Bang theory involving the once-only explosion of a primordial atom extruding all matter into space to expand forever, (b) the steady-state theory involving the spontaneous occurrence of matter in direct proportion to its annihilation, and (c) the pulsating-universe theory involving the explosion of a single atom containing all matter, followed by its extrusion into space, followed by its retrieval gravitationally into a single atom, followed by another explosion, and so on, world without end, a Big-Crunch existing for ever Big-Bang and a Big-Bang for every Big-Crunch. Partisans of each view have defended it more or less spiritedly while attacking rival views with relish. Furthermore, controversies have ebbed and flowed as to what is evidence and what the evidence, such as it is, implies, but at no time have the adherents of any one view seen their opponents as more than blind, muddled, mistaken, or perhaps, a bit bullheaded. Certainly they have not discerned the hand of the Bible-devil in rivals' theories, nor have they believed postmortem weal and woe to result from cosmological theorizing (also see chapter 2 on the demise of the dinosaurs). It is here, however, that the "Scientific Creationists" add something new to science, as they understand it, for to them the cosmologies above (together with the general theory of evolution) are not merely mistaken but are satanically inspired ideas used by the faithless to brainwash and pervert the innocent, including schoolchildren, the souls of perverter and perverted alike being imperiled by the very ideas at stake. So much for axiom 10.

It must be presumed that the Bible-god can save whomever he will, even a theistic evolutionist or other heretic. Still and all, damning knowledge is perilous, and neutral knowledge is useless to salvation; hence the modest declaration of axiom 11.

Axioms 12 and 13 are fraternal twins and should be treated as such. The seventeenth chapter of Acts records St. Paul's vexation over the idols of Athens. Encountering him in the marketplace (still fuming over the abundance of idols, no doubt), some Stoic and Epicurean philosophers, wanting to hear what the visiting "seed picker" (in the Greek, literally) would say (v. 18), took him to the Areopagus to address them. Judging from the report that some mocked him while others deferred judgment (v. 32), it cannot have been a thoroughly successful day. But Paul took vengeance on such people in the first chapter of 1 Corinthians, and by implication, on today's secular scientists and philosophers. Therein, one is led to believe that the Bible-god finds boasters insufferable, particularly those who boast of worldly wisdom (vv. 26–30). Citing Isaiah (in v. 19) to the effect that the Bible-god will destroy the wisdom of the wise and thwart the cleverness of the clever, Paul puts wise men (i.e., philosophers, broadly conceived) and rhetoricians (including logicians) on notice that their wisdom is foolish (v. 20). Since in the Bible-god's wisdom the worldly wise did not know him through natural knowledge, it pleased him to save believers through the foolish (i.e., moronic in the original Greek) message of the cross of Christ (v. 21), which message Paul had delivered on the Areopagus and elsewhere. Indeed, the Bible-god chose that moronic message for the very purpose of shaming the wise (v. 27). In 1 Corinthians 3:18, the saint avers that if anyone is wise in (and of) his time, he should become a fool that he may be (truly) wise, and thus become a candidate for salvation (also see chapter 1). The moral is obvious: The boastful wise of our age (evolutionists, for example) ought to become as morons, for then the two creation stories in Genesis, for example, would make sense to them and they could qualify for salvation.

Axiom 14 does not mean that the unaided Bible reader could have divined entropy prior to Clausius's introduction of the term in 1850 (or in ignorance of it today), nor that such a reader could spontaneously intuit $S = K \log W$ (Boltzmann's formulation of the measure of disorder) merely by reading Genesis 3:17b, wherein it is said that the Bible-god cursed the earth (following the fall of man). Axiom 14 merely means that the Bible-god knew that increasing entropy was to be a fact from that time forward (until his creation of a new heaven and a new earth) and that progressive randomness and the simultaneous loss of available energy would deprive natural processes of the power to evolve, i.e., to go from the simple to the more complex and from the disorderly to the orderly. That the Bible-god chose to reveal his knowledge of entropy (even if darkly in Genesis) long before Clausius and Boltzmann attests not only to the inerrancy of the scriptures but also to their prescience, thus heartening the "Scientific Creationists" in their lonely battle with legions of profane scientists who see no inconsistency between entropy and evolution.

Although axiom 15 does not date the Noachian flood relative to the creation or to these latter times, "Scientific Creationists" put the creation at no more than about ten thousand years ago, making the flood relatively recent. Profane science, on the contrary, has suggested such mind-boggling time spans as twelve to twenty billions of years as the age of the universe, four and a half billions of years as the age of the earth, and two or more millions of years as the age of hominids. Although these dates have been arrived at in a variety of ways, they share a common assumption, namely, that certain physical processes occurring today occurred at roughly similar rates in remote times. But this assumption presumably founders on the flood, which was so catastrophic (according to the "Scientific Creationists") that extrapolation from today's uniform processes to anything that happened prior to that time is impossible. For example, carbon-14 dating of human remains back to the time of the flood may be reliable in some cases, but no techniques indicating dates prior to that alleged event are reliable. Thus all hopes for a pre-deluge geology or archaeology must be abandoned, the Bible alone furnishing information about such times. Scientific doubts about the flood itself or about the alleged catastrophic effects of it are unfounded. After all, when the Bible-god tells a story, any part of it confirms any other part of it.

Unlike other sciences, "Creation Science" cannot be disconfirmed, according to axiom 16, nor does it require more confirmation than it already enjoys, the Bible-god himself certifying its truth. Thus, whereas other sciences are relative, dubious at times, modifiable, and of human or even of satanic origin, it is absolute, certain, static, and divine.

Of the four corollaries, three observations suffice. First, "Scientific Creationism" shares the mentality underlying the religious division of humankind into Jew and Gentile, Christian and heathen, Shi'ite Moslem and infidel, true believer and all others. Thus, the Christian evolutionist is read out of the true faith and lumped together with the atheistic or agnostic evolutionist whether that is appropriate or not, agreeable or not, to the individuals involved. The "Scientific Creationists" could not care less, for theirs is the true religion, all others being false.

Second, there is no occasion in the "Scientific Creationist's" life more triumphant than the one when his theory is confirmed (he thinks) through successful prediction. "If the Bible-god created each species by fiat and commanded it to breed true, there would not be any fossils of transitional life-forms, would there?" he asks rhetorically, and then continues, "And there are none, so that proves the point." "Scientific Creationists" do not appear to know, or to acknowledge, that deductive arguments in the form of "If p is true, then q is true; q is true, therefore p is true," are all invalid. One might as well argue, adopting Plato's creation myth in the *Protagoras* dialogue (320c–322d) as axiomatic, that if Epimetheus rather than Prometheus (hindsight rather than foresight) had been left in charge of distributing such attributes as great speed, natural armor, or such built-in weapons as sharp teeth or claws and such integuments as feathery, furry, or scaly skin to the animals and humans, then humans would be left "naked, unshod, unbedded, and unarmed." And, sure enough! That is the natural condition of human beings. So it must have been Epimetheus, or somebody as bad, who bungled the distribution of attributes and integuments at the time when humans were created (see chapter 2 for a much fuller exposition of this point). To return to the original example, the alleged absence of transitional forms in the fossil record could also be used as plausibly to support panspermia (the idea that life came to earth from a natural but extraterrestrial source) as to support the "Scientific Creationists' " position.

If the idea of divine creation by fiat is to be taken as an empirical hypothesis and held to be confirmable, then one must know what would constitute unambiguous evidence for it and for no other hypothesis. Even if it were true that no transitional forms exist either in the fossil record or elsewhere, one could still not conclude that the Bible-god (why that one and not another?) had probably created each species of living thing by fiat, only that it might have been the case that some deity or other did it. Furthermore, if that hypothesis is really subject to confirmation, then it is also vulnerable to disconfirmation. In short, one would need to know what would serve as evidence against the idea as well as what would serve in favor of it. Here the "Scientific Creationist" shows his true colors (i.e., the antiscience in his makeup), for as corollaries 1 and 2 show, he has rejected in advance any possibility of disconfirmatory evidence. If any is offered, such as a fossil taken by some experts at least to signify evolution, he will automatically deny that it is a transitional form and will also cast aspersions on its dating if it is said to be older than the Noachian flood.[9]

Third, "Scientific Creationists" do all in their power to make evolutionists pay the full price of their paradigm. Without defending evolution (with or without abiogenesis) any more than defending panspermia (directed or undirected), or any other conceivable means for life's earthly origin, this piece has attempted, rather, to make the "Scientific Creationists" pay the full price of their paradigm. Nowhere is this price higher than in corollaries 3 and 4. To learn the age of the earth, for example, one has but to date the Noachian flood (a most dubious occurrence, much like the amazing beanstalk that Jack climbed) and then reason back using the ages of the antediluvian patriarchs (very shadowy figures at best, if individuals at all) toward the days of the miraculous creation of humankind. Finally, having established that date, one reckons back three more days and presto! There is the answer, the sun, moon, and stars, of course, being one day younger than the earth and two days older than humankind. This should astound all noncreationist astrophysicists, geologists, paleontologists, and physical anthropologists. But let the lost be astounded—and confounded!

Such, in conclusion, is the paradigm of "Scientific Creationism," and such is the new and improved "Brand So-and-So" being offered for public consumption in general and being promoted in particular for forced feeding in the elementary and secondary schools, and even in higher education. Is the product really new and improved? No, it is the same old tripe that so exercised William Jennings Bryan in Dayton, Tennessee, in 1925. Is it, then, that the package alone is new? Yes, due in particular to that eye-catching, bewitching word 'scientific' in "Scientific Creationism," which would seem to distinguish it from plain old biblical creationism. Does this mean that the package is misleading? Yes, by proclaiming it to be scientific, the package makes the product a fraud.

The questions and answers above raise other questions, questions whose answers will be fraught with significance for our civic and religious lives. In constitutional terms, who may buy this product and use it on children as the buyer sees fit? Has the state no legitimate concern that creationist fictions are now being taught as scientific facts to credulous children in private Christian schools? Respecting the public schools, who may or must buy this product and use it equally with its chief rival? Who may disregard it safely, or must reject it decisively, teaching as science, rather, that which results from natural human inquiry alone, inquiry innocent of revelations and of the miraculous, to say nothing of the supersensuous and the divine? Such are the questions (moral, legal, and pedagogical) that "Scientific Creationists" are forcing the rest of us to ask—and to answer. (Temporarily, at least, the Supreme Court answered no to the legal question in *Aguillard*.) It is not the sort of product that one can simply take or leave on a private basis. For Americans it affects profoundly the body politic and the education afforded therein.

Notes

1. There is, of course, no fixed, permanent number of creationist groups. Moreover, some groups, associations, or alliances are small, local, ineffective, and short-lived. Through it all the Creation Research Society and the Institute for Creation Research have been towers of strength and have guided the forces of "Creation Science" very effectively. To learn about the situation as of the late 1970s, see *The Interstate Compact for Education* (of the Education Commission of the States) (Winter 1981): 32. For the most extensive account as of the early 1980s, but without stinting on the history of the movement, see Henry M. Morris, *History of Modern Creationism* (San Diego, Calif.: Master Book Publishers, 1984), chapters 4–9. For a recent account, by outsiders, see Raymond A. Eve and Francis B. Harrold, *The Creationist Movement in Modern America* (Boston: Twayne Publishers, 1991), chapter 7. Keeping track of the organizational, sociological, and political sides of "Creation Science" is not my primary concern here. This book is highly recommended for such purposes.

2. Michigan State University is by any measurement a major, comprehensive American university. That Moore should have gotten a foothold for "Creation Science" there is astonishing. See Henry P. Zuidema, "Less Evolution, More Creationism in Textbooks," *Educational Leadership* (December 1984): 211 and 217.

3. The aerospace engineer in question is Malcolm Cutchins, Ph.D., identified by the Institute for Creation Research (in *Impact*, no. 86, August 1980) as a prominent ICR scientist. Fortunately, nothing came of Cutchins's suggestion, but he did coauthor a 24-page document called "Seminar Notes on Scientific Creationism." My copy of it is undated, but it probably appeared in the late 1970s to early 1980s. Cutchins's coauthor is John E. Burkhalter, Ph.D., a colleague in aerospace engineering at Auburn.

4. The "Scientific Creationists" have made much of secular humanism as a nontheistic (i.e., godless) religion having evolution (which according to them is based on faith alone) as its principal "dogma." "It has become our unofficial state-sanctioned religion," says Duane T. Gish in his *Evolution: The Fossils Say No!* (San Diego: Creation-Life Publishers, 1972): 11–12. Henry M. Morris endorses the idea that secular humanism is a religion in his *History of Modern Creationism* (see note 1 above): 73–74. Most contemporary secular humanists would say that Morris, if honest in the matter, is really confusing religious humanism with secular humanism. Secular humanism is not a religion, because it does not take anything to be intrinsically sacred or holy. A sacred-less (sic) religion is incomprehensible. See the Introduction for a fuller treatment of secular humanism. It should be noted that the "Scientific Creationists" also have difficulty in recognizing the difference between secular humanism and secularism. By the same token, they would have difficulty keeping the category 'hound' separate from the category 'dog.' There are many religious people who believe in keeping

what goes on in public education completely secular. The secularity of such people, however, does not turn them into secular humanists.

5. For a time success for "Creation Science" seemed possible in Arkansas and Louisiana, but hopes for it were dashed in Arkansas in 1982 and in Louisiana in 1987. See the following reference for more information about what happened in these states; also see the opening paragraphs of chapter 2 for more on the Louisiana situation at the time; also see chapter 10.

6. See also Bird's "Freedom from Establishment and Unneutrality in Public School Instruction and Religious School Regulation," *Harvard Journal of Law and Public Policy* 2 (1979): 125–205.

7. Bird's argument, developed in great detail and with a great display of learning in his piece in the *Yale Law Journal*, was given embarrassingly short shrift by District Judge William Overton in the celebrated case of *Rev. Bill McLean, et al.* v. *The Arkansas Board of Education, et al.* With a flick of the judicial wrist, Judge Overton wrote tersely of Bird's 55-page article as follows: "The argument has no legal merit." See DCArk, 592 FSupp. 1255 (1982). This was a major legal blow to the "Scientific Creationists" and a harbinger of the even more devastating decision written by Justice Brennan in *Edwards* v. *Aguillard*, mentioned in note 5 above and elsewhere.

8. The "Scientific Creationists" reason as follows: Most contemporary scientists and science educators take evolution to be a fact, and all secular humanists believe in evolution; therefore, most contemporary scientists and science educators are secular humanists. Logicians, universally, take this kind of reasoning to be invalid, because, technically, it contains an undistributed middle term. Put in ordinary language, even if it is true that all secular humanists believe in evolution, it does not follow that all (or even most) who believe in evolution are secular humanists. Most or all scientists and science educators could, therefore, fall into the class of those believing in evolution but who are not secular humanists. Since this argument is invalid, it is dubious that its conclusion can serve as the basis for the further argument: Most contemporary scientists and science educators are secular humanists, and all secular humanists are religious in a godless way. Whether or not most scientists and science educators are secular humanists is an empirical, not a logical matter. This is not the sort of case that can be settled by syllogistic reasoning. If the "Scientific Creationists" want to know the truth about this, they have but to retain a reputable polling organization that can prepare a valid instrument for determining the percentage of scientists and science educators who are secular humanists. The "Scientific Creationists," of course, do not want to know the truth about this and do not want the American people to know it either. The knowledge that most scientists and science educators are not secular humanists would destroy one of their favorite arguments.

9. Gish, *Evolution: The Fossils Say No!* esp. chapter 7. Also instructive of the mind set of the "Scientific Creationist" is Thomas G. Barnes, "Oceans of Piffle in Evolutionary Indoctrination," *Impact*, no. 142 (April 1985). Dr. Barnes is Professor Emeritus of Physics at the University of Texas El Paso.

4

The Fiction That Saves

Introduction

The name of this chapter is purposely lifted from the longer, more comprehensive name in the last section of chapter 2 and should be read in tandem with it. The principal area of overlap concerns what Matthew's gospel reports Jesus to have said while he (Jesus) was revising the Mosaic law at certain points. The approaches, however, are different. The material toward the end of chapter 2 is more nearly a catalogue of biblical contradictions, inconsistencies, and curious lapses in knowledge than what appears herein.

For the children of the West, the Bible has been and continues to be of all books the most bewitching, and none there be with a greater appetite for its bewitchments than biblical inerrantists, whether Fundagelicals in general or the "Scientific Creationists" in particular. Such folk would not be bewitched any more than the rest of us if they were not sure that what they call salvation unto everlasting life depends on believing in the Bible's inerrancy. Where, one wonders, did they get this idea? Following St. Augustine (on Christianity in general) they are convinced, it seems, that they must have faith in the Bible before they can fully understand it. So, convinced at the outset that it contains no mistakes and that belief in this claim is essential to their (presumed) salvation, they read the Bible and immediately fall to rationalizing what they find that is disagreeable, false, or absurd until every piece fits their preconceived notions about it.

If, however, one strives at the outset to understand the biblical text and puts off believing any of it until later, if at all, it is clear that the Bible does not assert its own inerrancy, cannot assert it, and never predicates salvation on any such acceptance. To believe otherwise, as the inerrantist does, is to delude oneself with an elephantine fiction. Since no American can deny any other American the right to be deluded, the question is this: Must we suffer such people to take an active role in influencing, if not in dominating, what is taught in science classes in the public schools?

* * *

Consider the following assertions: (1) If I feel inspired, then I feel inspired; (2) If I feel saved, then I am saved; and (3) If I feel myself to be immortal, then I am immortal. Philosophers call such assertions as these *conditionals* (or hypotheticals). All such assertions share some characteristics in common. However, in this set of three, some interesting differences emerge. Statement 1 is a tautology (from the Greek meaning to repeat what has been said). Except for the "if" and the "then," each part is identical with the other. Deny such a statement and out pops a self-contradiction. Self-contradictions are taken to be false. Imagine the weirdness of a world in which one did not feel inspired when one felt inspired! Tautologies are taken to be necessarily true, even if uninformative.

Quite different is assertion 3, even though it is also a conditional. Most of us would probably be inclined to brush it aside, saying something to the effect that if wishes were horses, beggars might ride. It strains one's credulity too much to think that feeling immortal could cause one to be immortal or could guarantee that status in any way. Accordingly, most of us would probably think it false.

Statement 2 is the most intriguing for our purposes. The best initial approach to it is through the similar statement, If I feel forgiven, then I am forgiven. Doubtless all of us have offended others on occasion only to be forgiven *and* to feel forgiven, the slate having been wiped clean as it were. But what about those times when all anxieties and guilt (or shame) over some offense or other have drained away, leaving the offender to feel forgiven even though the offended party has not, in fact, been forgiving? The offended party could presumably still speak to the offender as follows: You may feel forgiven, *but* I have not forgiven you.

If we substitute "saved" for "forgiven," a subtle shift can be sensed. "Scientific Creationists," it must be remembered, are Fundagelicals, and Fundagelicals, typically, bear heavy loads of guilt, because they believe themselves to be depraved in their natural condition, having *no* good thing in them, and being unworthy of salvation unto everlasting life, a prize for which they yearn mightily. Imagine what happens when such people undergo religious conversion, second birth, or whatever one wishes to call it and suddenly feel all their anxieties and guilt over their very being and their dark deeds washed away.

As noted above, the individual in this world who feels forgiven but is not may suffer a confrontation with the offended party who says, "Regardless of how you feel, I have not forgiven you." In terms of the psychology of religion, let us ask ourselves if any supernatural savior (unto everlasting life for example) has ever come forward publicly to announce to those who feel saved, "Ah, but you are mistaken; you are not saved." No, this does not happen. Those who believe themselves saved unto everlasting life never run the risk of being told by their savior (or their reputed savior) that their feeling of salvation is delusional. By the same token no supernatural savior ever comes forward publicly to announce to those who feel saved that their assurance is valid. This is left to the emotional experience of the individual. So, for all any objective observer can tell, *feeling* saved may be all there is to *being* saved, i.e., it may be entirely psychological. Given this situation, the statement, "If I feel saved, then I am saved," takes on the characteristics of, "If I feel saved, then I feel saved." Indeed, in psychological terms, Fundagelicals proclaim their salvation with the same certainty as that experienced by logicians when asserting the truth of tautologies. This is a fact of religion that may baffle those who feel no such certitude, but it is a fact that must be reckoned with, if people like the "Scientific Creationists" are to be understood.

These people have yet another surprise up their sleeves for those outside their fold. Out of the blue and with no logical connections at all, they add gratuitous content to the assertion, "If I feel saved, then I am saved." The surprising new content is that *belief in the inerrancy of the Bible is crucial to salvation!* Nobody can identify the first Christian to entertain this curious notion, nor should its history from then (whenever it happened) until now concern us. The point is this: The Bible never requires anybody to believe in its inerrancy, "inerrancy" being a word that never occurs in the Bible. Indeed, no part of the Bible is aware of the Bible as a whole, the word "Bible" never appearing in the Bible as the name of a particular collection of religious writings. To be more specific, no part of the Old Testament is aware of the Old Testament as a *whole,* nor does any part of the New Testament know the New Testament as a *set* of writings. Anybody who reads the Bible with half an eye can verify these contentions.

At this point we can envision millions upon millions of Fundagelicals rising to their feet as one to announce that the Bible-god wrote the Bible, the human participants in its production being nothing but recording secretaries. If this is the case and if the Bible-god is all-powerful, all-knowing, and intent on revealing his will, then it ought to have been easy for him

84 THE MYTHMAKER'S MAGIC

to have shown in *every* book of the Bible an awareness of *every other* book. In short, the Bible could have been the be-all and end-all of cross referencing, but it is not. What a golden opportunity to have gotten the message across that the Bible is inerrant. Alas, it never claims this for itself. The reason why no book of the Old Testament knows anything about the Old Testament as a whole is that the writings constituting it (written over a thousand-year span of time) were not finally collected and made authoritative for Jewish faith and life until the Council of Jamnia, which convened in A.D. 90. After that time the canon of the Hebrew Bible was fixed, neither losing nor gaining any books.[1] In Jesus' day, in Palestine, the Hebrew Bible contained fewer books than does the Old Testament now. However, individual books of various sorts grouped as Law and Prophecy did exist as scripture.[2] There were also other religious writings that were revered. These were viewed as having different degrees of sacredness.[3] Much the same can be said of the New Testament. The set of twenty-seven books we now have did not exist as such before the middle of the fourth century.[4] Very early in the fifth century the translation by St. Jerome called the *Vulgate* brought the Old and New Testaments together into the Bible we now have.[5] No wonder no book of the Bible knows anything of the Bible as a whole (whether in Hebrew or Greek translations) or anything about its alleged inerrancy.

Legions of Fundagelicals are absolutely bound to ask, "But, what about 2 Peter 1:20–21?" Indeed, what about this passage? It says, "Knowing this first, that no prophecy of the scriptures is of any private interpretation. For the prophecy came not in old time by the will of man: but holy men of God spake *as they were* moved by the Holy Ghost." Let us grant (for the sake of the argument) that no prophecy is a matter of private interpretation. Let us go one better and grant that the Bible-god *is* the source of all genuine scriptural prophecy. Several points touching on inerrancy arise immediately. Whoever the "recording secretary" was, whether St. Peter himself or someone using his name,[6] the prophetic scriptures being referred to most likely existed in some writing(s) eventually to be gathered into what we now call the Old Testament. The words "in old time" (v. 21) indicate that no part of what is now the New Testament was being referred to, even the part being written (or written down) by the human author of 2 Peter. What a pity the Bible-god did not identify by name the Old Testament book(s) in which the scriptural prophecies of "old time" were recorded. Assuming that the issue of prophecy has been settled, assuming that none of it is to be interpreted privately, what does this tell us about inerrancy in the *rest* of the Old Testament, most of which is *not* composed of prophetic literature? Nothing at all. In short, inerrancy for the bulk of the Old Testament cannot be claimed on the basis of the prophecies, which are not to be interpreted privately, however many there were.

It should also be noted that, strictly speaking, the stricture against private interpretation is not tantamount to a claim of inerrancy, if by that one means the absolute truth. In 1 Kings 22:23 we read, "Now therefore, behold the LORD hath put a lying spirit in the mouth of all these thy prophets. . . ." Moreover, Ezekiel 14:9 says, "And if the prophet be deceived when he hath spoken a thing, I the LORD have deceived that prophet. . . ." Finally, 2 Thessalonians 2:11 says that on one occasion, at least, the Bible-god sent a "strong delusion [on some people] that they should believe a lie. . . ." One gains the impression from these verses that the Bible-god, occasionally at least, used deception to gain his ends. What better way to deceive than to put deceptions into the mouths of holy prophets? Merely avoiding the *private* interpretation of a deceptive prophecy could not make that prophecy inerrant. It would remain deceptive when properly interpreted and, therefore, false. Neither we nor any other recipient could tell from the text alone which prophecy was deceptive and which was not. So 2 Peter 1:20-21 cannot be used to establish the inerrancy of what to the early Christians was scripture, namely, parts of what we now call the Old Testament.

If 2 Peter cannot do the job, what about Revelation 22:18-19? It says:

> For I testify unto every man that heareth the words of the prophecy of this book, If any man shall add unto these things, God shall add unto him the plagues that are written in this book: And if any man shall take away from the words of the book of this prophecy, God shall take away his part out of the book of life, and out of the holy city, and from the things which are written in this book.

Fair enough, but what does this say about inerrancy? Very little. In the Bible as we now have it, Revelation concludes the New Testament, and in a way (for Christians at least) the New Testament concludes the Old Testament, so at first glance, the "plagues" mentioned in Revelation might seem to refer to any and all plagues mentioned anywhere in the whole Bible. Even so, what would this have to say about the inerrancy of all those parts of the Old Testament that have nothing to do with plagues? Nothing at all.

Since Revelation did not, in fact conclude the Old Testament and since at the time of its writing it did not conclude the New Testament either, the New Testament, as such, not yet being in existence, the plagues referred to in "this book" can only have referred to the plagues mentioned in the Book of Revelation itself. Whoever wrote Revelation did not want it tampered with and decided to frighten any would-be tamperers with dire threats. Such threats cannot guarantee their own inerrancy let alone all those parts of the Bible having nothing to do with plagues.

There is yet another passage that might seem to claim inerrancy for the whole of the Bible but upon analysis cannot be taken to do so. It is 2 Timothy 3:16, which says, "All scripture is given by the inspiration of God, and is profitable for doctrine, for reproof, for correction, for instruction in righteous." The Greek word translated by "inspired" is *Theopneustos,* literally God-breathed. However, we have already seen that the Bible-god sometimes breathed falsehoods, which simply cannot be depended on to establish inerrancy in any text in which they might appear. Moreover, we do not know when the author of 2 Timothy wrote (or wrote down) his letter and, thus, cannot know how many of the books of the Old Testament (that we now have) constituted his Old Testament, i.e., his scriptures. Was he, for example, including such books as Esther, the Song of Solomon, and Ecclesiastes? This seems unlikely. To continue, lacking a date for his letter, we cannot know which book(s) or letter(s) that were eventually to become parts of the New Testament he might have had available to him and, thus, in mind as scriptural—if any. So, we are left with the question, Which religious writings of his time did he take to be scriptural and which did he not? Finally, the scriptures in question are merely *profitable* for doctrine, reproof, correction, and instruction, not *mandated.* One would think that inerrant scripture should be mandated for the accomplishment of these "spiritual" goals.

Respecting inerrancy, what are we to make of a collection of writings (the New Testament) one part of which may call into question another part(s)? The prologue to Luke's gospel (vv. 1–4) may do just that. Herein we learn that the author is writing to a certain Theophilus so as to provide him with an orderly (or straight) account of the goings-on among the earliest Christians. The "many" who had already attempted this, according to Luke, apparently did not please him, having produced disorderly (crooked?) accounts, one must presume. Could it be that Matthew's gospel is one of these disorderly accounts, or what about John's? There is no way to tell from the *undated* text of Luke which writings he had in mind. Certainly there is nothing herein excluding Matthew and John from Luke's displeasure. This leaves us quite at sea as to whether we can put complete confidence in all four gospels in the New Testament.

The birth and genealogy of Jesus make this uncertainty painfully clear. John 1:45 identifies Jesus as the son of Joseph but fails to identify a virgin named Mary as his mother. Quite the opposite, Luke 1:26–38 identifies Mary as the virgin mother of Jesus, conceived of the "Holy Ghost," his true father, and in 3:23 identifies Joseph only as the *supposed* father of Jesus. On these points John and Luke clearly contradict each other.

Moreover, the genealogy of Jesus in Luke (3:23-38) cannot be reconciled with the genealogy in Matthew 1:2-16, these genealogies being contrary to one another. At best only one can be true at all points and maybe neither. To make matters worse, 1 Timothy 1:4 says, "Neither give heed to fables and endless genealogies." Could the author of this letter have had one or both of these genealogies in mind? Nothing in the text can rule this out. Worse yet is the reference in this connection to fables. Which fables?

Could the story in Matthew of the three wise men (magicians really) following the star to the place where the baby Jesus lay be a fable? Of course it is. Nobody can follow a star to any particular spot on earth. Could the story in Luke of an announcing angel, of the heavenly host praising the Bible-god, and of curious shepherds seeking a prodigy be a fable? Yes, for there is not one scintilla of historical evidence that any such things ever occurred. Similarly, Titus (a minor New Testament letter) reaches out (in 1:14) to include material that may be in the Old Testament when he urges Christians to have nothing to do with Jewish fables. Could there be Jewish fables in the Old Testament? Yes, assuredly there are! Such fables could hardly be taken to be inerrant.

In Matthew 5:21-48 Jesus is portrayed as making alterations in the Mosaic law, the most sacred material in the Old Testament (see also chapter 2). He extends the sanction against murder to include anger and insulting behavior toward one's brother (vv. 21-22), broadens adultery from the commission thereof to the mere thought thereof associated with lustful glances (vv. 27-28), narrows the conditions for divorce down to adultery alone (vv. 31-32), abolishes sworn oaths (vv. 33-37),[7] changes *Lex talionis* (an eye for an eye, etc.) to nonresistance to evil (vv. 38-42) and to extraordinary compliance (going the second mile), and changes the admonition to love one's neighbors and to hate one's enemies to love even for the enemy (vv. 43-48). Fundagelicals, of course, would not view these alterations as an argument against inerrancy. Rather, they would insist, Jesus was merely inaugurating the New Covenant between the Bible-god and man, the Old Covenant with the Jews having been superseded. The problem with this is that many, if not most, of the earliest Christians seem to have been observant Jews, not believing themselves to be living under a New Covenant at all but living, rather, at the time of the fulfillment of the old one.

When St. Paul arrived in Palestine at the end of his third missionary journey, he went to see James (the brother of Jesus) who was a (if not the) leading figure in the initial, primitive, mother church of Christianity (Acts 21:17). James wasted no time in saying to Paul (in v. 20b), "[T]hou seest, brother, how many thousands of Jews there are which believe; and they are all zealous of the law [of Moses]. . . ." James then announced to Paul that the thousands of Jews who were Christian, alive at that time in that place, had been told that he (Paul) had been teaching converts to forsake Moses (v. 21). Shortly thereafter a riot broke out over Paul's non-Jewish (or even anti-Jewish) conduct (vv. 27-36). This episode does not indicate that any new agreement between the Bible-god and the Jews who were Christian had been ratified or even recognized. Quite the contrary, their convenant-relationship (such as it was) seems to have been unchanged.

Another indication that the earliest Christians did not change their ways as though they had suddenly begun to live under a new or different agreement with the Bible-god can be seen in 1 Peter 2:12 wherein we read that Christians should keep their conversation honest among the Gentiles, a clear indication that Jews who were Christians were being admonished about their behavior in pagan lands rather than Gentile converts about their conduct among their own kind. Whether or not such Jews in the original Jerusalem Church had ever heard of Jesus' alleged alterations in the law (attested to in Matthew 5:21-48) is anybody's guess, though it seems unlikely. That, however, is not the point: The point is that Jesus can hardly have altered the Mosaic law if he had believed it to be inerrant. Additionally, it is dubious that he was intent on instituting any New Covenant, despite later church teaching to that effect. Finally, how could inerrant scripture have caused Christians (whether Jews or Gentiles) to have to choose sides between James and Paul? Such choosing actually took place in the early church, inerrant scriptures or no inerrant scriptures.[8]

Not only can the Bible not be shown to be inerrant, the possession of an inerrant book(s) was not and is not essential to salvation. Those Jews who were also Christian who confronted Paul over his non- or anti-Jewish misdeeds among the Gentiles believed in Jesus and were, presumably, saved thereby, but they had no New Testament. Moreover, they were not called on to believe in the inerrancy of any Old Testament book(s) then available to them. It should also be noted that none of twenty-seven books that were eventually to make up the New Testament is ever mentioned in reports of preaching in New Testament times.[9] Moreover, these documents were almost certainly not all to be found at any one center of Christianity until centuries later. Certainly they had not yet been collected into what we now call the New Testament. St. James needed no book, inerrant or otherwise, to become a Christian and to assume the mantle of Jesus, nor did St. Peter require a book to become the "rock upon which the church is built." St. Paul, though he knew the Greek translation of the Old Testament (the *Septuagint*), did not demand of his converts that they believe in its inerrancy.[10] Throughout the first generation or two of Christianity, people were converted and saved by *hearing* the gospel preached, not by reading anything claimed to be inerrant. The living tradition of Christian preaching does not require dependence on any inerrant book. Theologically speaking, Karl Barth made the proper point when he wrote, "Revelation in the Christian sense is the Word of God, the Word *spoken* [italics mine] in divine Majesty." The New Testament, he pointed out, is but a tiny "sheaf of news" about Jesus Christ, the true Word of God (see John 1:1-5).[11] In sound theology, the New Testament is certainly not the Word of God, but merely a witness to it.

The purpose of this chapter is to make the point that the Bible is not inerrant; we need not belabor the point. There is no need here to catalogue every falsehood in it to make this case. Nor do we need to list all of its inconsistencies and contradictions, others having already put their hands to this task.[12] The point is this: The various writings (largely ignorant of each other) that were eventually to be collected into our Bible put the lie to the notion of inerrancy. Biblical inerrancy is, in short, a fiction, an enormous article of make-believe.

A classic case against inerrancy can be found in Ezekiel 18:2-3 where it says, "What mean ye, that ye use this proverb concerning the land of Israel, saying, 'The fathers have eaten sour grapes, and the children's teeth are set on edge?' As I live, saith the Lord GOD, ye shall not have *occasion* any more to use this proverb in Israel." Though the Old Testament never quotes any Eli, Joel, or Obadiah who actually used this proverb on any particular occasion, there was plenty of reason in what were olden times to Ezekiel to have done so. In Exodus 20:5 the Bible-god says, "For I am a jealous god, visiting the iniquity of the fathers upon the children unto the third and fourth *generations* [italics mine] of them that hate me." In short, the father who sinned brought both his children and his even more distant progeny into rack and ruin with him. This is well illustrated by the story of Achan in Joshua 7. For the sin of this father and head of household the following was done to him and his family according to verse 25b: "And all Israel stoned him with stones, and burned them with fire after they had stoned them with stones." We must also assume from Exodus 20:5 that Achan's great-great-grandchildren (if there were any) also suffered for his sins. This is the sort of draconian punishment that led to the proverb that Ezekiel says is no longer to be heard in Israel. Ezekiel 18:20 puts the new position succintly: "The soul that sinneth, it shall die. The son shall not bear the iniquity of the father, neither shall the father bear the iniquity of the son: the righteousness of the righteous shall be upon him, and the wickedness of the wicked shall be upon him." Corporate punishment (of an entire family) for an individual's sins is to be abolished.

Did the Bible-god change his mind about punishments for sin? If so, what happens to biblical inerrancy? How can one have it both ways? Or, did Ezekiel change the Bible-god's mind for him as it were? In other words, did Ezekiel find the earlier practices respecting punishment abhorrent and enunciate a new, more just and humane position on his own and then proceed to certify it with the prologue, "Thus saith the Lord"? If so, what happens to inerrancy? Or, perhaps the Bible-god sent a lying spirit to Ezekiel who, unaware of the deception foisted on him, made his pronouncement about the sour grapes proverb. If so, what happens to inerrancy? How could we tell from the text itself which of the preceding possibilities is the case? There is no way.

The foregoing criticisms of biblical inerrancy, decisive though they are, do not speak to its greatest weakness, which is this: Why should the Bible-god, who is said to be all-powerful and all-knowing, have had to wait upon the uncertain services of the "recording secretaries" whose names appear on the various books of the Bible to get his revelations across? Why could he not simply have said, "Let there by an inerrant Bible," and produced one instantly as he is supposed to have produced the heavens and the earth? Why could he not have produced one every part of which is cognizant of every other part? The "Scientific Creationists" like to talk about "original autographs" by which they mean the biblical books as they were initially written down. Why do we not have these now? Where are they that we may look upon them? Could an all-powerful deity not have preserved these most precious of writings in their pristine form just as they were divinely dictated? Why are we in these latter days stuck with copies of copies of copies of the original into whose transmission human errors have, presumably, crept in or in which the Bible-devil has been at play? Where is the all-powerful Bible-god when he is needed most? What kind of revelation is it that can be handed down perfectly but cannot be preserved intact?

This is reminiscent of a similar problem in Mormonism (or, better yet, *with* Mormonism) for the rest of us. Joseph Smith, the prophet of that faith, testified that he was led (on September 22, 1827) to a certain place near Palmyra, New York, where his guiding angel showed him plates (having the appearance of gold) whereon were engravings of characters in "Reformed Egyptian." Miraculously, he was able to dictate the contents of these plates to certain copyists nearby who took the material down sentence by holy sentence, the result being the Book of Mormon. Biblical inerrantists who are not Mormons have as much difficulty believing this as do the most secular of unbelievers. Fundagelicals, religious liberals, atheists, and agnostics all would like to see the golden plates, but, alas, they are no more available than are the "original autographs" of the Bible. "Scientific Creationists" cannot seem to get the point of this, but my readers, I believe, can.

What I have shown in this chapter, and to some extent elsewhere, is (1) that the Bible is not inerrant, (2) that it never claims inerrancy in any chapter or verse for the whole of itself, (3) that many people have become Christian and been saved, as this is commonly understood, without possessing the Bible or knowing that it is supposed to be inerrant, and (4) that salvation today is no more dependent on an inerrant book than it ever was. Fundagelicals in general and "Scientific Creationists" in particular are at liberty, of course, to believe anything they like (or to try to believe anything they like), but if they believe in the inerrancy of the Bible (which is not a biblical doctrine), they put themselves in the camp of Tertullian who believed in the resurrection because he took it to be impossible. The extent to which the assurance of "salvation" is tied to belief in an inerrant book is the extent to which "salvation" is tied to a fiction and to a whopping big one at that. It cannot be reassuring to others that people who believe in religious fictions and absurdities wish to have a role in making public policy, but in a nation that prides itself on its religious freedom, there is no way this kind of mischief can be stopped. It would be enough, perhaps, if we could keep such people as the "Scientific Creationists" from having an influential role in the content of school texts, in curricula in the public schools, in the classrooms of America, and in library acquisitions.

Notes

1. 'Canon' means 'measuring rod.' Hence, a canonical book is one that has measured up to certain standards such as legitimacy of authorship, authority, and religious value to the communicants of a particular religion. When we speak today of the canonical Hebrew Bible we mean the thirty-nine books found in what Christians call the Old Testament. It is important to note that religious writings do not become canonical at the time of their writing. They have to prove themselves first, becoming canonical within a religion based on their perceived value to that religion at later (often much later) times. For an excellent description of the formation of the canonical Hebrew Bible, see Harry M. Buck, *People of the Lord* (New York: The Macmillan Company, 1966), chapter 20. For a much more detailed exposition, see the entry, "Canon of the OT," in the *Interpreter's Dictionary of the Bible,* vol. 1 (Nashville, Tenn.: Abingdon Press, 1962): 498-520. Or, see the entry on the Old Testament in any modern comprehensive encyclopedia.

2. According to Buck (ibid., p. 445) the canonical scriptures available in Jesus' time contained the Torah (Genesis, Exodus, Leviticus, Numbers, Deuteronomy) and the Kethivim (the former prophets, Joshua, Judges, Samuel, Kings [works we now regard as primarily historical] and the later prophets, Isaiah, Jeremiah, Ezekiel, and the Book of the Twelve, i.e., the minor prophets such as Hosea, Amos, Micah, etc., but not Daniel). A careful comparison of this list with the thirty-nine books in today's Old Testament shows that much had not yet been made canonical.

3. All Jews would have agreed that the Torah was sacred and authoritative for Jewish faith and conduct. However, the Jewish historian, Josephus, wrote that the Sadducees (the High Priesthood) accepted only the written law but not the prophets (which were also accepted by the Pharisees) as authoritative. Buck writes (on p. 444): "The historical writings of the Chronicler, some psalms and proverbs, the Books of Ruth and Lamentations were certainly known and used, but there is no evidence that anyone regarded these as scripture." Other

books, such as Esther and Ecclesiastes, had a difficult time becoming canonical.

4. For an extensive treatment see, "Canon of the NT," in the *Interpreter's Dictionary of the Bible:* 520-32. Also see Morton Scott Enslin, *Christian Beginnings,* 4th ed. (New York: Harper and Brothers, 1938), chapter 45, "On the Way to a Canon."

5. See any entry on St. Jerome and/or the *Vulgate* in any comprehensive encyclopedia, including the one-volume *New Columbia Encyclopedia,* which has a short article on each.

6. It is commonly believed by New Testament scholars nowadays that 2 Peter is quite late (around A.D. 125), that it is most definitely not the product of the Apostle Peter nor of the author of 1 Peter. See Steven L. Davies, *The New Testament: A Contemporary Introduction* (San Francisco, Calif.: Harper and Row, 1988): 204.

7. Matthew's gospel reports Jesus to have said (in 5:17-18), "Think not that I am come to destroy the law, or the prophets: I am not come to destroy but to fulfil. For verily I say unto you, Till heaven and earth pass, one jot or tittle shall in no wise pass from the law, till all be fulfilled." Just a few verses later, however, Jesus is portrayed as abolishing oaths (v. 34) as they were to be sworn under the law (see Lev. 19:12, Num. 30:2, and Deut. 23:21). Clearly Jesus did not fulfil the law at this point in any way, at least as recorded in Matthew's gospel.

8. The so-called Jerusalem Council (in Acts 15:1-21) records just such a dispute and the attempt to patch things up through a compromise.

9. See, for example, Jesus' sermon on the mount in Matthew, chapters 5-7, or Peter's sermons in Acts 2:14-36, 3:12-26, or Paul's sermon on Mars Hill in 17:22-31.

10. The version Paul had was called the *Septuagint,* a translation into Greek of all thrity-nine books of the present Old Testament plus some other books that failed to become canonical and are now part of the apocryphal (i.e., noncanonical) Old Testament. The *Septuagint* was the version used by the Jews of the dispersion, i.e., of those who lived in the Gentile world outside Palestine, in many parts of which Greek was the *lingua franca.* Any comprehensive encyclopedia will have an entry on this translation. Since the *Septuagint* was readily available, there is no reason why Paul should not have known the commandment in Genesis 1:28 to be fruitful and multiply, a commandment he openly chose to ignore in 1 Corinthians 7:7, 38. Worse yet, he encouraged others to follow his example.

11. Karl Barth, *Against the Stream,* ed. Ronald G. Smith (Student Christian Movement Press, 1954): 210-16.

12. A good book to begin with is William Henry Burr, *Self-Contradictions of the Bible* (Buffalo, N.Y.: Prometheus Books, 1987); also from the same publisher, Randel Helms, *Gospel Fictions* (1988). Those interested in attacks on the Bible by Robert G. Ingersoll, Joseph McCabe, Joseph Lewis, Clarence Darrow, and many others may contact Book Service-AR, 2001 St. Clair Ave., St. Louis, MO 63144.

5

Of Pandas and People: A Logical Analysis

Introduction

In August of 1989 there appeared a book called *Of Pandas and People,* its subtitle being *The Central Question of Biological Origins.* It was written by Percival Davis and Dean H. Kenyon, under the academic editorship of Charles B. Thaxton, and was published by the Haughton Publishing Company of Dallas, Texas. It was quickly submitted to the State Textbook Committee of Alabama (also to a similar committee in Idaho) for possible inclusion on the recommended list for science text adoptions.

Recognizing immediately a work of "Scientific Creationist" pseudoscience, Professor Scott Brande, a geologist at the University of Alabama Birmingham, sounded the alarm and solicited the support of various scientists in Alabama to testify against its adoption in any shape or form. My only contribution at the time was to write a letter (September 29, 1989) to Dr. Wayne Teague, Superintendent, Alabama Department of Education, attacking the book for its numerous and serious illogicalities. On October 2, 1989, the Alabama Textbook Committee rejected this book. It suffered a similar fate the following month in Idaho. Subsequently the publisher withdrew it from consideration.

In January of 1990 I expanded my rather long letter to Superintendent Teague into an article I believed, at the time, would appear in the journal *Creation/Evolution.* For reasons beyond my control, it has not yet appeared.

In any case, this would-be article seemed to me to be most appropriate for inclusion in this book. What appears here is an edited, slightly expanded

93

version of what I had initially prepared for *Creation/Evolution*. Since the "Scientific Creationists" may try again to succeed with a school text, and since any future attempt will, most likely, commit the same logical blunders as does *Of Pandas and People*, it seemed good to me to expose and explain these errors once and for all.

* * *

Of Pandas and People (hereinafter, *Pandas*) represents itself as a fair-minded book (of biology) worthy of adoption as a supplemental text (preface, ix). It was written with states such as Alabama in mind, states that permit the local adoption of supplementary texts. At no time does this book see itself as a primary text in biology at the high school level, nor does it dare to hope for statewide adoptions in bellwether states such as California and Texas.[1] Even as a supplementary text, it is unworthy of adoption. The reasons are simple: (1) It is an exercise in question begging and is thus illogical, (2) it establishes a completely false antithesis between the ideas of evolutionary descent and what it calls intelligent design, (3) it misunderstands and misuses reasoning by analogy, and (4) it muddles certain concepts such as chance, cause, and spontaneity. The balance of this chapter takes these points up one by one.

From a logical point of view the two nagging problems of theology are (1) its usual starting point and (2) the prevailing direction of its thought. Taking the "supernatural" on faith as though it were an undisputed fact, theologians, all too often, move on from it to try to explain the natural. There is seldom a serious attempt at starting with the natural and only then asking whether or not correct theory *demands* the supernatural. The same is true with thought beginning with the "spiritual" and moving on to the material or physical, rather than vice versa. Put differently, it is as though one were to try to move from the unknown (and perhaps the unknowable) to the known, rather than proceeding from the known theoretically toward the unknown. *Pandas* uniformly commits these errors in starting point and flow of thought. It simply assumes a divine artificer (the Bible-god) from the outset (thus making the universe into an artifact) without giving adequate reasons for doing so. Moreover, *Pandas* avoids all reasons for approaching the universe as natural, i.e., as not being an artifact or in any way resembling one. Nor does it ever show how matter/ energy are insufficient to explain the universe without also invoking "spirit" and the "supernatural." In short, it makes no attempt at being evenhanded and fair. It is, rather, a case of special pleading.

Science, as such, never addresses the issue of whether or not the universe is an artifact. On the contrary, it proceeds to treat nature as though it were to be explained exclusively on its own terms. This worries a great many religious people. They worry for themselves. They worry about their children, and they worry about students in general in the public schools where science is introduced to them. Limiting itself to the natural, as it does, and never presuming the universe to be an artifact, science can be seen to place itself in the camp of the agnostics or, worse yet, of the atheists. This appearance becomes reality in the minds of those who remember Matthew 12:30, which reports Jesus to have said, "He who is not with me is against me. . . ." Thus, naturalistic science, which refuses to reinforce the faith of theists (in the idea that the universe is a divine artifact), becomes the enemy. To tame the enemy, many religious people, led by the "Scientific Creationists," have sought to insinuate their brand of supernaturalism into the public schools to give what they call balance in science education. The problem with this is that a naturalistic method cannot be balanced by non-naturalistic or supernaturalistic assumptions or subject matter. If science were to accommodate religious claims on this point, it would have to forfeit its own naturalistic method and thus cease being science. To represent science as being untrue to its method(s) would be to engage in the false education of children in science classes.

* * *

Just as there are noses with which to scent odors and odors to be scented with noses and just as there are ears with which to hear sounds and sounds to be heard with ears, so human beings discover that they have intelligent brains with which to know and an intelligible order in nature to be known. Instead of marvelling at this (as did Einstein)[2] and attempting to learn how far the compatibility between human intelligence and intelligibility in nature goes and how it may be explained, those who wrote *Pandas* jump the gun by announcing not that human brains are intelligent but that the universe itself is (or exhibits) an intelligent design (preface, viii, and pp. 6, 7, 154, 155, and elsewhere).

Whence this intelligent *design* in nature rather than merely an order intelligible to brains like ours? Our authors hasten to assure us that it comes from an "intelligent cause," the artificer of theistic faith! This, of course, begs the question. It forecloses any sort of open-minded investigation as to whether (and if so how) the universe alone might have produced varying degrees of intelligence through evolutionary adaptions in earthly animals, most conspicuously in *Homo sapiens*. It is no accident that *Pandas* fails to distinguish between an intelligible order (to brains like ours) and objective, intelligent design in nature. Order for all we know may be intrinsic to matter, whereas design must be superimposed upon it. In this way theism is smuggled into the picture, something scientific method cannot permit and still be true to itself.

If we encounter something whose design shows considerable intelligence, we are prepared to ask questions of—perhaps even to meet—the intelligent designer thereof. This is not at all like asking whether or not the compatibility between intelligible patterns in nature and intelligent human understanding thereof are themselves both the products of an intelligent designer. *Pandas* assumes from the outset that the order that we humans experience in nature must have been *superimposed* upon matter/energy by an external agency. It does not wish to entertain the possibility of what the early Greek philosophers called *entelechy*. This is the idea that order (or developmental direction) is intrinsic to matter and not superimposed upon it. So, *Pandas* conveniently ignores this possibility just as though it did not exist. While the contraband of intelligent design is being smuggled into the picture, *Pandas* simultaneously and necessarily introduces teleology. The presumed artifact, which it calls the universe, is (or exhibits) an intelligent order, because the intelligent artificer *wants* it to be as it is for his own *purposes*. What wondrous accomplishments the authors can point to just by ignoring the conceptual differences between intelligible order and intelligent design. To ignore these differences is, if innocent, a major intellectual blunder; if calculated, the devious ploy of the propagandist.

Having begun by begging the question by ignoring all conceptual distinctions between intelligible order and intelligent design, *Pandas* compounds its illogicality by setting up a completely false antithesis between what it calls "evolutionary descent" and "intelligent design." It is often said that 90-plus percent of all the scientists who have ever lived are alive today. Of these the overwhelming majority take organic evolution to be a fact.[3] However, a poll of these experts would almost certainly indicate that many, if not most, of this majority also believe in a deity, at least in a vague (i.e., deistic) way. It is not now and never has been the business of science to prove that the universe is definitely not an artifact, nor does science prove that the universe can have had no artificer. Theistic metaphysics is logically possible, even respectable, provided that it is neither self-contradictory nor based on known falsehoods. In short, scientists who take evolution to be factual can study and attempt to explain nature on its own terms and still, in personal faith, relate the whole of it to the presumed purposes of an artificer. As long as one limits oneself to that which is beyond all possibility of falsification, one can say of the universe whatever one wants to say of it. One such saying is that it is the way it is, because this is the way it was *meant* to be. In this fashion an overarching teleology can be married to science without inconsistency. Many scientists, including biologists, are, in fact, religious, being in personal faith teleologists of the deistic sort indicated. Why is this not good enough for the "Scientific Creationists"? Why do they demand much more? Why cannot people be evolutionists and Christians at the same time?

What is true of theistic scientists is also true of millions of theists who are not scientists. During the past 130 years, educated theists have found it not only possible but agreeable to their faith to believe in intelligent design metaphysically and also in the evolutionary descent of all organisms physically.[4] Since there are multitudes of people, scientists and nonscientists alike, Jews, Christians, and others who believe evolution to be a fact while also believing in the "divine origin" of (and purpose for) the universe, why do our authors pretend that this is not so? Why do they try to make it seem that "intelligent design" and "evolutionary descent" must, logically, exclude one another? Clearly, they do not. What are the "Scientific Creationists" trying to conceal? To answer this we must take a peek at the secret agenda of the kind of people who write such books as *Pandas*.

To the fatherhood of the Bible-god, a dogma proclaimed by Jews and Christians alike, and to the "redeeming mission" of Christ, a dogma proclaimed by Christians alone, our authors add another dogma as essential to true religion, but do not state it categorically. This other dogma is the doctrine of biblical inerrancy or infallibility. There are, in fact, millions of American Christians who contend (in faith) that the Bible contains the dictates of the one true deity and that these dictates have been handed down essentially free of error, in all fundamental matters at least. To the biblical inerrantist, what the Bible says is absolutely true not merely in religion and sacred history but in science too. Moreover, whatever contradicts the Bible is of necessity false, no matter how up-to-date or scientific. Since the Bible does not teach evolution in any of its creation narratives (Genesis 1:1–2:4a, 2:4b–25; Proverbs 8:12–36; Psalms, 74:13–14, 89:10–11; Isaiah 51:9–10; 2 Peter 3:5–13) or elsewhere and since Darwin's *The Origin of Species* does teach evolution, the latter must be wrong, perhaps even demonically inspired. To the "Scientific Creationist," this is not a matter for inquiry. It is, rather, the logical outcome of taking the dogma of biblical inerrancy on faith and faith alone. Chapter 4 shows that the Bible does not require this doctrine of Christians. In so doing it shows that the "Scientific Creationists" have deluded themselves.

It would be insufficient and perhaps counterproductive for a book such as *Pandas* to lay all of its cards on the table at the outset. The reasons are two: First, it will just not do in today's world to say that evolution never occurred, simply because the Bible does not say that it did. *Pandas* announces, to the contrary, that all *kinds* of living things came into being suddenly and recently (Gen. 1:24). Second, neither will it do to announce openly that all Jews and Christians who accept evolution are apostates and that the only true Christians (i.e., the only people who are candidates for salvation) are biblical inerrantists. Yet this is almost certainly what the authors of *Pandas* believe.

Respecting the first point, the ploy is to contend that no data (from biology, geology, paleontology, etc.) confirm anybody's theory of evolution. According to the "Scientific Creationists," evolution has to be seen happening to be believed. Since such observation, presumably, has never occurred (in nature, outside a laboratory), evolution is a nonevent, a mere article of faith. According to the "Scientific Creationists," the data at issue, when properly understood, confirm their own position. This, of course, is a position concerning origins that just happens to be consistent, if not identical, with the biblical view of creation. The biblical view, it must be remembered, is of a creation recent and static. The general run of theists, however, would have no reason to require creation to be recent. To them it could have happened an indefinitely long time ago.

Respecting the second point above, the ploy of the "Scientific Creationists" is to ignore all religious people who are evolutionists and to claim, when pressed, that biblical inerrantists are the only true Christians. Christians who espouse evolution are taken to be apostates by the "Scientific Creationists." So much for the hidden agenda, which explains why "intelligent design" and evolutionary descent must be taken to be antagonistic to one another, when in point of fact they are not.

* * *

To its initial question-begging approach and to the false antithesis it sets up (explained immediately above), *Pandas* falls into muddles involving reasoning by analogy. This is a method of reasoning involving likenesses between what are taken to be analogues. The problem is to decide when the two entities or processes being proposed as analogues are sufficiently alike to warrant further reasoning based on their alleged likenesses. Reasoning by analogy is commonplace and often insightful but never valid in the strict sense of the word. The authors say (p. 149), "We saw how biological structures exhibit the characteristics of manufactured things." The intent of this assertion is to establish the following analogy: As the intelligent human is to manufactured things, so ——— is to nature (or the universe) which shows the same kind of objective intelligence. Carefully avoiding the word spelled with a capital "g," a lower case "o," and a lower case "d," our authors fill the blank above with 'intelligent designer.' They seem to think that in this way they can avoid the charge of introducing religion and the supernatural into their supplemental text for science students. They are, however, mistaken.

At this point a thought experiment may help. Let us imagine that we have acquired a spaceship that can greatly exceed the speed of light. Let us also imagine that techniques for putting people into suspended animation and bringing them out again after a long time in space are well-advanced, effective, and safe. The object of this prologue is to help us imagine that we have sped so far beyond all galaxies, quasi-stellar objects, nebulae, etc., that we can look back at what we have left behind to see *what it is like*. Let us imagine further that we have not only sped beyond the still-expanding universe but that we can circumnavigate it, so to speak, so as to determine what the universe is like—seen whole and from the outside. Indeed, what might it be like? Would it be like anything in our experience? Would it even vaguely resemble any work of human art or artifice? To use a biblical analogy, would the universe as a whole be like something ceramic a potter might have thrown, shaped, fired, and glazed (see Isa. 45:9, 64:8)? Would a slice of it (or a whole galaxy from it) be like a shard of pottery, so to speak? Those who smash atoms for a living cannot be depended on to see in the debris thereof the hand of a wise and benign potter. Some may have such faith; others most certainly do not.

We have, doubtless, all heard of the theologian who went walking on a meadow one day only to find a watch lying before him in the grass.[5] Closely examining the fabrication and function of his discovery and recognizing that such things do not grow from seeds or on trees, the bishop quite rightly discerned (he did not infer anything at all) that what he had found was a human artifact. The question is this: What would it be like to come upon the universe, suitably shrunk, lying in the grass of one of its own meadows? It would be impossible to tell, because the universe, no matter how miniaturized for our convenience, could hardly lie in the grass of one of its own meadows awaiting discovery by one of its own conscious, organic parts. Since human beings *do not know* what the universe is like, if anything at all, we are prevented, logically, from likening it to anything within itself. By the same token, it may be as a whole (and most likely is) radically different from any of its parts. Except insofar as human art imitates life and technology imitates nature, *Pandas* cannot maintain that biological structures and manufactured goods exhibit the same characteristics for identical reasons (or purposes). It tries in vain to do this.

Even if *Pandas* could maintain that manufactured goods and objects in nature resemble one another enough to use analogical reasoning, the results might be far less than happy. People who resort to analogical reasoning may find themselves paying a much higher price than they had bargained on. Consider the following analogy: As lack of knowledge and skill in human artificers stand in relation to the works of their hands, all of which are less than perfect, so ——— stands in relation to the creation of animals, none of which is perfect—as can easily be seen in the case of *Homo sapiens*. *Pandas* would have us fill the blank above with 'intelligent designer.' But just how intelligent, how competent, and just how much like the all-knowing potter in the theology of the biblical inerrantist? The Scottish philosopher David Hume wreaked havoc on this kind of analogical thinking when he wrote the following:

> This world, for aught he [any theist] knows, is very faulty and imperfect, compared to a superior standard, and was only the first rude essay of some infant deity who afterwards abandoned it, ashamed of his lame performance; [or] it is the work only of some dependent, inferior deity, and is the object of derision to his superiors; [or] it is the production of old age and dotage in some superannuated deity, and ever since his death has run on at adventures from the first impulse and active force which it received from him.[6]

Hume concludes his observations by saying, "And I cannot, for my part, think that so wild and unsettled a system of theology is, in any respect, preferable to none at all." Our authors cannot abide the thought that no theology at all is preferable to the "wild and unsettled" speculation they would foist upon school children.

Apparently unaware of the perils of analogical reasoning, our authors assert (p. 6) that there are two kinds of causes, "natural" and "intelligent." Then (on p. 7) they continue as follows:

> To say that DNA and protein arose by natural causes, as evolution does, is to say complex, coded messages arose by natural causes. It is akin to saying "John loves Mary" [written in the sand] arose from the interaction of the waves, or from the interaction of the grains of sand. . . . [S]cience tells us that the message encoded in DNA [which is like Morse Code, p. 6] must have originated from an intelligent cause.

What science is asserted above to tell us about the similarity of DNA and the Morse Code should come as a great surprise to many scientists. However, the problem posed here for the "Scientific Creationists" is greater than their misstatement of the fact about the likeness between DNA and Morse Code. What human beings call intelligence, whether in animals or in ourselves, is always found in the most intimate association with some living brain or other, its nervous system, and a supporting body. A mind can be lost without the annihilation of its brain, but any time a brain is destroyed, so too is its mind, as far as anybody can tell. Accordingly, if we argue that somebody named John stands to, "John loves Mary," as ——— stands to the creation of DNA, and if we fill the blank above with 'intelligent cause,' then we must ask where the intelligent cause's brain, supporting nervous system, and body are to be found. We know nothing of disembodied minds nor of deeds they might do. Only embodied minds can be shown to exist or to do anything. Would our authors have us believe that the 'intelligent cause' they speak of is physical? Would they say that the Bible-god has a brain, a supporting nervous system, and a body? Probably not, for that would not suit their Christian theology very well.

Furthermore, the John who wrote, "John loves Mary," would appear to have emotions and to be a person, but we know of no person not socialized by other persons. Even the feral children of India were said to have lived with wolves, a most sociable species indeed. Are we to believe that a *family* of intelligent causes exists or is responsible for the universe, including DNA and the man named Morse who invented the code bearing his name? If so, we have fallen into Hume's clutches again. To refuse to recognize that the natural and the intelligent are not to be set at odds in every way and to refuse to recognize that intelligence, as we experience it, is also natural is to open a can of worms.

In what might, loosely speaking, be called its more philosophical passages, *Pandas* compounds its logical blunders by failing to clarify what it means by the following terms: (1) "mere probability" as opposed to "intelligent design" (preface, viii), (2) the "spontaneous" organization of particles of sand to spell out a message (preface, ix), and (3) the "chance production" of biological structures (p. 149). It is one thing to contend that there are no uncaused events or happenings in nature. It is a very different thing to declare that some events occur without needing a sufficient cause or without requiring any necessary conditions. This would be what philosophers call an acausal (or noncausal) position.[7] It is a third thing to take no stand on either of the foregoing but simply to muddle the two. This is what *Pandas* does. When contrasting what it calls "the opposing explanations of *natural* or *evolutionary* descent and *intelligent design*," *Pandas* seems to be giving two alternatives each of which would be *equally causal* in its mode(s) of operation. However, when upholding its favored explanation of nature (i.e., "intelligent design") it never opts for acausality for obvious reasons, but when degrading the natural or evolutionary explanation, it revels in such terms as "chance production" or "mere probability," just as though these were causal agents but of an inferior sort to the causality of an "intelligent designer." It cannot be emphasized too strongly that chance and probability are not causal agents of an inferior sort, nor of any sort whatsoever for that matter.

To illustrate the muddle here, imagine a person who appears to have an infectious disease. This person goes to a physician who, after appropriate tests, announces that he/she can do nothing for the invalid because the infectious disease at issue was caused neither by a bacterial, nor a viral, nor any other known agent but, rather, by chance, as though chance itself were a pathogen of some weird sort.[8] To fail to distinguish between chance as an agent and chance as inadvertence or misadventure is to sow the seeds of confusion. Chance refers neither to a concept of causality in modern thought nor to an agent, or kind of agent. Chance has to do with randomness, with unpredictability, or with lack of intention. *Pandas* seems not to know this.

Take another example. You have gone for a drive on a country road and come up behind an old truck whose nameplate and logo are missing. You begin to speculate as to its make. Is it a Chevrolet, a Ford, perhaps a Dodge, or maybe an International, or could it be a Volvo, or even a Mercedes, or what? If mathematically inclined, you may enjoy trying to calculate the probabilities involved with the different makes. Finally you pass the truck hoping to identify it in your rearview mirror. Failing this, you flag the driver down and take a closer look. You are astounded to learn that it is a Reo, an antique Reo, a truck invented by R. E. Olds, a man whose name is familiar to us from the "Oldsmobile." Imagine the probabilities nowadays against coming upon a truck whose kind was never very numerous and whose manufacturer went out of business in the 1940s. They would be astronomical, but what force would these probabilities have against an actual Reo truck still in use? None whatsoever. The universe is filled with things and happenings that are most improbable from a human perspective or rare as we predict such things or happenings. Lack of probability, however, does not prevent the existence of anything that exists nor does overwhelming probability cause anything to be that has being or to happen that happens. *Pandas* never makes these important points.

The terms "spontaneous" and "spontaneously" get the same kind of confused treatment. If, on the one hand, a person were to claim that hydrogen atoms are spontaneously popping into existence throughout the universe at various, unpredictable times and were to mean by this that the atoms in question issue from no source and have no cause, that would be one position, a position denying causation. If, on the other hand, a mass of vegetable matter were said to have been ignited by spontaneous combustion, this would be quite a different kind of contention. In the latter case one would not be denying causation at all or holding it in any doubt. All one would be saying is that no external agency ignited the vegetable matter in question. *Pandas* never bothers to get straight on the various meanings of 'spontaneous.'

Ralph Alpher, a distinguished American scientist, once wrote on the topic of "Theology and the Big Bang." Here is some of what he said:

I would also reject the argument put forth by many fundamentalists that science has nothing to do with religion because God is not among the things making up the business of science. It is, in fact, the ultimate job of science to understand the universe in which we live. Surely if a necessity for a god-concept in the universe ever turns up, that necessity will become evident to the scientist. Meanwhile it seems to me to be undignified and unworthy to hide the sum total of our ignorance in a god-concept.[9]

To conclude, science has never needed and does not now use or in any way rely on a divine constant, so to speak, in any of its research strategies or protocols for testing hypotheses. To fail to represent science to school children as it really is or to misrepresent it, as the "Scientific Creationists" do repeatedly, is to foist a fraud upon them. *Pandas* is a fraud of the sort at issue and belongs in no classroom anywhere, but on the rubbish heap.[10]

Notes

1. The circumstances surrounding the writing of *Pandas* were very odd. Its forthcoming birth was announced in National Center for Science Education *Reports* 9, no. 2 (March–April 1989): 21. See also the same journal, 9, no. 6 (November–December 1989): 5–7, and 10, no. 1 (January–February 1990): 3 and 8. The latter two entries tell the story of its short life. For more, including an outright accusation of fraud on the part of *Pandas*, see footnote 10 below. California and Texas are bellwether states because their text adoptions are statewide, and their student populations are very large, guaranteeing lucrative markets. Hence textbook publishers pay close attention to what is acceptable in those two states.

2. Einstein said, "The most incomprehensible thing about the world is that it is so comprehensible." These words appear on a poster in the office of a colleague of mine who is a physicist. But, alas, she does not know the exact source of the quotation, I do not know it, and any number of scientists whom I asked for help in tracking it down do not know where it first appeared. It is, however, common knowledge that he said it.

3. Whenever biology comes up, it is not too much to say that all the leading universities of the world, together with all the leading research institutions, accept evolution as a fact. Exactly how the process(es) happens is still open to dispute and continued theorizing.

4. See C. E. Raven, *Science, Religion and the Future* (New York: Cambridge University Press, 1943).

5. William Paley, *Evidence of the Existence and Attributes of the Deity* (1802), quoted in E. D. Klemke (ed.), *To Believe or Not to Believe* (New York: Harcourt Brace and Jovanovich College Publishers, 1992): 32, and in numerous other anthologies in the philosophy of religion.

6. David Hume, *Works*, vol. 2, *Dialogues Concerning Natural Religion*, end of Part V (Scientia Verlag Aalen, 1964).

7. Acausality is one interpretation given (in the 1940s) to the alleged spontaneous appearance (and disappearance) of hydrogen atoms in the "steady-state" theory of the universe popularized by the British astronomer, Fred Hoyle. See Isaac Asimov's *Guide to Science* (New York: Basic Books, 1960): 56.

8. I would like to attribute this example to the Princeton philosopher, Leger Wood,

but look though I may, I cannot find the original reference, a reference that goes back twenty-five years. In any case, I cannot claim originality for it.

9. *Religious Humanism* 17, no. 1 (Winter 1983): 12.

10. William J. Bennetta, in his article, "Fundamentalists Launch Bogus 'Supplemental Text,' " *The Textbook Letter* (March-April 1990): 1 and 11, suggests fraud on a grand scale in producing *Pandas*. The academic credentials of the authors, Percival Davis and Dean H. Kenyon, are not given, nor those of the academic editor, Charles B. Thaxton, nor is any of the three listed in *American Men & Women of Science*. To continue, the publisher Haughton Publishing Company does not appear in *Literary Market Place*, "a comprehensive guide to book publishers operating in the United States." Moreover, the publisher does not own the rights to the book but, rather, the Foundation for Thought and Ethics of Richardson, Texas, an organization that promotes creationism. Curiouser and curiouser, Bennetta found that the publisher seems chiefly to be in the business of "printing agricultural labels and catalogs plus a magazine for operators of cotton gins." Finally, no critical reviews produced by legitimate experts in the field have ever been produced. At the time of writing this article, Bennetta was the president of the California Textbook League and a member of the California Academy of Sciences. Although I concur fully with his belief in the fraudulent nature of the book in question, I wanted to avoid such charges until now in favor of a straightforward analysis of how *Pandas* convicts itself because of its logical blunders. Even if its authors were completely innocent, these errors would convict their book.

6

Science, Creationism, and the Constitution

Introduction

On March 17, 1983, a symposium was held at the Florida State University in Tallahassee during the Southeastern Sectional Meetings of the Geological Society of America. The symposium was called "The Evolution-Creation Controversy: Perspectives on Religion, Philosophy, Science and Education." One of the co-convenors was my colleague, Robert A. Gastaldo, Ph.D., Professor of Geology at Auburn University. Respecting the symposium's purpose, Professor Gastaldo wrote, "This symposium was designed to introduce colleagues in the southeast of the untenability of 'creation science' over a spectrum of disciplines and subdisciplines in, and relevant to, the geological sciences. In this way it was hoped that colleagues would become better aware of 'creationist' arguments and become motivated to involve themselves in the controversy at the state and local levels."

The proceedings of the symposium were published in the form of a handbook by the Paleontological Society, Special Publication, no. 1, 1984, edited by Kenneth R. Walker, and produced at the University of Tennessee. These proceedings were not copyrighted.

My solicited contribution, "Science, Creationism, and the Constitution," was one of ten papers presented at this symposium. It has been edited slightly and updated here and there for inclusion in this book. Although now a decade old, it remains as true today, I believe, as when it was first written. It will become clear in the following pages that, religiously speaking, the Constitution is not the kind of document Fundagelicals in general and

"Scientific Creationists" in particular would like it to be. Nor is it the kind of document they would like the average American to take it to be. The Constitution's total secularity, however, has not been able to shield science education from concerted attacks on it by Fundagelicals. Our Founding Fathers did not foresee the extent to which advancing science might threaten religious belief, nor did they envision the degree to which religious forces might attempt to make science into an ideology inimical to certain manifestations, at least, of religion.

* * *

It pleases many Americans to believe that our government is founded on Christianity. However, the Treaty of Tripoli of 1797 states:

> As the government of the United States of America is not in any sense founded on the Christian religion,—as it has in itself no character of enmity against the laws, religion or tranquility of Musselmen [i.e., Muslims],—and as the said States never have entered into any war or act of hostility against any Mehomitan [Muhammedan] nation, it is declared by the parties that no pretext arising from religious opinion shall ever produce an interruption of the harmony existing between the two countries.[1]

By what the Constitution *does not say* makes the same point. Its Preamble aims exclusively at secular goals in aiming "to form a more perfect union, establish justice, insure domestic tranquility, provide for the common defense, promote the general welfare, and secure the blessings of liberty to ourselves and our posterity." Moreover, the main body of the Constitution does not name, presuppose, nor acknowledge any deity. Neither does it mention nor acknowledge any divine law above the laws passed by Congress and upheld by the Supreme Court. Futhermore, the Constitution utilizes neither biblical language nor theological concepts. Finally, neither prayer nor any ritual act is mentioned or recommended. In short, this thoroughly secular instrument of government has nothing to do with a kingdom not of this world.

The only time the word 'religious' appears (Article VI) is in a passage prohibiting any religious test for office holding. Likewise, the world 'religion' appears but once and then in a generic sense. The First Amendment states, "Congress shall make no law respecting an establishment of religion, or prohibiting the free exercise thereof. . . ." The Supreme Court has taken this to mean that no branch of American government may promote religion, or any aspect thereof, nor detract from religion or impede any citizen's belief therein.[2]

The Constitution (Article I, Section 8) says that Congress shall have the power to "promote the progress of science and useful arts by securing for limited times to authors and inventors the exclusive right to their respective writings and discoveries. . . ." But nowhere does it mandate a public school system or other mechanism for advancing science. Of the two, religion fares better constitutionally than science, for the free exercise of religion *must* be protected, whereas Congress (and by extension other branches of government) may or may not promote science. Let us ask what the constitutional remedy might be if an arm of government were to detract from religion or to infringe upon its free exercise by promoting science or science education. This is not an idle question. We are in the midst of such an entanglement now (see also chapters 7 and 10).[3]

Stephen Jay Gould spoke for multitudes when he wrote, "True science and religion are not in conflict."[4] As already noted (in chapter 1), it must be assumed that he meant that true science and *true* religion do not conflict. If so, he can only mean by true religion faith in an overarching cosmic purpose (or telos, for which the word 'teleology' is derived) that is permanently compatible with advancing science and in no danger of being disconfirmed by it. Expressed this way, true science and true religion (which can only be deism) do not conflict, but *real science* and *real religion* have often conflicted, conflict now, and will continue to conflict. It must be noted that our Constitution does not recognize *true* religion or *false* religion; it speaks merely of religion. Thus, should conflicts arise in our country between science and religion, we are left no alternative, legal or otherwise, but to contend with some *real religion* or other.

The resurgent religion we now confront in our schools, libraries, and courts is one in which faith in biblical inerrancy is as important a doctrine as is belief in the Bible-god's creation of the universe and/or trust in the presumed redemption of Jesus Christ as preached in Christianity. Its adherents are not content, as religious liberals may be, with confidence in an overarching divine purpose or final cause. Inerrantists also believe in a deity who busied (and still busies) himself with efficient causes. In synopsis, he made heaven and earth in a day. He made light, vegetation, sun, moon, and stars. He made birds, fish, and land animals. Then he ravaged his newly created earth with a cataclysmic flood and began again with a human remnant. Eventually, he gave his Law and, thus, laid down an absolute morality for his people. Subsequently, he often intervened in the affairs of men and nations and performed abundant miracles, singularities with which science cannot deal (see for example Gen. 1:1–2:4a; Exod. 19:16–20:17; Isa. 10:5–6, 44:28, representative of countless other passages).

Although belief in "divine" purpose of the most general sort is logically compatible with science (even with Darwinism), scientific progress often attenuates this belief.[5] For example, consider biblical faith in relation to the following: Not only does modern astrophysics not confirm the existence of any deity, it tells a very different story than does Genesis. So it is with geology, which knows nothing of a "divine" act in creating this earth a scant ten thousand years ago, or of the Noachian deluge. Or consider the biological sciences, which know nothing of the six days of biblical creation with their topsy-turvy order of life forms (see chapter 2) but much about the eons of organic evolution. Modern anthropology and linguistics also tell different stories than does the Bible. As for absolute moral law, science knows nothing of it. In view of this procession of negativities, one can confidently predict that the attenuation already noted will go on. Biblical literalists, such as the "Scientific Creationists," are (and can only be) profoundly aggrieved by this.

In scientifically inspired notions of cosmic, planetary, and biological evolution, "Scientific Creationists" perceive satanic threats to true religion.[6] In keeping with their trust in scriptural inerrancy, they view these ideas not merely as nonbiblical, but as *antibiblical*. Accordingly, they must do what they can to impede or destroy these (to them) perfidious ideas, especially in public schools and libraries. The potential consequences of their various legal and extralegal attacks on evolution and concepts thereof are as ominous to science and science education as they are vast. At least one planetary astronomer has asserted that the creationist threat to astronomy is at least as great as it is to the biological sciences. He estimated that were it true, he would have to delete 50 percent of the content of his introductory course in astronomy.[7] Geologists and paleontologists involved in classroom teaching hardly need this author to tell them how much of their course content (including radiometric dating techniques) would also have to go. The same would be true of much in anthropology, archaeology, and to a lesser but still significant degree in linguistics. In Alabama a textbook was banned because it said that language developed over long centuries in the old Stone Age. This was done because Genesis 2:4b and 19 tell us that Adam was able to name all the animals on the day of creation itself.[8]

A Gallup poll taken in 1991 showed that 47 percent of Americans believe that the Bible-god made human beings less than ten thousand years ago, essentially as we now are.[9] Another 40 percent believe that the Bible-god created us during millions of years of evolution. Suppose that some or all of the 40 percent who have reconciled themselves to evolution were to become progressively aggrieved by what are, or at least are perceived to be, scientific developments casting doubt on their favorite religious themes. For example, suppose that powerful new evidence in chemistry were to support the abiogenesis of all life (i.e., its emergence from nonliving materials), or that future research in genetics were to question the Bible-god's purposiveness (as some think it already has),[10] or that ethology were to confirm that humans are aggressive by nature, not by nurture and deliberate choice. In short, suppose that the process of attenuating religious beliefs were to continue alarmingly and were even to alienate many religious liberals from science. A case in point appeared in a popular news magazine in an article entitled, "How the Brain Works."[11] The authors note, "Now some neuroscientists are beginning to suspect that everything that makes people human is no more than an interaction of chemicals and electricity inside the labyrinthine folds of the brain." At another point, the authors quote the eminent Dr. Paul MacLean of the National Institute of Mental Health to the effect "that the raw stuff (even) of emotion is built into the circuitry of the brain." Such ideas as these are a sword of Damocles hanging over the traditional ideas of free will, the soul, and the mind (as an entity in its own right) distinct from the brain, ideas cherished by the general run of religious people, including well-educated liberals, ideas in whose defense they will fight strenuously.

That has already happened with the 47 percent who believe in recent creation by divine fiat. Religious rightists who maintain that view have tried repeatedly to pass legislation mandating "balanced treatment for the scientific creation model of origins" (i.e., for the scenario based on a literal reading of the account in Genesis), if and when evolution is taught in the public schools. In the important case of *McLean* v. *Arkansas Board of Education* (1982), District Judge William R. Overton made two points worth noting here.[12] First, "The two-model approach of the creationists is simply a contrived dualism which has no scientific factual basis or legitimate educational purpose." Second, "The defendant argues that the teaching of evolution alone presents both a free exercise problem and an establishment problem [in reference to the First Amendment] which can only be redressed by giving balanced treatment to creation science, which is admittedly consistent with some religious beliefs." Judge Overton was not persuaded (see chapter 3, n.7).

Despite this ruling, which gave hope to scientists and science educators (at the time), it was to become clear that another reason for concern existed, a reason that has not dissipated with the passing of the 1980s. The concern is that courts will involve themselves in deciding what is and what is not science, a task for which they are clearly not qualified.[13] An example of (if not the full extent of) court involvement can be seen in a suit filed in U.S. District Court in Mobile, Alabama, in June of 1982 (see also chapter 7). There a local attorney asked that teachers be restrained from "maintaining or allowing the maintenance of regular religious prayer services or other forms of religious observances" in the Mobile public schools. He then broadened his complaint to include the (at that time) new Alabama prayer law, also of 1982.[14] U.S. District Court Judge W. Brevard Hand, before whom these cases came, encouraged prayer advocates with his observation to the press that "the religions of atheism, materialism, agnosticism, communism, and socialism have escaped the scrutiny of the courts throughout the years, and make no mistake these are to the believers religions; they are ardently adhered to and quantitatively advanced in the teaching and literature that is presented to the fertile minds of students in the various school systems."[15]

That a federal district judge should entertain such muddled notions was alarming at the time (and remains alarming), for it is patently absurd to take agnosticism to be a religion. Atheism (in the sense of an affirmative declaration of the nonexistence of any god) does contain an element of faith, but it does not divide the world into the sacred and the profane as does religion. What kind of religion, we may well ask, recognizes nothing sacred? Much the same can be said of philosophical materialism, but having mentioned it, why should Judge Hand not have included naturalism? Ignorance is the most likely reason. In any case the physical sciences operate on naturalistic assumptions. They also proceed agnostically in that they question both *a priori* notions (i.e., notions formed prior to or apart from experience) and opinions based on authority. Moreover, they systematically question their hypotheses through rigorous testing until one, having survived probing attempts at disconfirmation, eventually emerges as the closest approximation to the truth thus far attained about whatever is at issue. In light of this, does Judge Hand, perhaps, believe that science is religious or a species of religion? Do other federal judges believe such nonsense? Could a Supreme Court justice believe it? A careful reading of Justice Scalia's dissent in *Edwards* v. *Aguillard* leaves one fearing that the answer is yes (see chapter 10).[16]

Yes to this question is what "Scientific Creationists" yearn to hear from the High Court, if not now, then in the not-too-distant future. Defining true religion to suit themselves (being sure to include scriptural inerrancy and to leave religious liberals out) in just such a way that true religion and true science do not and cannot conflict, "Scientific Creationists" have contended all along that when evolution is taught in the public schools, it is not science that is being taught but "the religion of secular humanism" (see the Introduction for a characterization of secular humanism). Judge Hand's comments indicate that he subscribes to this view. How would science fare, one wonders, if as many as five justices of the Supreme Court were at some future time to adopt this viewpoint? One trend to be feared here is that of ideologizing science, of emphasizing its philosophical assumptions, and then of transmuting these into religion or quasi-religion.

Currently, "Scientific Creationists" have been stopped legally in trying to make evolution seem to be a doctrine of the "godless religion of secular humanism."[17] In short, to put it in legal terms, whenever religion is taught in the public schools, the state is innocent of establishing religion. Hence, there is no justification for neutralizing such teaching through balanced treatment by permitting "Scientific Creationism" to be taught. The "Scientific Creationists," however, have also tried to make a free-exercise-of-religion issue out of their position. It is worth the time to understand how this argument goes, because at some future time, depending on the make-up of the High Court, the argument may be trundled out again and become appealing.

Wendell R. Bird, an attorney, once wrote on behalf of the "Scientific Creationists" as follows:

> Exclusive public school instruction in the general theory (of evolution) burdens free exercise. It can undermine religious belief in creation and can inculcate a contrary belief. It can violate separatist practices of creationist religions. Exclusive instruction also can compel unconscionable declarations of belief, because creationist individuals object to affirmation of the general theory for test questions or class discussion. These restraints become substantial through operation of the various forms of coercion present in public schools.[18]

To burden the free exercise of religion to this extent, attorney Bird thinks the state must have a *compelling* interest in the reason for the burden imposed on dissenting believers of whatever stripe.[19] What, he wonders, is the state's compelling interest in teaching anything about the origins of the universe, the earth, or life? Reading, writing, arithmetic, and civics can be taught with no reference to origins—as can much of science.

Bird identifies three legally acceptable ways of alleviating this alleged burden: (1) exemption of students from hearing, reading, or responding to anything hostile to their religion(s); (2) neutralization of offensive materials by balanced treatment for contrary but acceptable views; and (3) elimination of the offensive materials from courses or curricula. Bird rejects the first as unworkable in this case, and Judge Overton's ruling (mentioned above) rejects the second, denying the need for neutralization through balanced treatment for "Creation Science." That leaves the third alternative, the elimination of course content deemed offensive because of its hostility, or perceived hostility, to the religious persuasions represented in the public schools. Bird writes, "The state has authority to remove instruction in a particular topic (such as sex education) from a public school's course." Says he:

The state furthermore holds power to eliminate teaching in the academic disciplines from public school curricula. The Constitution does not require states to institute public schools. Upon creating public education government may choose not to present some areas of human knowledge, and indeed must. After presenting a discipline the state can decide to cease teaching it.[20]

To the question, Is teaching evolution in the public schools worth the bother? some may answer no. To a considerable extent, elimination of offensive materials respecting origins is already occurring by extralegal means as textbook publishers cave in to the pressures applied by the Fundagelicals. At various times Texas has been a bellwether state in this regard.[21] Why not just cooperate with the compliant revisers of textbooks and help remove anything and everything from texts, public school courses, and curricula inconsistent with a literal reading of the Jewish scriptures, the Christian scriptures, the Muslim scriptures, or any other scriptures believed in by any public school child? A news item once quoted some self-styled "creationist extremists" as follows: "Heliocentricity, or general Copernicanism, is an anti-biblical notion and is the precursor of Darwinism."[22] What better way to begin educating twentieth-century school children than by making them go back to Ptolemy? The "Scientific Creationists" are more than happy to pay this price, if only they can get to live forever in bliss (or to save their souls as they might prefer to put it).

Despite the efforts of peacemakers who would reconcile all differences amicably, some areas of *real science* (the sort of thing Gould has in mind when he talks about true science) and some elements of *real religion* (the very thing being peddled by the "Scientific Creationists") are now in *real conflict* in the United States and have been since the 1960s in particular, nor is any end in sight. Powerful social forces (religious, scientific, and political) will see to that. Since the Constitution is secular, science and science education might have been expected to fare better therein than they have, but the Founding Fathers did not foresee how ideologically sensitive future science would become. Aware on the one hand of the value of religion (and its free exercise) to our society and on the other of the evils that can occur when government and religion become excessively entangled, they focused their efforts on trying to find a lasting constitutional solution of church/state relations. Largely, they succeeded, but not altogether, and, so, we must now try to find our way without their guidance.

The "Scientific Creationists" have revealed just how inimical science and their brand of religion can be and have in the process impaled us on the horns of a dilemma. If we introduce public school children to modern science, we introduce them to ideas of cosmic, planetary, and biological evolution. These ideas are not merely contrary to creationist religion but are also perceived as hostile to it (see chapter 7). Note well, the First Amendment has been interpreted to mean that the public schools may not be hostile to religion.[23] If to treat religion neutrally we expunge from the schools everything scientific that conflicts (or might conflict) with a religion of scriptural literalism, then at many points we must, indeed, go back to Ptolemy, and beyond. To do this would not only make us the laughingstock of the technically advanced world (something we might learn to bear) but could also cripple us in scientific and economic competition.[24] Again, not too high a price to pay for those bent on saving what they take to be their souls and who can see no other way than to believe in biblical inerrancy! To make matters worse, denying an introduction to the basic scientific ideas of our time would have the same effect as lying to children by deliberately keeping them in ignorance.[25] In no case would such treatment enhance their cultural literacy.

If my readers believe as I do that the removal of much of modern science from the public school curricula is too high a price to pay to resolve our dilemma, then certain prescriptions as to what to do may be in order. First, concerned citizens, professional educators, scientists, and professional scientific and educational organizations must become involved in ways both massive and vital in matters involving curriculum development in order to strengthen science education across the board in public education. Second, we should do all in our power to guarantee and enhance the academic freedom and integrity of science teachers in primary and secondary education. Third, we should attempt to create a more favorable climate for the acceptance of science by the American people. Since compromise in solving the dilemma at issue is, for all practical purposes, impossible, let us now choose up sides and prepare to fight.

Notes

1. H. Miller (ed.), *Treaties and Other International Acts of the United States* (Washington, D.C.: U.S. Government Printing Office), 2: 365. See also Rob Boston, "Myths and Mischief," *Church & State* (March 1992): 10.

2. *Epperson et al. v. Arkansas*, 393 U.S. 103–104 (1968). Herein, the Court quoted *Watson v. Jones*, 13 Wall 679, 728 (1872) as follows: "The law knows no heresy, and is committed to the support of no dogma, the establishment of no sect." By virtue of knowing no heresy, the law can know no orthodoxy either, yet Chief Justice Burger in *Lynch, Mayor of Pawtucket et al v. Donnelly et al.* 465 U.S. 668, 673 (1984) wrote for the Court as follows: "Nor does the Constitution require complete separation of church and state; it affirmatively mandates accommodation, not merely tolerance, of all religions, and forbids hostility toward any." At 683 he also wrote, "We can assume, *arguendo*, that the display [of a Nativity scene in a public park] advances religion in a sense; but our precedents plainly

contemplate that on occasion some advancement of religion will result from governmental action." Strict separationists in constitutional issues involving church/state have reason to worry about the accommodationism of the Burger Court and now of the Rehnquist Court.

3. Wendell R. Bird, "Freedom of Religion and Science Instruction in Public Schools," *Yale Law Review* 87 (1978).

4. "Genesis vs. Geology," *The Atlantic* (September 1982): 14.

5. John Stuart Mill, "Theism," in *Collected Works* (Toronto: University of Toronto Press, 1969), vol. 10: 432, 450.

6. Henry M. Morris, *The Twilight of Evolution* (Grand Rapids, Mich.: Baker Book House, 1964): 93.

7. D. Morrison, "Astronomy and Creationism: The Evolving Universe," *The Skeptical Inquirer* 7, no. 1 (Fall 1987): 5-7.

8. M. Perry, "Banning a Textbook," *The New York Times* (May 31, 1981).

9. *U.S. News & World Report*, in its issue of December 23, 1991, carried the results of a recent Gallup poll containing these percentages. Compare these with those in a Gallup Poll released on August 29, 1982, which showed that 44 percent of Americans believed in the recent creation of human beings by the Bible-god, and 38 percent believed in the creative activity of this deity but using the mechanisms of evolution.

10. Peter B. and Jean S. Medawar, *The Life Science* (New York: Harper and Row, 1977): 17. Also see Richard Dawkins, *The Blind Watchmaker* (New York: W. W. Norton and Company, 1986), the entire volume (see also chapter 10).

11. *Newsweek* (February 7, 1983), especially pp. 40, 43. *Newsweek* has returned to a similar subject in its article, "Is the Mind an Illusion?" in the issue of April 20, 1992: 71-72. At one point (p. 71), this article asks, "If we are essentially defined by neurons, what about the little matter of soul?" To suggest as this article does that the human mind is an illusion because it is a function of the brain is to suggest that sights, sounds, scents, and tastes are illusions, because they are functions of eyes, ears, noses, and tongues respectively. Those who write for *Newsweek* are not quite up to the task of writing intelligibly on the subject of contemporary philosophy of mind. In the same issue, pp. 66-70, there appears an article entitled "Mapping the Brain."

12. The full title is *Rev. Bill McLean et al.* v. *The Arkansas Board of Education et al.*, DC ARK 529 FSupp 1255.

13. Robert M. O'Neil, "Creationism, Curriculum and the Constitution," *Akademe* (March-April 1982): 22.

14. The attorney in question was Mr. Ishmael Jaffree (a personal acquaintance for whom I gave testimony in Judge Hand's court) who eventually won his case. See *Wallace, Governor of Alabama et al.* v. *Jaffree et al.* 472 U.S. 38 (1985).

15. ddddSee my article "Science vs. Religion in Future Constitutional Conflicts," *Free Inquiry* 4, no. 3 (Summer 1984): 17, n.14.

16. See *Edwards, Governor of Louisiana et al.* v. *Aguillard et al.* 482 U.S. 578 (1987). Herein Justice Scalia, after a great show of legal learning, falls quickly into scientific ignorance and engages in what amounts to apologetics helpful to the "Scientific Creationists." He was joined in dissenting by Chief Justice Rehnquist. This, no doubt, gives us a foretaste of decisions to come (see chapter 10 for a much fuller statement).

17. See my "Creationism and the First Amendment," *Creation/Evolution* 7 (1982): 30-32.

18. Wendell R. Bird, "Freedom of Religion and Science Instruction in Public Schools," see also especially pp. 523, 525, 531, and 538.

19. I am indebted to my colleague Clifton Perry, an expert in the philosophy of law, for the following statement regarding compelling state interest: "In general, if a state statute precludes all individuals from the exercise of a protected right, said statute will be subject to judicial scrutiny under due process. On the other hand, if a state statute precludes only

some individuals from the exercise of a protected right, said statute will be subject to judicial scrutiny under equal protection. The tests under which judicial scrutiny is conducted for alleged governmental violations of the federal constitution depends upon whether the issue involves due process or equal protection and in the former case, the weight of the right infringed upon and in the latter case, the type of class of individuals excluded. In the area of due process, there are generally two tests. According to the first test, the so-called 'Rational Relationship' test, which arises when considering economic and social welfare legislation, the statute need only manifest a rational relationship to a legitimate state interest in order to survive. However, if the legislation infringes upon a fundamental right, the state must demonstrate a compelling interest and the statute must be so narrowly drawn as to constitute the least restrictive means of achieving the compelling interest. The 'Strict Scrutiny' test is much more difficult to pass than the rational relationship test, as the means test under the rational relationship analysis allows the legislation to be both over- and under-inclusive, whereas the means test under strict scrutiny allows the legislation to be neither over- nor under-inclusive and permits no less restrictive means to be extant."

20. Wendell R. Bird, "Freedom of Religion and Science Instruction in Public Schools": 565-66.

21. Henry Zuidema, "Less Evolution, More Creationism in Texts," *Educational Leadership* 39 (1981): 217-18.

22. R. Schaeffer, "Creationist Cosmology," *The Skeptical Inquirer* 7, no. 1 (Fall 1982): 7-8.

23. See note 2 above; also *Lemon et al.* v. *Kurtzman, Superintendent of Public Instruction of Pennsylvania et al.*, 403 U.S. 602 (1971).

24. J. Opel, "Education, Science and National Competitiveness," *Science* 27 (1982): 1116-17.

25. See my "Religion, Separation, and Accommodation," with Clifton B. Perry, *National Forum* 68, no. 1 (Winter 1988), esp. pp. 5-7.

7

"Scientific Creationism" and Sour Prongs of Lemon

Introduction

In bringing forth a new nation, our Founding Fathers did not quite know what to do about religion. On the one hand they prized it and wanted Americans to be as free as possible in the exercise of it (consistent, of course, with law). On the other hand they wanted American society (including government) to be free from the evils of religion. We twentieth-century Americans have, in general, formed such a good opinion of religion that it is hard for us to link it with evils of any sort.

Our seventeenth- and eighteenth-century ancestors, however, had no trouble in identifying the evils of religion. These ancestors knew of intolerant state churches in Europe, of the widespread persecution of so-called heretics, and of vicious religious wars. During our early history, some of the same evils persisted here. The established church (Episcopal) in Virginia, for example, made life very disagreeable for certain Baptist sectarians; Protestants were anything but benign toward Catholics in Maryland; Christians were usually intolerant of Jews; and many a person, like Roger Williams, had to flee one state for another.

Nevertheless, the wisdom of the Fathers in writing a secular constitution together with the good sense of our ancestors in breaking cycles of religious intolerance have served us well until recently. Religious animosities today are rising. The primary arena for these animosities is in the public schools, particularly in science.

118   THE MYTHMAKER'S MAGIC

In *Lemon* v. *Kurtzman* (1971) the Supreme Court requires that the primary intent of public school activities shall be secular. The fifty secular states making up our Union intend that school children shall know something about the world as modern science sees it. The Court also requires that nothing the schools do shall have the effect of inhibiting religion. The Court seems not to have noticed that some of the contents of science inhibit some religious doctrines of some students on a regular basis. Thus are the prongs of *Lemon* sour.

* * *

In 1971, in *Lemon* v. *Kurtzman,* the Supreme Court handed down a decision containing a certain test, the famous *Lemon* test, often cited and highly regarded as definitive in church/state cases involving public education.[1] This test, however, is not without its problems. One of these consists of the differences between how our justices view "hostility toward religion" and how the "Scientific Creationists," for example, view these closely related matters. Another consists of differences in evaluating the effects of what the Court calls "primary intent" and permits the schools to try to accomplish. Due to these differences, the "Scientific Creationists," without meaning to do so, have exposed *Lemon*'s otherworldly ineptitude as a test.

The Lemon test did not, of course, materialize out of the blue. On the contrary, it has deep roots in certain legal attitudes and traditions common to Americans, attitudes and traditions that are both judicial and nonjudicial. The judicial root of *Lemon* lies in an assumption that is as unjustifiable as it is unspoken, the assumption being that Supreme Court justices are expected to become deists when ruling in church/state controversies.[2] They never say so themselves, and, as far as I know, nobody else has remarked on this peculiarity. Certainly the Constitution does not require that it be so, the Constitution being an utterly secular document. Perhaps our justices confuse it with the Declaration of Independence, clearly a deistic document. Whatever the case, they routinely interpret the Constitution as though it were a deistic document and as though they were authorized somehow to hand down deistic decisions in church/state disputes.

The nonjudicial root of *Lemon* goes back at least as far as 1875. In that year President Ulysses S. Grant worked (though unsuccessfully) for a constitutional amendment "to establish and forever maintain free public schools . . . for all children . . . forbidding the teaching in said schools of religious, atheistic, or pagan tenets; and prohibiting the granting of any school funds or school taxes . . . for the benefit or in aid, directly or indirectly, of any religious sect or denomination."[3] Although a great deal of public money has flowed into the coffers of various religious organizations, indirectly at least,[4] most of the rest of what President Grant sought above or tried to prevent has been accomplished through law and/or judicial opinions. Deistic justices of the Supreme Court have done their part to accomplish this, even though their unofficial deism has blinded them to real religion (which is not an attenuated deism) and to the problems it poses for secular education.

In *Lemon* the Court handed down a three-pronged test in light of which the public schools can know when they are treating religion(s) properly under permissible state statutes. Chief Justice Burger, in delivering the opinion of the Court, wrote:

> First, the statute must have a secular legislative purpose; second, its principal or primary effect must be one that neither advances nor inhibits religion, *Board of Education* v. *Allen*, 392 U.S. 236, 243 (1968); finally, the statute must not foster "an excessive governmental entanglement with religion." *Walz, supra,* at 674.[5]

He also made it clear in *Lemon* that the schools must accommodate religion.[6] The Rehnquist Court seems strongly disposed to agree.[7]

Neither to aid nor to inhibit religion, but always to accommodate it while simultaneously restraining all hostility to it and refraining from advancing the "religion of secularism" (see *Schempp* 1963) is a recipe of perfection that the public schools cannot achieve in light of the real religion(s) their students represent.[8] The Court has given us a recipe that can be followed only if the real religion(s) at issue are boiled down to their lowest common denominator, namely, the deism of the justices. Given this situation, it is easy to see how the prongs of *Lemon* become sour.

Lemon's First Prong

Lemon's first prong seems at the outset to be straightforward and unobjectionable. Information about religion(s) may be taught in the public schools provided that the context is academic, not confessional or dogmatic. Contrary to popular *misperception*, this issue had already been settled in favor of religion and the Bible in *Schempp*, where it says:

> In addition, it might well be said that one's education is not complete without a study of comparative religion and its relationship to the advancement of civilization. It certainly may be said that the Bible is worthy of study for its literary and historic qualities. Nothing we have said here indicates that such study of the Bible or of religion, when presented objectively as part of a secular program of education, may not be effected consistently with the First Amendment.[9]

The secular goals to be achieved with such instruction are obvious: (1) General cultural literacy in students can be enhanced thereby, (2) an accurate knowledge of history in its relationship to the role(s) of religion can be gained, and (3) tolerance for religions other than one's own may be promoted, an important civic virtue in a country as diverse religiously as the United States. Such at least is the theory behind *Schempp* and *Lemon*. Unfortunately, the facts are quite different, so different that *Schempp* and *Lemon*, however sound they may be constitutionally, are naive in the extreme.

Remembering that the Court has merely *permitted* academic instruction in the schools (for a variety of secular intentions) and has at no time *mandated* such instruction, let us look at what would happen if the schools were to take advantage of the permission granted. Millions upon millions of fundagelical parents, including the "Scientific Creationists," would be up in arms should their children have to take a unit of comparative religion, because that would force a captive audience to encounter religions that, to the parents, are heathenish at best, satanic at worst. To such parents, an even-handed, sympathetic presentation of other religions would have at least three deplorable results. First, it would tend to elevate other religions to the level of the favored religion (in our case Christianity) and, thus, blur the distinction between what is perceived as true religion and what is taken to be false religion. Second, it would cause students, potentially at least, to become critical of their own religion as a result of comparing and contrasting it with other religions, some of which might be appealing. In academic circumstances, there is no guarantee that students would always find their own religion the best in all ways, however best is to be measured. Third, it might cause students to distance themselves from their own religion, if for no other reason than to study it objectively rather than confessionally or dogmatically as would be the case in the home, church, or Sunday school. Whatever the virtues might be of a course in comparative religion at the college level, such instruction in the public schools would be explosively counterproductive. The "Scientific Creationists" have already given a preview of how they would react. They have claimed, for example, that a fundagelical student having to give a Darwinian answer (even if not believed by the student) to a question in biology would be engaging in corrupt communication, a practice forbidden by Ephesians 4:29. Imagine the corrupt communications about pagan religions that might be called for in a comparative religion class![10]

It is true to say, as *Schempp* does, that the "Bible is worthy of study for its literary and historic qualities," but hopelessly naive to think that this could be done with *academic integrity* in the public schools. The Court of 1968 did not seem to know that it is precisely at the point of literary and historical studies that the kind of Bible scholars who could and would teach at Harvard, Yale, and Princeton are separated by an impassable gulf from those who could and would teach at Bob Jones, Oral Roberts, or the Criswell Institute. To reiterate, it is precisely at the points of literary and historical studies that German scholarship initiated the process (more than two hundred years ago) that has led to modern biblical studies, studies that have shattered orthodoxy at a thousand points and denied magic and mystery to the various religious writings that, over time, first coalesced into the Old Testament, then into the New Testament, and finally into the whole Bible as we now have it.[11] There is probably not a teacher in ten thousand in the public schools prepared to teach the literary and historical qualities of the Bible with academic integrity, nor are any being prepared in religion departments and colleges of education in our secular universities. If any such teachers were so to teach, the Fundagelicals would be in an uproar far greater than anything Darwin and evolution have ever occasioned. Moreover, they might be joined by more than a few religious liberals.

The "Scientific Creationists" and their multitudinous ilk reject Mark 9:40 in favor of Matthew 12:30, a nicety lost on the Court. The former says, "For he that is not against us is on our part," and the latter, "He that is not with me is against me; and he that gathereth not with me scattereth abroad." Public school teachers adhering to the standards of academic integrity would, of necessity, have to recognize and make clear to students the difference between articles of faith and matters of fact in the Bible, would have to teach in a neutral rather than in a proselytizing way, and would not even need to be believers themselves, let alone born-again zealots, in order to reveal the meaning of the biblical texts. Such teachers would be viewed as the *enemy* by Fundagelicals and not simply as neutral teachers posing no threat to the faith. Fundagelicals do not want the Bible read for its literary and historical qualities; they want it read dogmatically for its presumed soteriological and moral values.

Nor would accurate instruction in public schools in the history of religion(s) fare any better. Religion serves as the basis for some of the most intensely partisan activities in human history. Such activities frequently involve extremes in behavior as well as in belief and often produce deplorable results that many think better to conceal than to make known. Making the barbarisms of religious strife known to school children may be of dubious value indeed. But to leave out the barbarisms is to present a one-sided story amounting to propaganda. One of the first truths of history is that history is not always edifying. Those who know something, at least, of the history of religion(s) will know, for example, that religion is not automatically a good thing always and everywhere. The Roman Catholic Church, for instance, has not found it edifying (in high school textbooks) to have the whole story behind Huguenot immigration to the United States told.[12] Protestant responses to Irish immigration during and after the potato famine are not always uplifting. Christian responses to Jewish immigration in general do not make for inspiring reading, and the biblical justifications (in both the Old and New Testaments) for slavery (in our case the slavery of blacks kidnapped and brought here against their will) do not ennoble the reader. This minuscule and highly focused list is, of course, but the meltwater at the tip of an iceberg of deplorable doings in the history of religion(s). Christians in general, as well as Fundagelicals in particular, are quick to take umbrage when negative comments (perceived to be hostile) are made about their religion whether in the name of the unvarnished truth, of academic integrity, of secular value, or whatever.

Lemon's Second Prong

The second prong of *Lemon* says that the principal (or primary) effect of a statute (or of a congruent public school policy) must be such that religion is neither advanced nor inhibited thereby. The advancement and the inhibition of religion should be treated separately and can be taken to be the lesser prongs of a single larger prong. Respecting the effect called the advancement of religion, it is probably safe to say that there are no Americans who think that this is the proper business of the public schools. Religion *is* advanced in the public schools in varying degrees in various parts of the country with, perhaps, secondary intent on the part of individual teachers, but that is not our concern here.

Respecting the effect called the inhibition of religion, it is equally certain, no doubt, that Americans do not want the schools to inhibit religion. Surely, school children should not be singled out, harassed, or made to feel inferior or peculiar because of the religious persuasions which they have, in most cases, simply inherited from their families. Surely, Protestant teachers in the public schools should not make fun of Catholic kids, nor Catholic teachers of Protestant kids, nor Christian teachers of Jewish kids, nor Jewish teachers of Christian kids, nor Fundagelical teachers of liberal Christian kids, nor liberal Christian teachers of Fundagelical kids, nor any kind of teachers of Muslim or Buddhist kids, nor any kids from American Indian or Eskimo religions, and so forth.

Though the record in this regard is not perfect, the most serious issue associated with the second prong of *Lemon* has to do with the inhibitions that invariably occur in the public schools on a daily basis. It is these inhibitions of religion (having to do with secular intent) that constitute what may well be the sourest prong of *Lemon*. The Court, quite simply, failed to notice the effects on religion of achieving *permissible* secular goals in the public schools. In essence, the first prong of *Lemon* is inconsistent with the second part of *Lemon*'s second prong.

The major force inhibiting religion in today's public schools is lodged in the curriculum itself or in activities allied with it. Americans engage in sloganeering when they say of public education, "We don't teach kids what to think; we teach them how to think." Most American schools, in fact, are conspicuous in their failure to teach children how to think. The extent to which critical thinking components are lacking in the curriculum is the extent to which the slogan above is nothing but a slogan. However, the extent to which children do learn the rudiments of critical thinking in the public schools is the extent to which religion *is* put in jeopardy, for logic trespasses upon the sacred as readily as upon the secular.

A bright student with half an eye (who is not stricken with fear) can see that nearly the whole of theology is based upon questionable assumptions and is in essence a question begging enterprise. This is easy to illustrate. Whether the example comes from biology, geology, chemistry, or some other science, the expert in the field must come in contact with living organisms, with rock formations, with chemicals, or with whatever is being studied as well as with the literature of the field in question. In theology, however, one comes in contact only with the literature of the field, i.e., only with what other theologians have thought, spoken, or written. In short, one never comes in contact with any theological facts—only with what are believed to be facts. Taking alleged facts to be demonstrable, but failing to demonstrate them, and then proceeding as though the demonstration had taken place is question begging, an elementary fallacy in informal logic so obvious that grade school children can recognize it. Legally, this amounts to no more than hearsay.[13] The same should be true in pedagogy.

The foregoing does not suggest that opportunities for religious faith ought to be denied to any American, nor does it mean that the free exercise of religion (within permissible law) should be withheld from any schoolboy or girl. It simply means that critical thinking is the potential enemy of dogmatic faith, especially of an ignorant or stultifying faith maintaining such an absurdity, for example, as the doctrine of biblical inerrancy (see chapter 4). This gives us a clue as to why the "Scientific Creationists" and other Fundagelicals have been so aggrieved by public education for so long. Elements of the secular curriculum itself pose a serious threat to the dubious facts of religion and to the vagaries of theological method, so-called. Nothing as esoteric as "the religion of secularism" (whatever the Court might have had in mind) is called for to accomplish the kinds of inhibitions at issue. The point is transparently simple: In carrying out its primary *intent* to achieve secular educational goals, the public school *inhibits* religion which is an *effect* its activities are forbidden to have.

The extent to which the public schools attempt to educate children from homes where some brand of scriptural literalism or other intensely dogmatic religion is espoused is the extent to which the curriculum itself is the enemy inhibiting religion. It must be remembered that no known scriptural literature is updated from time to time to keep it congruent with the discoveries of advancing science. This is certainly true of Judaism and Christianity (and of Islam, too) whose scriptures are all archaic in their outlook on the nature of humankind, on the habitat of humankind (our planet), and on the cosmos in general when these are compared with the modern scientific world view. The following examples should make this crystal clear.

1. Over the last three decades the "Scientific Creationists" have given ample evidence of how much they think the secular curriculum inhibits their brand of religion. The curriculum does this whenever it broaches the subject of evolution, whether biological, planetary, or cosmic, or whenever it suggests dates for any occurrence more ancient than the ten thousand years that they believe the Bible allows. Removing 'biblical' from biblical creationism and substituting 'scientific,' thus providing a smoke screen, they have attacked the presumed "religion of secularism" that has, in their view, taken over the public schools rather than focusing on the secular curriculum itself as the real cause of their concern.[14] Since *Edwards* v. *Aguillard* (1987), they have downplayed the evil machinations of the "religion of secularism" but have remained as aggrieved by the secular curriculum as ever, betraying that it was this that really bothered them from the beginning even if they were not fully aware of it and in no mood to acknowledge it.[15]

2. Viewing the world from the Olympian height of deism, the Court has never understood how varied the grist really is for the different mills of religion. Take the extreme biblical literalists, for example, who accept on good scriptural grounds the geocentric model of the universe (Gen. 1:14, Josh. 10:12-13) rather than what the secular curriculum teaches as fact about the relation of the planets in our solar system to the sun.[16] Two points need to be stressed: First, the acceptance of the fact that our planet revolves around the sun is not an article of faith in any "religion of secularism," and second, geocentrists do not need the Court to tell them what inhibits their religion. They know perfectly well what inhibits it, secular teaching to the contrary. The same is true of those who, on biblical grounds, think that the earth is indeed round but round like a plate rather than round like a ball and that it is, therefore, not globular as the globe presented to children in geography classes indicates it to be (see Isa. 40:22, 1 Thess. 4:16-17). The globe that we are all familiar with from our secular education has no ends (as Isa. 40:28 indicates that the earth has), or corners (as Rev. 7:1 would have it), or pillars upon which to sit (as

Job 9:6 and Ps. 75:3 claim) but, rather, orbits the sun with no fixed supports at all.

3. Christian Scientist parents will know the effect of inhibition on their religion if and when their children are taught in hygiene classes (or in good health components of biology classes) to avoid or otherwise to protect themselves from the agents of infectious diseases. Instruction in the prevention of AIDS, for example, will hardly proceed in the public schools on the idea that it results from bad, negative, or impure thoughts (à la Mary Baker Eddy), but as though it results from the HIV virus. No Christian Science practitioner has succeeded to date (through spiritual counsel) in delivering anybody from AIDS. Jehovah's Witnesses will also find their religion inhibited if and when the therapeutic uses of blood transfusions are taken up approvingly in the public schools. To Jehovah's Witnesses blood transfusions are tantamount to eating blood, a practice prohibited in the Bible (Gen. 9:4, Lev. 3:17). The inhibitions above have little or nothing to do with a so-called "religion of secularism," alleged to be present in the public schools, but much to do with modern, scientific knowledge and successful medical practice.

4. Nowhere, as Fundagelicals see it, is the inhibition of religion greater than in textbooks presumed guilty of promoting secular humanism or the "religion of secularism," whichever one prefers. In 1985 Fred Hechinger wrote an article entitled "Religion as Issue in School" for the *New York Times*.[17] In it he made extensive reference to a report entitled *The Attack on Public Education: North Carolina's Experience* by Jodi Wallace. She wrote that a distinction should be made "between parents who want only the best education for their own children and those parents who want to mold the schools to conform to their own religious beliefs." She also wrote, "Teachers are being frightened away from classroom discussion about dozens of topics, books are being censored and whole curricula are being attacked and in some cases withdrawn."

At about the same time, Paul Vitz, a psychologist at New York University, was busy writing an article to be entitled "Religion and Traditional Values in Public School Textbooks."[18] At first blush this would seem to have little to do with Jodi Wallace's report, but at certain points the two converge. Among other things, Vitz noticed in the "ten sets of six books each" (for grades 1–6) that he examined that "[t]raditional roles for both men and women receive no support, while role-reversal feminist stories are common." Indeed, "[b]y far the most noticeable ideological position in the readers is a feminist one. . . ."[19]

Meanwhile the federal courts were being entangled in disputes involving education, but not of the sort *Lemon* hopes to preclude; disputes, rather, having nothing to do with any policy of the schools to inhibit religion but much to do with the concerns raised by Wallace and Vitz above. Into federal court (in 1986) came Robert B. Mozert, Jr., of Church Hill, Tennessee, complaining about the kind of school books children were reading in the public school.[20] Mozert was upset, because in one book a boy named Jim pops bread into a toaster (thereby cooking) while his little girl companion reads a book, a clear violation of God-given sex-roles laid down in scripture. A Mrs. Vicki Frost, who was to gain national notoriety for her complaints, joined Mozert. Believing that "Our children's imaginations have to be bounded," she was afraid that a story called "A Visit to Mars" might lead to excessive imaginative activity on the part of school children (here one discerns in the background the "wicked imagination" of Prov. 6:18). She was also disturbed that children were reading *The Wizard of Oz*, because "it portrays witches as good," and *King Arthur* and *Cinderella*, because "they contain magic and supernatural acts." In her view reading Hans Christian Andersen might be perilous as well, for it could "foster acceptance of occult practices and diverse religious beliefs." Books promoting (or allegedly promoting) "pacifism, child rebellion, situation ethics, and feminism" also alarmed her. And, then, too, there was the perennial bugaboo of evolution![21]

While matters were coming to a head in Tennessee, there were similar goings-on in Alabama. There a federal district judge, W. Brevard Hand, was blithely incorporating the roles of prosecutor and jury into his judicial activities. Reorganizing a case that had once concerned prayer in the schools into one investigating various public school texts and, simultaneously, transforming the defendants in the prayer case into the plaintiffs in the school text case, Hand managed for a time to ban from use in the public schools forty-odd books.[22] His finding was that they "unconstitutionally neglected the role of Christianity and other theistic religions in American society and promote the 'religion of secular humanism.' "[23] How, he wondered, could schools not ban Anti-Christ if they were going to ban Christ?[24] The offensive material in question was included in such bland books as *Today's Teen* (Bennett, 1981), *Contemporary Living* (Goodheart-Wilcox, 1975), *America: Past and Present* (Houghton-Miflin, 1980), and *Homemaking: Skills for Everday Living* (Goodheart-Wilcox, 1981).[25] The last named book above was viewed with more than a little alarm on the ground that it could lead to confusion (if not worse) concerning sex-roles, roles "divinely ordained" in scripture, in the minds of many. Paul Vitz, the aforementioned psychologist, testified against the books in question, finding, no doubt, more instances of feminist ideology in them.[26] Whatever the evils of these forty-odd books, it is noteworthy that Judge Hand did not accuse these of setting out to inhibit religion (as might be expected from secular humanists in the schools), nor did he accuse the schools of using these books for this purpose. The effect of the secular curriculum as such seems to have escaped him. It was the presumed effect of the secular humanists allegedly behind it all that excited his judicial wrath.

5. Buddhists, extremely conservative Seventh Day Adventists, and others who may practice vegetarianism for religious reasons would experience some inhibition of their respective religions were the public schools to include in the curriculum a component on good nutrition in which meat is recommended. This is not a major consideration at present, but the American Buddhist population is growing, especially in California, and may one day be aggrieved by public school practices in ways never dreamed of by the Court.

6. To course content that has the effect of inhibiting (or potentially inhibiting) religion(s), one must add certain practices and activities, allied to the teaching function of the schools, that do the same. These range from innoculations required for admission to school, to the dispensing of condoms, to any use of pork products in the school lunch program, to physical education classes in which immodest dress (in the view of some religionists) is worn, to, of all things, the American practice of allowing boys and girls to sit next to each other in the classroom. In 1987 a Mr. Talat Sultan wrote in the *School Administrator* asking that Muslim students not be required to

> sit next to students of the opposite sex in the classroom; participate in physical education, swimming, or dancing classes (unless classes are held separately for boys and girls); participate in plays, proms, social parties, picnics, or activities that require free mixing of the two sexes; participate in any event or activity related to Christmas, Easter, Halloween, or Valentine's Day.

He also asked that Muslim

> students be excused from classes to attend off-campus special prayers on Friday (approximately 1:00 to 2:00 P.M.); students be excused for 15 minutes in the afternoon to offer a special prayer in a designated area on the school grounds; all items containing meat of a pig in any form or shape should be clearly labeled in the cafeteria; at least one properly covered toilet should be available in each men's and women's room. Also a separate and properly enclosed shower stall should be available for use after physical education classes.[27]

Lemon's Third Prong

Little needs to be said about the third prong of *Lemon,* the prong that prohibits any statute or congruent school practice that would "foster excessive entanglement" between government and religion. It is hard to imagine that any sane person would want excessive entanglement of this sort, but entanglement there is, because the other prongs of *Lemon* do not work as they were intended to work. In fact, there may have been as many entanglements with the *Lemon* test in place as there would have been without it. The origin of some of the entanglements at least is to be found in the Court itself (see note 1).

Feeling the imperative to rise above all hints of denominational affiliation, feeling the need even to rise above Christianity and Judaism, the Justices of the Supreme Court have, typically, assumed the lofty stance of deists (i.e., of minimal theists). Their decisions relative to church/state issues reveal this again and again.[28] Thus, the Constitution (which gives no hint of deism) has been interpreted deistically from the beginning of church/state entanglements until now. It should come as no surprise, then, that the Justices were espousing a deistic overview when they permitted the public schools (with *Lemon*'s first sour prong) to offer academic study in comparative religions and in the literary and historical qualities of the Bible. The same is true of the two little prongs of *Lemon*'s second sour prong. Respecting the first little prong, no denomination is to be advanced at the expense of another. Going even further, perhaps, no form of theism, such as Christianity, is to be preferred to another, such as Judaism. If the Court means to see matters this broadly, we are led to wonder how Islam will fit in. With respect to the second little prong, deistic religion is not to be inhibited in any way. In short, the schools may not advocate atheism or agnosticism which, no doubt, make up what the Court has in mind when referring to the "religion of secularism."

How differently Fundagelicals in general and "Scientific Creationists" in particular view the matter! Hoping to claim all good things for their religion, while simultaneously trying to be patriotic Americans, they naively believe the Constitution to be a Christian document and look to the Founding Fathers as great exemplars of Christianity.[29] Moreover, they have no intention of rising above their brand of dogmatic theism to the lofty deism of our Justices, past and present. As pointed out above, Fundagelicals have no wish to have comparative religions taught in the public schools or to achieve secular goals, nor do they care a fig for the literary and historical qualities of the Bible apart from belief in it. Furthermore, they are perfectly happy to have religion advanced in the schools as long as it is *their* religion. To continue, a great deal more inhibits their religion than inhibits the deistic religion of our Justices as expressed in their decisions. Whereas the Court has naively limited itself to what it takes to inhibit religion (or to cause that effect), Fundagelicals have really experienced the inhibition of their religion in the public schools due to the secular intent permitted by *Lemon*'s first prong. Finally, excessive entanglements in church/state cases (touching on education) pose no problem for them as long as they can see the faintest glimmer of legal relief from their educational enemies, most of whom turn out to be liberal or moderate theists of various sorts.

Our Justices could, no doubt, have done worse than to adopt deism as their unofficial religion when interpreting the Constitution in church/state cases. Deism has elevated them above the strife of real religions as these combat the world, the worldly, and, more often than not, each other, but at the same time it has put them out of touch with reality. For constitutional purposes, whatever inhibits deism inhibits religion but not the other way around. Alas, very few religious people are merely deistic. Real religions are much richer in doctrine and more complex in faith and practice than anything afforded by the Court's standard of bare-bones deism. Accordingly, many more inhibitions of real religion can occur in the public schools than the Justices have foreseen, and these inhibitions may be perceived by a raft of believers as hostile, even though the Justices' deism remains unscathed. The *Lemon* test, in short, is ill-informed, and out of touch, and too inclined to accommodate religion for the educational well-being of our country. Unfortunately, in crafting this test, Chief Justice Burger chose to ignore *Epperson* v. *Arkansas* wherein Justice Fortas wrote:

> There is and can be no doubt that the First Amendment does not permit the State to require that teaching and learning must be tailored to the principles or prohibitions of any religious sect or dogma.[30]

He also quoted an earlier decision as follows:

> As Mr. Justice Clark stated in *Joseph Burstyn, Inc.* v. *Wilson*, "the state has no legitimate interest in protecting any or all religions from views distasteful to them. . . ."

Given the failure of accommodation in practice to prevent "excessive entanglement" in church/state cases involving education and given the chilling effect on a wide range of topics in public school curricula, it is time to promote vigorously in every way possible the kind of strict separationism implicit in the *Epperson* and *Burstyn* decisions. Few if any roadblocks could daunt the "Scientific Creationists" more effectively.

Notes

1. *Lemon et al.* v. *Kurtzman, Superintendent of Public Instruction of Pennsylvania et al.* 403 U.S. 602 (1971). *Lemon* can no longer be said to be held in high esteem universally, for then Justice Rehnquist has attacked it tooth and nail in his dissent to *Wallace, Governor of Alabama, et al.* v. *Jaffree et al.* 472 U.S. 38 (1985).

2. See my "Deism and the Supreme Court," *The Humanist* 52 (March–April 1992): 25–28, 48. The judicial root singled out by Chief Justice Burger, who wrote for the Court in *Lemon*, consists of two cases: *Board of Education* v. *Allen*, 392 U.S. 236, 243 (1968) and *Walz* v. *Tax Commission of the City of New York*, 397 U.S. 664, 668, 674 (1970).

3. Quoted in John M. Swomley, *Religious Liberty and the Secular State* (Buffalo, N.Y.: Prometheus Books, 1987): 65–66.

4. See *Voice of Reason*, Newsletter of Americans for Religious Liberty, no. 10 (Fall 1983): 4. Here one reads, "Over one billion dollars in state and federal tax aid goes annually to parochial and private elementary schools," according to a study recently completed by Americans for Religious Liberty executive director, Edd Doerr. Also see Elaine Sciolino, "Millions in American Financing Aiding Religious Schools Overseas," *The New York Times* (January 24, 1988).

5. *Lemon*, pp. 612–13.

6. In *Lynch, Mayor of Pawtucket, et al.* v. *Donnelly et al.* 465 U.S. 668, 673 (1984), Chief Justice Burger wrote that the Constitution "affirmatively mandates accommodation, not merely tolerance, of all religions and forbids hostility toward any."

7. On the back page of each issue of *Church & State* in recent years there has appeared the following quote from Chief Justice William Rehnquist, "The 'wall of separation between church and state' is a metaphor based on bad history, a metaphor which has proved useless as a guide to judging. It should be frankly and explicitly abandoned." This direct quotation is taken from *Wallace* v. *Jaffree*, note 1 above. For more of this sort from the chief justice, see chapter 10.

8. *School District of Abington Township, Pennsylvania, et al.* v. *Schempp et al.* 374 U.S. 203, 225 (1963). *Schempp* says, "We agree of course that the State may not establish a 'religion of secularism' in the sense of affirmatively opposing or showing hostility to religion thus 'preferring those who believe in no religion over those who do believe.' See *Zorach* v. *Clauson*, at 314." Also see my "Religion, Separation, and Accommodation" (with Clifton B. Perry) in *National Forum*, The Phi Kappa Phi Journal 68, no. 1 (Winter 1988): 2–7.

9. *Schempp*, p. 225.

10. See Wendell R. Bird, Institute of Creation Research (ICR) *Impact Series*, no. 69 (March 1979), p. ii. In the same place Bird notes that the "Court has stated that public schools cannot require objectionable declarations of belief," as though merely answering a question from classroom instruction would be a corrupt communication or an objectionable declaration.

11. See, for example, "Biblical Criticism" and "Biblical Criticism: sketch of history of" in Vergilius Ferm, *Encyclopedia of Religion;* "Form Criticism" and "Higher Criticism" in *The Oxford Dictionary of the Christian Church;* and "Biblical Interpretation" in *Dictionary of Christianity in America*. Articles under these or very similar headings can be found in any of the leading encyclopedias, such as the *Britannica*.

12. During the academic year of 1959–60, Samuel Terrien, a professor of Old Testament Archaeology (and a Huguenot) at Union Theological Seminary in New York City told a class that included the author the following: The Macmillan Company had produced an American history text for secondary schools that was so good that Catholic parochial schools in New York City and elsewhere were interested in adopting it as well as were many public schools. The Archdiocese of New York City, however, was disturbed, because the author(s) of the history text in question had written that one of the reasons for Huguenot immigra-

tion to America was vicious persecution at the hands of the Catholic Church (see any encyclopedia entry on the St. Bartholomew's Day massacre). When it was pointed out to Macmillan that this was disturbing and that the Archdiocese could see its way clear to adopt the text if the offensive material were altered or removed, the company, seeing great financial gain, obliged by having the Huguenots come here because they wanted a nice cruise on the Atlantic and a change of scenery. History is often rewritten for reasons no better than this.

13. I am indebted to my colleague Clifton B. Perry, who is an expert in the philosophy of law, for the following note on the legal nature of hearsay: "According to the Federal Rules of evidence (Rule 801), hearsay evidence is that evidence which depends upon the credibility of someone (the declarant) who is unavailable for cross-examination and the evidence is offered to establish that to which the evidence attests. Thus, in order to determine whether some statement is hearsay, one simply looks to the content of the out-of-court statement (oral or written) and sees if it is identical to the issue for which the statement is offered as evidence. If one wanted to demonstrate the truth of a proposition uttered by God, one would have to rely upon the evidence of others' spoken and written reports of that proposition. In a word, such evidence would be hearsay. It is not that hearsay is categorically evil but only taken to be presumptively untrustworthy. In a court of law, unless the hearsay evidence falls within an exception, i.e., a category which attenuates the untrustworthiness of the hearsay, the evidence is simply inadmissible. To allow hearsay evidence is arguably to assume as true what stands in need of being established as true."

14. Raymond A. Eve and Francis B. Harrold, *The Creationist Movement in Modern America* (Boston: Twayne Publishers, 1991): 58. Here, among other materials, one finds a quote from the well-known Fundagelical, Tim LaHaye, who said, "Much of the evils [sic] in the world today can be traced to humanism, which has taken over our government, the UN, education, TV, and most of the other influential things in life."

15. *Edwards, Governor of Louisiana, et al.* v. *Aguillard et al.* 482 U.S. 578 (1987).

16. Some "creationist extremists" still hold to the geocentric theory of the universe. See *The Skeptical Inquirer* 7, no. 1 (Fall 1982): 7. The Bible Science Association (founded 1963) that produces the *Bible Science Newsletter* promotes geocentrism.

17. September 20, p. 22.

18. See *The Public Interest*, no. 84 (Summer 1986): 79-90. See also *Newsweek* (July 28, 1986): 20.

19. *The Public Interest*, p. 88.

20. Dudley Clendinen, "Conservative Christians Again Take Issue of Religion in Schools to Court," *The New York Times* (February 28, 1986): 11.

21. *Time* (July 28, 1986): 68; *Newsweek* (July 28, 1986): 18-20; *The New York Times* (July 28, 1986): 7; also see the issue of October 25, 1986: 1 and 8.

22. Dudley Clendinen, " 'Humanist' Schoolbooks Go to Court in Alabama," *The New York Times* (October 6, 1986): 14; also see *Time* (March 16, 1987): 66.

23. See "Court Overturns a Schoolbook Ban in Humanism Case," *The New York Times* (August 27, 1987): 1 and 11.

24. Cathy Donelson, "Fundamentalists May Get Chance to Fight Humanism," *The Alabama Journal and Advertiser* (Sunday, February 16, 1986).

25. "Do Textbooks Foster 'Secular Humanism'?" *The New York Times* (October 19, 1986).

26. *Time* (October 27, 1986): 94.

27. Quoted in *Religion & Public Education* 14, no. 2 (Spring 1987): 151.

28. McKown, "Deism and the Supreme Court."

29. See especially "Deism in the United States," under the general heading of "Deism," in *The Encyclopedia of Philosophy*. Here E. C. Mossner, the author, singles out Benjamin

Franklin, Thomas Jefferson, George Washington, and Thomas Paine for special attention, lesser figures also being noted.
30. *Epperson* v. *Arkansas,* 393 U.S. 97, 106 (1968).
31. Ibid, 107.

8

"Creation Science": Newspeak Before Its Time

Introduction

In his novel *Nineteen Eighty-Four,* George Orwell makes his readers feel real foreboding at the threat of Big Brother's total takeover of Oceania, and by extension, of their own countries. Well, 1984 has come and gone, and Big Brother is on the run. A scant five years after that portentous date, the Berlin Wall began to fall, and now the Soviet Union is gone. Moreover, secret police files are being opened in country after country, and democracy is burgeoning.

The flight of Big Brother, however, does not mean that nobody is watching and trying to eavesdrop, that nobody is purging libraries and trying to expunge certain topics from school texts, that nobody is intent on curbing artistic freedom and preventing "blasphemy." Big Brother has a potential successor. Guess who? Keep reading.

At the end of *Nineteen Eighty-Four,* Orwell added an appendix giving the rules for "Newspeak," the verbal device Big Brother used to dominate people by confusing their minds profoundly. Among other things, Newspeak was used to alter what could be thought by changing the connotations of old words and by creating new ones. The word 'Christian,' for example, can be redefined so as to exclude from Christianity all who believe in the Bible-god *and* in evolution. This is the way Fundagelicals manage religious liberals. That which names a religious doctrine (creationism) can be compounded with 'science' to make a word that seems to name a position

133

both real and respectable. That which is inherently nonreligious, if not irreligious (i.e., *secular* humanism), can be called religious over and over again until this is taken for a fact. Such is Fundagelical Newspeak.

In 1981 the journal *ETC* (vol. 38, no. 4) published my article "Creationscience: Newspeak Before its Time." It now makes up the slightly edited content of this chapter. There could have been no more fitting outlet for it. *ETC* describes itself as a journal devoted to the role of symbols in human behavior. Symbols, it should be noted, can be used to deceive and create confused belief and behavior.

* * *

Orwell wrote (in 1949) that some of Big Brother's minions would be using Newspeak by 1984. Actually a religious variant of it appeared as early as 1963 with the founding of the Creation Research Society.[1] Following came the Institute of Creation Research and the Creation-Science Research Center.[2] Nor is that all. Some observers have detected as many as fifty creationist groups.[3] Each of these is zealously trying to smuggle biblical cosmology into the public schools under the honored guise of science. I propose hereafter to refer to the members of these groups and of such like-minded organizations as the Moral Majority (plus a host of television evangelists and legions of lay evangelists) as "Powerful Parson."[4] Powerful Parson and Big Brother are tempted similarly, succumb to temptations similarly, and act similarly, granted sufficient political power. Each has a totalitarian twinkle in his (or, collectively, its) eye, each knows what is *really* good for people, and each uses language deceptively to further his (its) ends.

It is imperative that we not use the words that Powerful Parson coins for himself, appropriates for his cause, or remodels for his own ends. To do so is to do Powerful Parson's work for him by mouthing his brand of Newspeak. For example, in using any pet term of his, one tends to legitimize what he takes on faith (and faith alone) to be its referent. Here I am reminded of a student who announced in one of my classes that trolls are "gross, ugly, mean, little things." It seems that this student had not theretofore distinguished between Kewpie dolls or other statuettes purporting to be of trolls and trolls in the flesh, as it were. The student appears to have thought that each statuette of a troll had been sculpted from a live model or that every picture of one had been painted from someone sitting for that purpose. One has only to think of "Creation-Science" in the Creation-Science Research Center to get the point. Moreover, remove the hyphen, and out pops "Creationscience," a perfect entry in the lexicon of Newspeak. "Creationscience," one supposes, is the same sort of thing as "the Science of Creation." "The Science of Creation," however, has no more meaning than the physics of metaphysics. There is no physics of metaphysics; neither is there any science of creation in the sense in which the "Scientific Creationists" understand the term and would have others understand it. Using the term, then, has us referring to nothing.

Presently, science allows us to regress no further than the Big Bang. Perhaps the primordial atom that then exploded was but an episode in the eternal (and perhaps cyclical) career of matter/energy. Possibly a supersensuous first cause created that atom just before it blew up. Perhaps the primordial atom came into existence spontaneously, i.e., out of nothingness without cause (acausally), or perhaps it was self-created, whatever that might mean when applied to a primordial atom bent on exploding. Although scientific sobriety would seem to counsel a suspension of judgment pending further information, people are obviously free to place their faith in whichever alternative is most attractive to them. But to call any of these metaphysical alternatives scientific is to misunderstand science and to misuse the word. Clearly, there are creationists and noncreationists respecting cosmology and scientists and nonscientists respecting expertise, but there are no scientific creationists in proper English, despite those who call themselves that in their brand of Newspeak (also see chapter 1).

"Scientific Creationists" believe in neither the Big Bang nor in its remote occurrence ten or more billions of years ago. They believe more nearly in a Big Wash (although they do not call it that) and think that it happened no more than ten thousand years ago.[5] I say Big Wash because according to Genesis, chapter one (a literal reading of much of which they covertly peddle), water was already present when the Bible-god began to create the heavens and the earth (Gen. 1:1–2). Then the firmament appeared, separating the waters above it from those below it (Gen. 1:6–7; Ps. 24:2, 148:4). Finally, the dry land emerged from the waters and set bounds to them (Gen. 1:9). Loath to believe nowadays that there is an ocean of water above the sky, Powerful Parson has created the term 'vapor canopy' expressly to explain where the rain originated for the biblical flood (of which more later).[6] But, alas, 'vapor canopy' is not scriptural. Thus, there is outright deception whenever Powerful Parson uses this term to refer to a supposed atmospheric source of that flood. More Newspeak!

To bolster this unbolsterable "science," Powerful Parson misstates the second law of thermodynamics (which still sounds scientific enough) and maintains a nonevent by continuing to name it as though the mere naming thereof could underwrite the alleged event.[7] Powerful Parson takes it on faith that evolution has not occurred, because Genesis says otherwise. The problem is to find a scientific reason for this article of faith. Taking evolution to be the spontaneous generation of life forms from the simplest and least ordered to the more complex and more ordered,[8] Powerful Parson casts about for anything with which to negate such a process and comes up with entropy according to which the universe is always and everywhere tending from the complex to the simple, from the ordered to the disordered (or is running down, so to speak).[9] Thus, evolution is made impossible—supposedly. Calling this a "kindergarten level" formulation of the second law, Isaac Asimov writes that our sun is indeed running down but that in the process it delivers more than ample energy for evolution to occur, and he is seconded by legions of thermodynamicists.[10]

It horrifies Powerful Parson to hear that Earth was formed about four and a half billion years ago, that life began around four billion years ago, and that evolutionary processes have been working on organic matter ever since.[11] Dr. Henry Morris, sometimes called the foremost "Scientific Creationist,"[12] has attributed the idea of evolution (together with its immense time scale) to the Bible-devil.[13] To combat this satanic lie, Powerful Parson utilizes another nonevent, the one known as Noah's flood. I call it a nonevent because geology knows nothing of a deluge occurring less than ten thousand years ago that inundated Earth's highest mountains.[14] The selection of the date for Noah's flood (which depends entirely on the ages of the biblical patriarchs and the times of their begetting) is as dubious as is the alleged event.[15] The patriarchs are plenty dubious, too.

Powerful Parson, nevertheless, clings to his nonevent because there has to have been a planetary catastrophe disruptive enough to nullify all radiometric or other attempts at dating anything prior to ten thousand years ago, the approximate date of creation according to "Scientific Creationists."[16] Any technique establishing much earlier dates would be a disaster, because Powerful Parson is committed to the doctrine of biblical inerrancy.[17] So, since Noah's flood is biblical and since it alone qualifies to render invalid the uniformitarian premises of science (together with the dating techniques based thereon), it must be maintained, despite a cacophony of scientific nays.

Such, in a nutshell, is "Creationscience," a nonempirical, miracle-laden system of beliefs expressed in a variant of Newspeak designed to make the ideas in question seem scientific rather than religious. How, you may wonder, is it doing? In the muddled minds of many Americans, it is doing fabulously well, all the way from the White House and the halls of Congress to state legislatures and on to individual churches and school systems nestled in the grass roots.[18] Consider the following four reasons for this unhappy, frightening situation.

First, Powerful Parson has us talking and writing pro and con about "Creationscience," has us voting for or against it, trying to get it into the public schools or trying to keep it out, and trying to block it in state legislatures or trying to ram it through. This national embroilment is a major achievement. It is as though the Flat Earth Society had suddenly revived (becoming rich, populous, and politically potent in the process) and had embroiled the country in geocentrism. This, too, is biblical and may be on the docket next, if current tendencies continue. Robert J. Schadenwald, denying that it is a parody, has already written a bill entitled, "The Balanced Treatment for Flat-Earth Science and Spherical Science Act."[19] It parallels "The Balanced Treatment for Scientific Creationism and Evolution Act," which Powerful Parson has been introducing into state legislatures.

Second, speaking of legislatures, 1981 was a banner year for "Creationscience." After a decade of frustration in a dozen or more states, Powerful Parson finally won in Arkansas and Louisiana (temporarily at least). There was also a close call in Alabama and an even closer call in Georgia in 1980. In 1978, South Carolina approved of local option leaving individual public school systems free to offer "balanced treatment" of origins. Similar triumphs can be expected elsewhere unless or until the federal courts quash "Creationscience."[20]

Third, Powerful Parson takes advantage of the scientific illiteracy afflicting the United States. Speaking glibly of paradigms (a term made famous by Thomas Kuhn, a prominent philosopher) and quoting Sir Karl Popper's opinion that evolution is merely a "metaphysical research programme" as though Popper (an even more eminent philosopher) were infallible or never changed his mind, Powerful Parson confuses all but scientific sophisticates.[21] The *Creation Research Society Quarterly* continues the bamboozlement. It comes from a society all of whose full members have at least a master's degree in some science or other, including (if not dominated by) engineering.[22] What wonderful mileage Powerful Parson gets out of credentials nowadays. John Q. Public can be depended on not to know how to distinguish between credentialed people. If David Boylan, former dean of the school of Engineering at Iowa State University, says that entropy prevents evolution and Isaac Asimov, formerly of the School of Medicine at Boston University, says that it does not, how can a scientific simpleton like John Q. tell the difference?[23] In addition to the aforementioned journal, there are also what look like bona fide textbooks of "Creationscience" pouring off Powerful Parson's presses.[24] If John N. Moore (Ed.D., Michigan State University) says in one of these that the universe is only about ten thousand years old and Carl Sagan (Ph.D., the University of Chicago) says that it is billions and billions of years old, how can innocents (including college graduates) be expected to know who tells the truth?[25] Meanwhile, Powerful Parson successfully censors offensive textbooks. One such book says that humans developed language over the long centuries of the old

Stone Age. This book was removed from use in Alabama on the ground that man possessed language from the outset; otherwise Adam could not have named the animals on the day of creation (Gen. 2:4, 19).[26]

Fourth, Powerful Parson appeals to much that is deepest in the American psyche. In addition to being scientific illiterates, we are anti-intellectual as a people—and pious. We also believe in democracy to a fault and in fair play. When these characteristics coalesce around an ideologically sensitive issue (such as creationism versus evolution), we choose up sides and vote on it, naively unaware that science is not an enterprise that can be determined by popular referenda (see also chapter 10). An English commentator (whom I can no longer identify) once remarked that though the industrial revolution originated in England, the English really do not like machinery, preferring, instead, horses and dogs. To speak of Americans in a parallel fashion, one would have to say that though we have carried technology to great heights and like the resulting gadgets, we really prefer the old-time religion. In light of recent tendencies in the United States, this observation should have a chilling effect on those who create the science behind the technology. Not only are they less honored than technologists, they are Powerful Parson's real enemy.

Currently, Powerful Parson is misled about this, whether due to ignorance or to the confusions of Newspeak I cannot say. In any case, Powerful Parson thinks that the enemy is secular humanism. Recently, *Newsweek* treated its readers to an exposition of this befuddled belief in its article, "The Right's New Bogeyman."[27] This article was enriched by a drawing and a caption, each deserving comment. The drawing was of an octopus identified as secular humanism. With one tentacle it encircled television, with another the Capitol of the United States, with another a church, with another a school, and with another an American family. More worrisome, perhaps, was the fact that three tentacles were left unoccupied, tentacles which, like idle hands, were no doubt seeking even then to do the Bible-devil's work. What next? one wonders. The caption in question, referring to a prominent "Creationscience" preacher, said, "LaHaye: Making humanism a dirty word." It suffices to note that changing the connotations of words was one of the original tasks of Newspeak as Orwell conceived it.

Even though secular humanism is the target of Powerful Parson's broadsides, it is science which will absorb the greater punishment. Even if secular humanism suffers a direct hit, the damage will be slight compared with the demolition science education will suffer. Despite the modernity of the United States and the power of American science and technology, our public schools have been unable to produce minds generally congenial to and appreciative of the basic assumptions and procedures of scientific inquiry. Surely, this borders on the disastrous! Given that we now produce hordes of scientific simpletons, imagine the greater disaster in the astrophysical, earth, and life sciences were "Creationscience" to be incorporated in the public schools as a valid model of origins. Then add the fact that private Christian schools endorsing "Creationscience" are currently pullulating like rabbits. It boggles the mind! One can see a time a decade hence when most, if not all, science during the first two years of college will be remedial. What an enormous waste of time and money that would be; what a crushing indictment of primary and secondary education! Moreover, science at the college level will be increasingly alienated from society in general. Nor will scientists at that level necessarily be safe. Presently, primary and secondary education preoccupy Powerful Parson, but it need not always be so. It does not even tax the imagination to foresee a time when research monies in ideologically sensitive areas may dry up in favor of what Powerful Parson takes to be theologically innocuous.

Orwell was wrong about Big Brother—in the United States at least. Big Brother is not going to take over here by 1984.[28] But Powerful Parson may. Orwell was more nearly right about Newspeak. It is flourishing, flourishing before its time, even though it is being accented more in holy tones than in the overtly political ones he expected. The "Scientific Creationists" will, of course, use any means (that they take to be morally permissible) to gain their ends. Political action is one of these permissible means. This does not mean, however, that politics is the key to understanding their movement. Religion is the key to understanding it; soteriology is its bottom line.

Notes

1. See any copy of *Creation Research Society Quarterly*.
2. Barbara Parker, "Creation vs. Evolution: Teaching the Origin of Man," *The American School Board Journal* 167, no. 3 (March 1980): 26 and David Milne, "How to Debate with Creationists—and 'Win,' " *American Biology Teacher* 43, no. 5 (May 1981): 235.
3. Parker, "Creation," p. 26.
4. The Moral Majority no longer exists as an organization. On January 4, 1986, the *New York Times* carried an article (whose dateline was January 3) concerning the Rev. Jerry Falwell's creation of a new, successor entity (subsuming the Moral Majority) to be called the Liberty Foundation.
5. Arthur F. Williams, "The Genesis Account of Creation," in Walter E. Lammerts (ed.), *Why Not Creation?* (Nutley, N.J.: Presbyterian and Reformed Publishing Co., 1970): 34.
6. Jody Dillow, "The Attenuation of Visible Radiation in the Vapor Canopy," *Creation Research Society Quarterly* 14, no. 3 (December 1977): 139–46.
7. Milne, "How to Debate with Creations—and 'Win,' " p. 236 and Henry M. Morris, "Entropy and Open Systems," *Impact* no. 40 (October 1976): 1.

8. Henry M. Morris and Martin Clark, *The Bible Has the Answer* (San Diego, Calif.: Creation-Life Publishers, 1976): 79.

9. Duane T. Gish, "A Consistent Christian-Scientific View of the Origin of Life," *Creation Research Society Quarterly* 15, no. 4 (March 1979): 199–200.

10. Isaac Asimov, "The Threat of Creationism," *The New York Times Magazine* (June 14, 1981): 94 and Stanley Freske, "Creationist Misunderstanding, Misrepresentation, and Misuse of the Second Law of Thermodynamics," *Creation/Evolution* 4 (Spring 1981): 9–16.

11. Carl Sagan, *Cosmos* (New York: Random House, 1980): 30.

12. Wendell R. Bird, "Freedom of Religion and Science Instruction in Public Schools," *The Yale Law Journal* 87: 515, 517, n. 12.

13. Henry M. Morris, *The Twilight of Evolution* (Grand Rapids, Mich.: Baker Book House, 1964): 93.

14. Milne, "How to Debate," p. 244.

15. Morris, *Twilight*, p. 56.

16. Duane T. Gish, *Evolution: The Fossils Say No!* (San Diego, Calif.: Creation-Life Publishers, 1972): 40–43.

17. See any copy of *Creation Research Society Quarterly*.

18. At the time this article was published there was a president about to occupy the White House who liked to associate himself with the Gipper of football fame. This gipperish president had already mouthed the creationist line in public saying, "the biblical story of creation ought to be taught in the schools as well as evolution, which was 'only a theory.'" See Anthony Lewis's "Cross and Flag" in *The New York Times* (October 8, 1984). A trenchant indictment of the association between this president, the religious right, and the "Scientific Creationists" can be found in Professor Lawrence S. Lerner's "Killing Darwin for Christ," *Freethought Today* 9, no. 3 (April 1992): 9.

19. *Creation/Evolution* 3 (Winter 1981): 38–41.

20. For an update, see *Creation/Evolution* 4 (Spring 1981): 27–34 and *Church and State* 34, no. 5 (May 1981): 9–14. Before the end of the decade, a stunning blow was delivered to the "Scientific Creationists" in *Edwards, Governor of Louisiana, et al. v. Aguillard et al.* 482 U.S. 578, 596–97 (1987) wherein Justice Brennan wrote, "The Louisiana Creationism Act advances a religious doctrine by requiring either the banishment of the theory of evolution from public classrooms or the presentation of a religious viewpoint that rejects evolution in its entirety. The Act violates the Establishment Clause of the First Amendment because it seeks to employ the symbolic and financial support of government to achieve a religious purpose. The judgment of the Court of Appeals is affirmed." For more concerning the aftermath of *Aguillard*, see chapters 2 and 10.

21. See the letters in *Science* 212 (May 22, 1981): 273ff.

22. See any copy of *Creation Research Society Quarterly*.

23. Asimov, "Threat" and Institute of Creation Research, *Impact*, no. 86. Asimov, it should be noted, is no longer actively associated with the School of Medicine of Boston University. In fact, he no longer lives, having died on April 6, 1992.

24. For example, *Of Pandas and People*. See chapter 5.

25. Sagan, *Cosmos*, p. 30 and John N. Moore, *Impact*, no. 86, p. vii.

26. Marvin Perry, "Banning a Textbook," *The New York Times* (Sunday, May 31, 1981).

27. July 6, 1981, p. 50.

28. Although Big Brother is in full retreat at the present time, Powerful Parson is alive and well in various places. Wherever any form of scriptural literalism reigns or there is a strong fundamentalist movement afoot, Powerful Parson waits to take over for the sake of his deity and "true" religion.

9

How to Dose the "Scientific Creationists" with Their Own Medicine

Introduction

In an earlier chapter I suggested that all honorable means should be used to fight "Scientific Creationism." The object, of course, is to neutralize its influence while simultaneously preserving freedom for Americans to be "Scientific Creationists." One honorable way, I believe, is through satire. This chapter is thoroughly satirical and not to be taken seriously in any other way. Perish the thought that it should make converts of my readers!

Nothing vexes dogmatists more than being out-dogmatized. It is easy to do this to the "Scientific Creationists" using the scriptural source of their faith plus their characteristic methods of interpretation and persuasion. What follows is a *bogus* tract attempting to persuade the reader to believe in a biblical teaching so absurd that even "Scientific Creationists" cannot stomach it.

In 1978, alarmed by the progress of "Scientific Creationism," I began to attack it in talks to professional groups and indirectly in my writing. Frustrated by the relatively few people I was reaching, I decided to remodel a who-done-it I had planned to write someday into a tragicomic novel one of whose principal purposes was to satirize "Scientific Creationism." The novel is *With Faith and Fury* (Prometheus Books, 1985).

In this novel I created a backwoods, charismatic, female evangelist who proceeds to develop a new sect. Religious sects, of course, distinguish themselves from related groups by finding a defining doctrine in scripture that has been overlooked or forgotten by those outside the fold. With such a doctrine they proceed to divide the world into the sheep (themselves) and the goats (everybody else) and soon come to see themselves as the only true believers. I called the new sect the Holy Nation Association of Churches of the Chosen. As the novel progresses, this bizarre sect develops into a full-fledged denomination. Its defining doctrine I called "Three-World Creationism." The following pages show how it all works out and how perfectly biblical it is.

* * *

Why has the Roman Catholic denomination, which claims it was built on the rock that is Peter, *ignored* for almost two thousand years his message of threefold (or triune) creation?

Why have Protestants, even those who search the Scriptures daily, overlooked the *indispensable* key to understanding the triune nature, not just of Holy God Himself, but of his creation as well?

Why have Scientific Creationists, who have done so much to get the saving knowledge of God's Word back into the public schools, *failed to recognize* that the creation model they teach and believe in refers only to God's first heaven and earth, and not to his second heaven and earth, the ones in which we today live, and move, and have our being?

We need not ask why liberals or *humanist-inspired dupes* have never noticed the true biblical doctrine of triune creation. Scoffers and skeptics like these people cannot be expected to read the Scriptures, let alone believe in them.

Albert Einstein once observed that "God does not play dice with the universe." If God does not play dice with the universe, neither would He play games with his children, asking us to believe in that first world which is scripturally documented in Genesis, *a world that is clearly not the one that we inhabit now.* This pamphlet is for those who up to now have heard only of God's original creation and have neither read of, nor been told of, the manifold truths of God's *Three-World Creationism.*

The New Testament has less to say about God's acts of creation than does the Old Testament, for God had already spoken of his *original* creation in many and diverse ways to Moses and the Prophets in the Old Testament. The New Testament does, however, often refer to God's creative powers and achievements. In John's Gospel 1:1 we read, "In the beginning was the Word, and the Word was with God, and the Word was God," and in 1:3, "All things were made by him; and without him was not any thing made that was made." In the Apostle Paul's Colossian letter we read (1:16–17) as follows: "For by him were all things created, that are in heaven, and that are in earth, visible and invisible, whether they be thrones, or dominions, or principalities, or powers: all things were created by him and for him: And he is before all things, and by him all things consist." In Hebrews 1:2 we learn that it is the Son of God, the heir to all things, by whom God the Father "made the worlds." *Notice that the word "worlds" is plural, not singular.* What could that mean? Prepare for a *surprise* as you read on.

From Matthew through Revelation, the New Testament refers often to God's creations but does not emphasize them, presumably because they had been explained in the Old Testament and were common knowledge. Thus, "the God who created all things" is mentioned in Acts 4:24, 14:15, and 17:24; in Ephesians 3:9; and again in Revelation 4:11 and 10:6. References to the phrase, "from the beginning," occur in Matthew 19:4 and 24:21, in Mark 10:6 and 13:19, and in Romans 1:20 (where it talks of "the creation of the world"). The phrase, "from the foundations of the world," also occurs often, for example, in Matthew 25:34, Luke 11:50, John 17:24, Ephesians 1:4, Hebrews 4:3, and 1 Peter 1:20. But, and this is important, in none of these New Testament books is world creation spelled out in detail. To learn the details of triune creation, that is, to learn about the *worlds* alluded to in Hebrews 1:2, one must turn to 2 Peter 3:4–13.

The conservative scholar, William Barclay, points out that 2 Peter is "one of the most neglected books in the New Testament," but that "it is a book of first rate importance."[1] Another conservative scholar, Gordon H. Clark, says, "The Second Epistle of Peter, like the First, has a message for the present age. In fact it is more obviously pertinent to our present age than it has been to some of the centuries intervening since its original date of publication."[2] Peter's inspired writing contains three often quoted messages of such spiritual brilliance that they leap out of the text, catching every eye, thereby consigning the rest of his work to lie neglected in the shade.

First, there is the oft-quoted passage (2 Peter 1:20–21) that says, "Knowing this first, that no prophecy of the scripture is of any private interpretation," and also, "For the prophecies came not in old time by the will of man: but holy men of God spake *as they were* moved by the Holy Ghost." Liberals, of course, have itching ears, as 2 Timothy 4:3 points out, and are all the time taking liberties with the Scriptures, distorting them to make them say what they like. We in the *Three-World Creation Society,* on the other hand, take the holy text as it stands, literally and objectively. We do not flinch or itch in our ears, as many conservative scholars do, but take God's Word as it stands, in faith, confident in so doing that we cannot go wrong.

Second, there is the wonderful passage, more wonderful than most of us may have imagined, that says (2 Peter 3:3–4), "Knowing this first that there shall come in the last days scoffers walking after their lusts, and saying, 'Where is the promise of his coming? For since the fathers fell asleep, all things continue *as they were* from the beginning of creation.' " The denial of the coming *third world* could only be expected from scoffers who deny God's creation of the present world in which they live, based on their accurate rejection of the first world that is described in Genesis.

The third great passage is in 3:8, "But beloved, be not ignorant of this one thing, that one day *is* with the Lord as a thousand years, and a thousand years as one day." With spiritual truths like these, it is no wonder that the rest of 2 Peter has been left a bit in the shade. But, oh, what treasures are to be found there when read with a discerning, truly spiritual eye!

We now stand on the threshold of the revelation of *Three-World Creationism,* a revelation that has been so overlooked it might as well have been locked up in the deepest, darkest dungeon for the last two thousand years. Thank God, it today sees the light!

Until now, we have quoted directly from the King James version of the Bible. At this point, however, we supplement the King James version with *The Interlinear Hebrew/Greek English Bible* translated, word for word, by the conservative translator, Jay Green.[3] No translator and no version have been more on guard against Satan's attempts, throughout the ages, at preventing Christians from getting the most accurate and objective translation possible of God's Holy Book. By all means compare it with your own King James version as we go along. We have also consulted the original Greek and have tried to smooth out the translation for our readers, but at no point have we changed or dropped any meaning.

For *Three-World Creationism,* the verses from 2 Peter 3 that are crucial are 5, 6, 7, 12, and 13. They read as follows:

Verse 5: "For this, they willfully ignore that fact that there were heavens from of old and an earth that had been formed, and by means of water formed by God's word."

Verse 6: "By means of which, the world that then was, perished, through being flooded by water."

Verse 7: "While the heavens and the earth that now are, by the same word, have been stored up for fire, being kept unto the day of judgment and the destruction of godless men."

Verse 12: "Looking for and hastening the coming day of God wherein the heavens shall blaze, being on fire, and the elements shall melt with intense heat."

Verse 13: "But new heavens and a new earth we are expecting, according to his promise, wherein uprightness will abide."

The words in the verses above are as plain, understandable, indisputable, and worthy of belief as *anything* in the Holy Bible. We can understand how a liberal professor like A. R. C. Leany could ignore this teaching,[4] but how could the conservative Michael Green, published by Eerdmans, say, "There is nothing here to suggest that the whole earth was destroyed by the flood, let alone the heavens as well."[5] How could the equally fundamental scholar, John Wick Brown, in *The Layman's Bible Commentary* try to make it seem that the first world was not really destroyed but was just in a passing condition of flood?[6]

What the verses in 2 Peter say, quite simply, is that the heavens and the earth that existed from the creation until the flood (as described in Genesis 1:1 through 8:5) constituted the creation of God's *first world* (or cosmos), the heavens and the earth and everything in them. Where it says, in verse 6, that the world that *then was* perished, the Greek word *apoleto*, translated as perished, also means *annihilated*. There you have it! The earth from which Noah's ark rose up on the first of the flood waters (Gen. 7:13) was not the same as the new (or *second*) earth upon which the ark settled down as the flood waters were dissipated (Gen. 8:13). Although this may seem strange and mysterious, we have our proof both from Scripture and from our common-sensible, sensory knowledge of this, the second earth and the second heavens above, created by a God who works in strange and mysterious ways.

Before examining these amazing matters further, a word needs to be said about the future of our present earth and our present heavens, i.e., this *second* of God's created worlds. As every Bible-believing Christian knows, this world in which we live is being stored up for fire at the final (nuclear?) meltdown, as is plainly prophesied in verses 7 and 12 of 2 Peter 3, and in Joel 2:30-31; Psalm 50:3; Isaiah 29:6, 30:30, 66:15-16; Nahum 1:5-6; and Malachi 4:1. Our major concern here, however, is not with the just fate of our present world, but with the fact that ours *is* the *second* world that God made.

Verse 13 of 2 Peter 3 above prophesies the coming of new heavens and a new earth wherein dwelleth righteousness. This, of course, is the *third* heaven and the *third* earth, the blissful everlasting world that God will create in the future for the saved of our *second earth* (see Rev. 20-22). So, in summary, God created one world (the first), which was annihilated by water. It is gone! It is no more! The second world He created, the one we now inhabit, awaits annihilation by fire. The third world, the heavens and the earth He has yet to create, will, of course, be everlasting. You can see now why we promote *Three-World Creationism* and where our society's name comes from.

As we turn to the Bible's proof of *Three-World Creationism*, we stand foursquare on the following principle: *The Bible means just what it says.* There is no reason why it should not! What does it say about the creation of the first earth? In Genesis 1:6-7 God created the firmament (or Heaven, see Gen 1:8) in the *middle* of waters. In other words, the firmament (of the first of God's three worlds, remember) was like a huge air bubble with waters above it and around it on all sides (except for the bottom about which we will speak later).

The barrier between this air bubble and the waters above is likened in many verses unto a tent or curtain stretched out (see Ps. 104:2; Job 9:8; Isa. 40:22, 51:13; Jer. 10:12). Psalm 148:4 confirms this when it calls upon the "waters that be above the heavens to praise him," i.e., God. Liberals, of course, just turn this into a big myth, and, sad to say, even our allies in creationism, the *Scientific Creationists,* are often less than candid when they talk about a vapor canopy above, but that is not what the Bible teaches.[7] Much of the water that flooded the world in Noah's day came from the windows of heaven that God opened at the beginning (Gen. 7:11) and closed at the end of the flood (Gen. 8:2). If you find this an incredible description of the world in which we now live, see also 2 Kings 7:2, Isaiah 24:18, and Malachi 3:10 where the windows of heaven of the *first world* are clearly mentioned as being real. *Of course our second world does not have such windows.*

The first firmament was the place where God put lights to rule the day and the night, the sun, moon, and stars (Gen. 1:14-17). Notice also that the fowl fly in, or through, the first firmament (Gen. 1:20). So, in the time of the first heaven and the first earth, the sun, moon, and stars were not set in outer space (as they are now) but in the same atmosphere that birds flew through.

At the bottom of that great air bubble, i.e., the first heaven, was the first earth founded upon waters below it as Psalm 136:6 makes crystal clear, and is confirmed by Exodus 20:4. So, Genesis 1:7 is by no means alone in referring to the waters under the firmament. The exact relationship between the pillars of the earth (Job 9:6, 1 Sam. 2:8) or the foundations of the earth (Job 38:4; Ps. 104:5; Prov. 8:29; Isa. 48:13, 51:13; Jer. 31:37) and the great deep need not concern us here except to note that these are founded upon water, the same water as that which broke forth, welling up, at the time of the flood (Gen. 7:11, Prov. 3:20) and was stopped up at the end of the flood period (Gen. 8:2).

Three things are clear. First, Noah did not realize, nor did God choose to tell him, the magnitude of the miracle that the Lord had performed while Noah and his family were adrift in the ark. They did not know that a *completely* new heaven and a *completely* new earth were being prepared for them and their posterity. Second, God did not choose to reveal this to the Jews of the Old Covenant but let them continue to believe that they were living in the same world as the one before the flood. In His wisdom, He reserved this revelation for Peter and for Bible-believing Christians in the age of the New Covenant. Third, what the Bible says of the first heaven and the first earth is not, and cannot be, true in all respects of this *His second world.*

Another principle on which we stand foursquare is this: True religion and true science do not conflict for those who are properly informed. What God has revealed about his first world in Scripture does, of course, conflict mightily with what he has let mankind learn about his second world through science. For *Three-World Creationism* there are no conflicts, but for ordinary creationists, including Scientific Creationists who have failed to read and understand Peter, the conflicts are dreadful and very unedifying. For example, is there an envelope of atmosphere around the second earth like the big hemispheric air bubble described in the Bible? No! Does rain today fall through apertures (or windows) in outer space beyond the orbit of the moon and the stations of the sun and stars? Heavens, no! The rain falls from moisture drawn up into the atmosphere as everybody knows. Do birds fly through outer space up around the sun, moon, and stars? Certainly not! Is the second earth basically a flat, roundish platform floating on foundations laid in watery depths? No, no, no; it is a sphere that sails through space in orbit around the sun. Does the sun today move from one end of an air-bubble heaven to another? No, our (second) earth revolves around our sun, which itself is in outer space. These apparent problems, which can cause the Bible to be held up to ridicule and unbelief, all disappear when the *truths* of *Three-World Creationism* are grasped and appreciated.

How You Can Help

If you accept and appreciate these truths, as we believe you will, upon prayerful consideration, you may wonder how you can help to spread this revealed word of the Lord. Here's how:

1. Feel free to photocopy this pamphlet and give it to as many friends as possible.
2. Leave a copy in the Gideon Bible the next time you stay overnight in a hotel or motel.

3. Call it to the attention of your school board members and to members of the state board of education; to your senators and representatives, state and federal; to the governor; and to our president and members of his administration.
4. Demand equal time for *Three-World Creationism* in the public schools whenever science instruction is perverted with evolutionism and whenever Christian schools are misled by ordinary scientific creationism.
5. Call it to your pastor's attention and to the attention of your favorite radio and TV preachers, and talk it up in Sunday School and Church.
6. Try to get news stories about it in your state and local papers. Remember, publicity is very important.
7. Help us continue our important work by sending your contributions to: Three-World Creation Society, 1208 Jenkins Drive, Auburn, AL 36830.

Notes

1. *The Letters of James and Peter*, rev. ed. (Philadelphia: Westminster Press, 1976): 283, 289.
2. *I & II Peter* (Phillipsburg, N.J.: Presbyterian and Reformed Publishing Co., 1976), iii, Preface to *II Peter*.
3. In four volumes (Lafayette, Ind.: Associated Publishers and Authors, 1979).
4. *The Letters of Peter and Jude* (Cambridge: At the University Press, 1967).
5. *The Second Epistle General of Peter and the General Epistle of Jude* (1968): 131.
6. Balmer H. Kelly et al. (eds.), *The Laymen's Bible Commentary*, vol. 24 (Richmond, Va.: John Knox Press, 1962).
7. Jody Dillow, "The Attenuation of Visible Radiation in the Vapor Canopy," *Creation Research Society Quarterly* 14, no. 3 (December 1977): 139–46.

10

What Now? What Next?

Introduction

Some summarizing occurs in this final chapter but only to establish the point that nowadays "Creation Science" has powerful friends at court—at the Supreme Court to be exact. How these friends may one day help this pseudoscience provides us with a possible answer to the question, What next?

The "Scientific Creationists" also have friends on all the highways and byways of America. They are everywhere where scientifically established fact runs counter to daily intuitions, depersonalizes the universe, threatens confidence in cosmic meaning and purpose, and undercuts faith in everlasting bliss for the "saved." Such friends, individually or collectively, may at any time and place use any of the devices the "Scientific Creationists" have already tried out, even if unsuccessfully. Fundagelicals of all stripes are conditioned to believe that their cause is just and that it will ultimately triumph. Failure at any given time is taken as a form of correction sent by the Bible-god to test the faith of his servants and to toughen their moral fiber. Herein we see more potential answers to the questions What now? What next?

Those who would neutralize "Creation Science" must expect failure if all they do is to present the wonders of science with wide-eyed enthusiasm. They will also fail if they expect "reason" to prevail or acceptable compromises to be possible. "Scientific Creationists" will not compromise with those whom they believe to be adversaries of the Bible-god. Such adversaries, to succeed, will have to go against the American grain and become real adversaries of the twin beliefs in scruptural literalism and biblical inerrancy. They will also have to reveal the egotistical, soteriological motivation behind these beliefs.

It is imperative to differentiate between respect for one's fellow citizens, as they exercise their constitutional freedom of belief, and respect for *what* they believe. Americans are not required to respect religious ideas that are false, invalid, or delusional.

* * *

Richard Dawkins (well-known for his books *The Selfish Gene* and *The Blind Watchmaker*) has written, "It is absolutely safe to say that if you meet somebody who claims not to believe in evolution, that person is ignorant, stupid or insane (or wicked, but I'd rather not consider that)."[1] Let us agree that wickedness is not at issue, nor is insanity a major contributing factor. Ignorance and stupidity are to be reckoned with, but not by themselves alone. What Dawkins fails to recognize is the fact of voluntary self-stultification for soteriological reasons. He has trouble it would seem (as do numerous intellectuals) in taking seriously the fact that unnumbered millions of people will demean their intellects to gain forgiveness and will murder their minds in order to be redeemed unto "everlasting life." Let us agree that this seems, nowadays, too childish, too egotistical, even too cowardly to countenance. Nevertheless, it is not at all below human dignity in Western culture to stultify the mind while bending the knee to the Bible-god, that sacred sovereign (of faith) who is presumed to save—or damns forever.

Seeing themselves as good soldiers in the "Church Militant" here below, the "Scientific Creationists" will fight on and ever on until they are translated into the "Church Triumphant" that they think awaits them beyond the grave. They will do whatever they can (that is not dishonorable in their eyes) to advance the hegemony of the Bible-god and will attempt to neutralize or destroy whatever they perceive as casting doubt on his existence or making light of his authority. Theirs is a never-say-die attitude because that is precisely what they believe, that they will never really die but will live on, world without end, either in joyous bliss or in utmost misery. The feeling of total forgiveness (even for one's very being) that Christianity so amply supplies is to the "Scientific Creationists" both a down payment on and a foretaste of the postmortem glories to come.

Intellectually, scientifically, the world, of course, has not developed as biblical inerrantists had hoped it would. Quite the contrary—and with more bad news coming! Dawkins is quite right when he says, "I don't think it is too melodramatic to say that [Western] civilization is at war," but he is wrong in saying that "it is a war against religious bigotry."[2] Bigotry is not the fundamental point; salvation is the fundamental point, and the price that must be paid for it in Christianity. What we call bigotry is simply part of the price. So, with respect to the "Scientific Creationists," we should ask, what now and what next? In short, with which absurdities will they engage us today and tomorrow as they pay the price of their (presumed) salvation?

A brief foray into the past generation may serve best as a prelude to answering the questions above. With the *Scopes* trial (and the 1920s) over and done with, a liberal period dawned in the 1930s.[3] It was to last until about the mid-1960s. During this period, the mainline Protestant denominations (e.g., the Methodists, Presbyterians, Episcopalians, Congregationalists, American Baptists, and Disciples of Christ) flourished. They also found themselves able to integrate a non-inerrantist biblicism with advancing science as science was then perceived to be from the liberal theological viewpoint. Indeed, evolution seemed to some liberal Christians a splendid way for the Bible-god to have created human beings. A boost was given to this cooperative, harmonious outlook when the World Council of Churches was formed in Europe in 1948, followed two years later by the National Council of Churches of Christ in the United States. The so-called ecumenical movement here and abroad was composed of liberal Protestant and Eastern Orthodox churches that sought to remove traditional creedal and structural barriers that were becoming increasingly trivial and obfuscatory in the eyes of well-educated Christians everywhere. With fascism effectively destroyed in Europe, the principal threat to the various churches involved in forming the World Council seemed not to lie in one another but in atheistic communism, then powerful and growing.

So enticing was the ecumenical movement that even the Roman Catholics (who knew themselves to belong to the one true church) entered into dialogue with representatives of it, sent some of their advanced, more dependable priest-students to study with such eminent Protestant theologians as Karl Barth, Emil Brunner, and Rudolph Bultmann, and went so far as to exchange certain seminary professors with their opposite numbers in Protestant seminaries.[4] Following this, Roman Catholic biblical scholars (something of a rarity earlier) began to emerge and to find employment in the leading graduate departments of religious studies, whether openly secular as are those in state universities or traditionally oriented toward Protestantism as are such institutions as Harvard's and Yale's divinity schools.

Many religious groups, of course, never joined the liberal, ecumenical movement that led to the World and National Councils of Churches. The Southern Baptists, the Missouri Synod Lutherans, the Churches of Christ,

Southern Baptists, the Missouri Synod Lutherans, the Churches of Christ, the Assemblies of God, the Church of God, the Seventh Day Adventists, the Nazarenes, and the Jehovah's Witnesses all come to mind, to mention but a few of the more prominent groups. The curious fact is that in the 1960s these groups and others began to coalesce into a new ecumenical movement in America but without intending to do so formally or structurally. The threats these groups perceived also led them to lower some of their theological barriers against one another. Furthermore, many an interdenominational congregation with a strong fundagelical orientation began to spring up.

Such denominations and interdenominational congregations (1) rejected modern biblical scholarship and the (to them) heretical interpretation(s) to which it led, (2) rejected the liberal churches that gave voice, even if only occasionally, to such scholarship, (3) feared atheistic communism and the socialism increasingly evident (to them at least) in the World and National Councils, and (4) perceived an ominous, pervasive threat in the naturalistic assumptions of science. To illustrate, take the wide-spread acceptance of evolution as a fact by scientists, science educators, textbook publishers, and secularists in general. United by so much to fear, how could the denominations mentioned immediately above not form a new, de facto ecumenical movement, even if they never called it that? The members of these groups are, of course, the people I have been calling Fundagelicals, among the foremost of whom are those doughty warriors, the "Scientific Creationists."

At the same time the mainline Protestant churches began to weaken while the fundagelical churches were becoming ever stronger, public school instruction in evolution was gaining legal strength.[5] *Epperson* v. *Arkansas* (1968) held that states could not forbid instruction in evolution by statute. The State of Tennessee, responding to *Epperson* by trying to get equal emphasis put on biblical creationism whenever evolution was taught, lost in a ruling of the Sixth Circuit of Appeals (1975).[6] By this time the "Scientific Creationists," more than a decade old as an organized group, were able to lead Fundagelicals in counterattacking. Let me reiterate briefly the shells they lobbed at their opponents. The creation stories in Genesis are scientific or are at least as scientific as is Darwinism, which is really based on faith. Evolution is a dogma of the secular humanists and cannot be taught in the public schools without an unconstitutional establishment of religion. If this violation is permitted, it can be remedied by balanced treatment for "Creation Science" by presenting it as the only rival "scientific model" of origins. Exclusive instruction in evolution in the public schools inhibits the religion of students, something not permitted by the Constitution. The State has no compelling interest in teaching children anything about origins.

States can expunge subject matter from the public schools' curriculum. The academic freedom of students is being violated if they are prevented from receiving instruction in "Creation Science" whenever evolution is presented. The academic freedom of teachers is also, perhaps, being violated whenever they are forbidden to balance evolution with "Creation Science."

Such attempts at counterattacking lost in a preliminary way in *McLean* v. *Arkansas* (1982) and then in a definitive way in *Aguillard* (1987). The ratification of these defeats followed in *Hazelwood School District* v. *Kuhlman* (1988), *Webster* v. *New Lenox School District* (1990), and, most recently, *Peloza*.[7] In view of this string of defeats, why do the "Scientific Creationists" not give up? There are two reasons: First, their religion forbids them to give up; second, changes in the make-up of the Supreme Court give them renewed hope. This new hope may answer, in part, the question, what next? Why this hope may one day be realized requires some explaining.

The barrier between American government and religion was not, is not now, and almost certainly never will be a *wall of separation*. It is much more like a picket fence. The point to notice in this metaphor is that pickets can be added, shutting more out, or removed, widening the gap between pickets and thus letting more or bigger things pass to and fro. Those who would add pickets are the strict separationists. Those who would remove pickets are the accommodationists. With the creation of the Burger Court in 1969, accommodationism came into favor. In *Marsh* v. *Chambers* (1983), Chief Justice Burger wrote:

> To invoke Divine guidance on a public body entrusted with making the laws is not, in these circumstances [prayers opening sessions in the Nebraska legislature], an "establishment" of religion or a step toward establishment; it is simply tolerable acknowledgement of beliefs widely held among the people of this country.[8]

In *Lynch* v. *Donnelley* (1984) he wrote:

> Nor does the Constitution require complete separation of church and state; it affirmatively mandates accommodation, not merely tolerance, of all religions and forbids hostility toward any.[9]

In the same decision he said that "our precedents plainly contemplate that on occasion some advancement of religion will result from governmental action."[10]

The Rehnquist Court has nurtured this accommodationist mood. In *Wallace* v. *Jaffree* (1985), a case involving prayer in the public schools, Justice Rehnquist wrote:

> The "wall of separation between church and State" is a metaphor which has proved useless as a guide to judging. It should be frankly and explicitly abandoned.[11]

He wrote moreover:

> [N]othing in the Establishment Clause [of the First Amendment] requires government to be strictly neutral between religion and irreligion, nor does that Clause prohibit Congress or the States from pursuing legitimate secular ends through nondiscriminatory sectarian means.[12]

He concluded his dissent as follows:

> Nothing in the Establishment Clause of the First Amendment, properly understood, prohibits such generalized "endorsement" of prayer [as was at issue in the Mobile, Alabama, public schools which occasioned Jaffree's complaint].[13]

Just how the mood of accommodationism, firmly established above, may one day aid the "Scientific Creationists" can be seen clearly in *Edwards v. Aguillard* (1987), a case not involving prayer but "Balanced Treatment" for "Creation Science."

Justice Scalia wrote a long dissent to this decision in which he was joined by Chief Justice Rehnquist. The two appear to have swallowed "Scientific Creationist" propaganda hook, line, and sinker. At no point do they give any indication of being aware of any of the refutations assembled in this book. Even though it was not available to them, many of the refutations it contains were and could have been consulted, if there had been any will to do so. It is not too much to say that the "Scientific Creationists" now have friends at Court.[14]

Justice Scalia was already favorably disposed toward accommodationism by the time of *Aguillard*. Therein he posits a significant difference between secular means (in the public schools) that have the effect of advancing religion to *tolerable* limits and secular means that advance religion *wholly,* or put differently, that *only* advance religion. To date the latter remains unconstitutional, but not the former. In this frame of mind Justice Scalia received the testimony (through the appeals process) of Bill Keith, the Louisiana state senator who introduced the "Balanced Treatment Act" in that state.

Since Justice Scalia at no time questioned Keith's sincerity, let us assume the same. Our justice based his dissent to *Aguillard* on the following seven points: First, "The witnesses repeatedly assured committee members [in the

Louisiana legislature] that 'hundreds and hundreds' of highly respected, internationally renowned scientists believe in creation science. . . ." In fact affidavits filed by appellants attest to the fact that two scientists, a philosopher, a theologian, and an educator "swear that it ["Creation Science"] is essentially a collection of scientific data supporting the theory that the physical universe and life within it appeared suddenly and have not changed substantially since appearing."[15] From this Justice Scalia concludes that "we must assume that the Balanced Treatment Act does *not* require the presentation of religious doctrine."[16] (An acid test for this conclusion will follow in due time.) Justice Scalia does not appear to have had the presence of mind to recognize that the hundreds and hundreds of highly respected, internationally renowned scientists who believe in "Scientific Creationism" are the "Scientific Creationists" christening themselves as such. One of the experts mentioned above by profession is the co-author of *Of Pandas and People* (refuted in chapter 5). Ah well, how is a Justice of the Supreme Court to know who's who in science?

Second, Keith and his witnesses testified that there "are only two scientific explanations for the beginning of life."[17] Justice Scalia in his innocence appears to have taken them at their word. The assertion above, however, is absolutely false. Plato's creation story involving Prometheus and Epimetheus (see chapter 2) is just as scientific as is "Creation Science." In fact, neither is scientific at all.

Third, "the body of scientific evidence supporting creation science is as strong as that supporting evolution. In fact, it may be even stronger."[18] Justice Scalia does not appear to have asked what this scientific evidence is nor who it is who is judging its strength. Certainly not the world's leading molecular biologists, nor the world's leading cell biologists, nor the world's leading evolutionary biologists! Who then? Why, the "Scientific Creationists," of course. But why not let a leading biologist speak as Justice Scalia could have done, but did not? Richard Dawkins has written that the fact of evolution is "proved utterly beyond reasonable doubt."[19] He writes:

> [W]e now know from the work of Mr. [Vincent] Sarich and his colleague, the molecular biologist Allan Wilson, that our common ancestor with chimpanzees lived astonishingly recently. Moreover, we are closer cousins to African apes (chimpanzees and gorillas) than those apes are to other apes (orangutans and gibbons). We are not, then, merely like apes or descended from apes; we *are* apes, and African apes at that.[20]

Fourth, "Creation science is educationally valuable."[21] If Justice Scalia really believes this, then teaching it in the public schools would constitute a *tolerable* religious means to a secular end. Being a secular end and not wholly a religious one and not prejudicial to any religious denomination, such a practice would be constitutional. Again Dawkins may be allowed to speak:

> To claim equal time for creation science in biology classes is about as sensible as to claim equal time for the flat-earth theory in astronomy classes. Or, as someone has pointed out, you might as well claim equal time in sex education classes for the stork theory.

Fifth, "Creation Science" is now being educationally censored from or misrepresented in the public schools.[23] The quote from Dawkins above can do double duty here.

Sixth, Senator Keith was apparently able to convince Justice Scalia of the following:

> The censorship of creation science has at least two harmful effects. First, it deprives students of knowledge of one of the two scientific explanations for the origin of life and leads them to believe that evolution is proven fact; thus, their education suffers and they are wrongly taught that science has proved their religious beliefs false. Second, it violates the Establishment Clause. The United States Supreme Court has held that secular humanism is a religion.[24]

These tired old charges have been refuted over and again in the preceding chapters.

Seventh, "the [Louisiana] legislature wanted to insure that students would be free to decide for themselves how life began based upon a fair and balanced presentation of the scientific evidence—that is, to protect the 'right of each [student] voluntarily to determine what to believe (and what not to believe) free of any coercive pressure from the State.' *Grand Rapids School District* v. *Ball* 473 U.S. at 385."[25] This point, as might be expected, is joined to the charge that the absence of "balanced treatment" is identical to the denial of students' academic freedom. To any "sincere" exponent of "Creation Science," whom Justice Scalia could easily believe, academic freedom means freedom from indoctrination.

If any indoctrinating about origins is to be done in the public schools, the "Scientific Creationists" want to be in a position to do it. It is, in fact, puerile to think that schoolboys and girls are going to be in a position to judge for themselves on origins, just because they are in a context permitting "Balanced Treatment." Schoolboys and girls are not in a position to make up their own minds, logically, in any context in which the evidence is beyond their intellectual capacity. Science, of course, should always be presented to children critically and as something tentative. They should be encouraged to suspend judgment until they are capable of assessing the evidence for any theory. Children are not being indoctrinated when they are presented with the facts of gravitation even though theoretical problems concerning how it operates remain to be settled. The fact of evolution is exactly parallel to the fact of gravitation (except that the latter is more obvious to daily experience). Theories explaining evolution, of course, remain as open as those put forth to explain gravitation.

Taking points one through seven above at face value, Justice Scalia had no difficulty in accepting Senator Keith's vehement denial that "his purpose was to advance a particular religious doctrine." This vehement denial plus the (to Justice Scalia) overwhelming evidence presented above brought him to say, "At this point, then, we must assume that the Balanced Treatment Act does *not* require the presentation of religious doctrine."[26] That "Creation Science" might just happen to coincide with certain religious tenets is no reason, to our justice, to think that its presence in the public schools would advance religion.

Earlier I mentioned an acid test that can bring this house of cards down. It could have been put to Senator Keith, if anybody had had the wit to do so, and it can be put to anybody now who agrees with him. Moreover, it can be put to anybody in the future, at any place or time, who advances such a position. To return to Keith, let us assume that he is as much a man of integrity as Justice Scalia believes him to be. If so, we may assume that he would answer honestly any relevant question put to him, even though the answer might expose the position above as a charade. "Scientific Creationists" dote on the notions that the universe appeared suddenly and recently and that nothing much has changed since.[27] Let us suppose that any one of those ideas or any combination thereof leads inevitably to agnosticism. Correspondingly, let us also suppose that because of these alleged facts, school children are encouraged to make no decision about origins but to suspend judgment. Would the very sincere Senator Keith want the sudden appearance of a recent, static universe taught in the public schools if it resulted in agnosticism and lack of belief? Let us make his shoe pinch a bit more. Let us suppose that the sudden appearance of a recent, static universe led, by logical necessity, to atheism. Would he then want these ideas taught in the public schools? Approached from the opposite direction, let us assume that only an ancient, slow-to-appear, evolving universe could lead with any probability to the idea that it is an artifact or sufficiently like one to require an artificer somewhat like the Bible-god. Would Senator Keith still cling gladly to the sudden appearance of a recent, static universe? No, of course not! Though it might come as a considerable shock to his system, he would change sides quickly.

So much for the *science* in "Creation Science"! The sole purpose of the "Scientific Creationists" is to get fundagelical religion, with its idea of biblical inerrancy, into the public schools. It is very worrisome that a Justice of the Supreme Court cannot see through anything as transparent as this.

If as many as three other justices were to be taken in by "Scientific Creationist" propaganda (as Rehnquist and Scalia seem to have been) and were to entertain similar negative views of the *Lemon* test (see chapter 7), a profound challenge to science education in the public schools would result. Moreover, we might find ourselves living in a place where and at a time when judges decide what is and what is not science (see chapter 6, n. 13). Or, they might allow greater leeway to state legistatures to decide such issues. Even local option policies could arise again.

In addition to having friends at Court, the "Scientific Creationists" have unnumbered friends in the American populace who are no better suited than Justice Scalia to judge what is and what is not science or what ought and what ought not to be presented in science education in the public schools. Among the hoi polloi and professionals in nonscientific fields alike, science has become its own worst enemy. A word of explanation is in order.

The "Scientific Creationists" have posed, all along, as admirable exponents of democracy in education. Let school children, they have urged, make up their own minds about origins after they have heard both the "Creation Science" and evolution models. In orded to throw this context for choice into the brightest light possible, let us visit an imaginary grade school anywhere in Europe after the mid-1500s. Though Copernicus was dead by this time, his heliocentric theory lived on. Let us imagine a component of natural philosophy in the curriculum taking up the "Bible-science" model of the universe and the Copernican model of our solar system. Copernicus had taught that the sun did not really come up in the east each morning, pass overhead, and set in the west. On the contrary, the earth, he taught, revolves around the sun and spins once each twenty-four hours on its axis. The sun only seems to come up, pass overhead, and set. Thus did Copernicus save the appearances.

Quite apart from the authority of the family and tradition, the Bible, and the Roman Church, which view would have gained the easiest acceptance among schoolboys of the time? The one closest to intuition, daily experience, and common sense, of course! "Bible science" in those days would have been to Copernicanism what "Creation Science" today is to Darwinism. How interesting it would have been if a teacher and his pupils could have gotten a papal travel grant to visit the north pole on or about the twenty-first of June of any year. There the sun would not have been seen to rise in the morning, pass overhead, and set in the evening, but to have remained above the horizon for twenty-four hours at a stretch. Even if the schoolboys witnessing this unexpected sight could have believed their eyes, they still would have had no direct, intuitive experiences of the earth's rotation on its axis or its revolution around the sun. As unfortunate as it may be, science is often counter-intuitive. As regrettable as it may be, "Creation Science" is quite intuitive, to scientific simpletons at least.

Without belaboring the point, let us imagine another school room, this time in Salem, Massachusetts, in the year 1692. Strange goings-on have been witnessed and reported. As one writer has put it, "the tongues of innocent children were yanked to their chins, their jaws snapped open and shut, their limbs corkscrewed like branches." Some seemed to be in trances, "hands frozen in place, uttering the most hideous gargles and growls."[28] A teacher of the time, let us imagine, is presenting his students with both the "Bible-science" and the ergot models of explanation. The ergot model, which our very advanced teacher presents, holds that a hallucinogenic fungus (found on badly handled rye) caused the bizarre phenomena at issue. The "Bible-science" model, of course, explains it all with reference to demonic possession, witchcraft, and satanism. (No disease theory available at the time, by the way, was able to explain the weird phenomena in question.) Even supposing that there had been a contemporary scientist available who could have explained the biochemistry involved, who else could have been expected to believe it? Who could have understood it? Who could have understood how to confirm or disconfirm the ergot hypothesis? Nobody, and that is very nearly the situation of most Americans today. The understanding of high energy physics, for example, is now as far beyond the ordinary person and the nonspecialist alike as would an understanding of the biochemistry of ergot have been beyond the understanding of the Salem clergy in 1692. Meanwhile, for the people of Salem there was the Bible, a great authority indeed in Western culture. For many then (as now) its teachings were (are) as certain as the content of personal intuition. Moreover, for the laity the clergy then (as now) could (can) claim more authority over the ordinary person than can even the most eminent scientists. Given the vast number of people, from the pope on down, who believe in the Bible-devil and his legions of imps, what better way to explain the witches of Salem (then and now) than through satanism, demon possession, and witchcraft (see Matt. 12:22–32, Mark 5:1–13, Luke 8:26–33 and 22:3 for passages referring to demons, and Matt. 4:5–11, Luke 10:18, 2 Cor. 11:14, 12:7, and 1 Peter 5:8 for passages referring to Satan; these, of course, are but a few of the passages that could be cited).[29]

In purely scientific terms, the alleged theorizing about origins called "Creation Science" cannot withstand the genuine theorizing of leading evolutionary biologists. But who among ordinary people can recognize this? To continue, there is no evidence at all for the "Creation model," whereas geologists, paleontologists, and molecular biologists have amassed mountains of data tending to explain how evolution has occurred. But who among ordinary people can evaluate the evidence? Moreover, the major premise of "Creation Science" is not falsifiable and thus cannot appear in a truly scientific explanation, whereas conditions can be specified that would cause consternation among evolutionary biologists and wreak havoc in their theorizing. But who among ordinary people can comprehend the significance for science of the falsifiability criterion? Much in evolutionary theory could be falsified, for example, if a fossilized human skeleton where to be found cheek by jowl with a fossilized dinosaur skeleton. The "Scientific Creationists" cannot and will not tell anybody what would falsify their belief in the Bible-god.

As I write these words I have before me the *New York Times* of April 24, 1992, p. 1, which says that NASA's discovery of "wrinkles in the fabric of space" supports the Big Bang theory. Temperature fluctuations "no more than a hundred-thousandth of a degree . . . signal primeval variations in the universe's topography a mere 300,000 years after its explosive birth." "Direct observations" of the expanding universe go back no further than the end of the first 300,000 years. We are told that there is still uncertainty concerning the nature of the matter creating "density ripples." Meanwhile, the search for dark matter goes on. Who understands this? Would it not take great "faith" to teach this to schoolboys and girls as the truth? Are our instruments good enough to detect what has been claimed for them? Is there but one interpretation of the data gained this way? Do cosmologists really know what happened during the first three-trillionths of a second after the Big Bang? What would disconfirm their conclusions? These and a thousand other questions arise that separate a handful of experts from all the rest of the earth's people. Worse yet, the experts do not all agree.

Meanwhile, speaking with sublime confidence, the "Scientific Creationists" make it easy for us. The Bible-god made the world miraculously. It is as it is, because that is the way he wanted it. Our lives have meaning in relation to his will in creating this world and not some other. He is interested in saving the "souls" of those who believe the foregoing. To continue, the world is recent. A big flood came along and made false all the findings of the instruments that indicate a universe billions of years old. The Bible-devil has confused the scientists who put their reliance in their instruments indicating great age. Kinds breed true. Cats have kittens, whereas dogs have puppies, and dinosaurs never bring forth birds.

The "Scientific Creationists" have very fertile fields, indeed, in which to work. Millions of ordinary Americans, thousands upon thousands of sympathetic public school teachers, and untold numbers of school administrators and school board members are, in fact, scientific simpletons. Such folk will want the Bible-god to have his say in the public schools. This is one area in which the American tradition of local control of public schools is manifestly bad. As a set comparatively fewer members of most state boards of public education, for example, will be persuaded by the specious arguments of the "Scientific Creationists" than will members of local school boards. In Alabama in 1992 a bill was introduced in the legislature to require school board members to be high school graduates themselves.[30] Well, what difference would that make when it comes to understanding "wrinkles in the fabric of space" or trying to fathom how a cosmologist can claim to know what was going on three-trillionths of a second after the Big Bang?

For the rest of our lives and beyond we and our descendants will have to battle with the "Scientific Creationists." It will be easy for them to introduce their own idea of "abrupt appearance," a euphemism for instantaneous creation by fiat on some day or other, that happened but a short time ago. It will be easy for them to question science detrimentally (in favor of their own position), since science questions itself as part of its proper business and since scientists are often critical of what their fellows are doing. Who among ordinary Americans will be able to assess whether the universe came into existence abruptly only ten thousand years ago or abruptly fifteen billion years ago? It will also be easy for the "Scientific Creationists" to make light of the weirdness of modern cosmology, a discipline just now coming out of its own "dark ages" according to the *Times* article. This unhappy litany could go on and on.

With powerful friends in the Supreme Court (and elsewhere in government) and with 47 percent of the American people affirming belief in the recent creation of human beings by "divine fiat," do the "Scientific Creationists" need any other friends? Clearly the answer is yes. The friends they also need and seek to cultivate are those who can legitimize their educational efforts. For example, the Institute for Creation Research (ICR), located in California, represents itself as having a graduate school. This school awards Master's Degrees in such subjects as astronomy, biology, geology, and science education.[31] However, the Western Association of Schools and Colleges (WASC), which accredits colleges and universities in the western part of the United States, has refused to accredit the Master's Degree programs of the ICR.[32] Failing to attain this desirable status, the ICR has responded by accrediting itself, for all intents and purposes, by a newly created agency called TRACS, the Transnational Association of Christian Schools.[33] TRACS accreditation "rests predominantly on whether Biblical inerrancy and literalism are foundations for course work."[34]

Even though the ICR claims that TRACS is officially recognized by the U.S. Department of Education (DOE), TRACS is academically beneath contempt in the eyes of WASC.[35] Until the ICR can be accredited by WASC, its graduates will be unable to obtain California teaching certificates.[36] Lacking this credential, ICR's graduates will be hampered in more ways than one.

As the result of a complicated lawsuit filed against Bill Honig, California's superintendent of public education, the ICR received a settlement of $225,000. It also received permission to teach "the creation model as being correct, provided the institution also teaches evolution," and it may operate under its old California license until 1995. At that time it must have its license reviewed by the newly formed Council for Private Postsecondary and Vocational Education.[37] Eugenie C. Scott, executive director of the National Center for Science Education, writes that "California *licenses* unaccredited schools, colleges, business schools, etc., to guarantee the public that the institution is financially reputable, and that the course of study is actually what is claimed" for it.[38] So, though the ICR is *not* accredited by the only agency that really matters (i.e., WASC), it is inching toward respectability. *Nature,* the eminent British journal of science, quotes Kevin Padia, a biologist at the University of California Berkeley, as follows: "It's a shocking and puzzling decision. . . . The state lawyers gave away the store." *Nature* continues by saying that "state officials were unwilling to do battle with religious groups" at a time when the licensing procedure in California is in transition.[39]

Neither the tangled skein of events leading to the ICR's lawsuit nor changes in how California licenses *unaccredited* schools needs to concern us further at this point. What concerns educators is (1) that evolution will almost certainly be caricatured, treated unfairly, and presented inaccurately to ICR graduate students; (2) that these students, once graduated, will be able to worm their way into science classrooms in California and perhaps elsewhere; and (3) that the principle applied to the ICR may be applied to other kinds of unaccredited schools. Scott writes, "Perhaps a 'College of Crystal Healing' will apply for degree-granting status based on the fact that it *also* teaches about 'real' medicine" (although certainly not seriously).[40] The opportunity for educational mischief is, indeed, staggering.

The ICR's failure to achieve accreditation by WASC should not be seen as a serious defeat. The Rev. Jerry Falwell's Liberty University (LU) has already surmounted this kind of problem—in Virginia at least. There it has found it possible to supply its graduates with a credential good enough to serve its purposes. As Eve and Harrold note, LU has a "Creationist-oriented Biology Program accredited by the Virginia Board of Education to train teachers."[41] Similar accreditation may one day be possible for other fundagelical colleges in a variety of states, especially if notions of alternative schooling continue to find favor in Washington.[42] Even in states not having teacher certification boards as compliant as Virginia's, ways can surely be found to place teachers trained in "Creation Science" in public classrooms. These ways involve some loss of control and a smidgen of duplicity, but these are not prices too high for the "Scientific Creationists" to pay.

With a little ingenuity, the ICR (or other creationist institutes, denominational colleges, etc.) could provide the dogmatic training necessary for teaching "Creation Science" and could then prompt students to transfer (where possible) to accredited schools or simply to enroll in accredited schools after their indoctrination in "Creation Science." Graduation from accredited schools opens the doors to teacher certification. The ICR could even subsidize this kind of Trojan horse. With the appropriate dogmatic preparation accomplished whether on a credit basis (as at LU) or on a noncredit basis (as at the ICR), students, once enrolled in accredited colleges, could simply major in science education, taking the fewest legitimate science courses allowed, and then enter the teaching profession upon graduation.

Once certified and hired, the teachers of "Creation Science" would have only to exercise a bit of discretion and not be too obviously zealous to pass on their particular variety of pseudoscience. To a very large degree it has been and will continue to be welcomed. Even with its high educational standards, California has not succeeded in keeping "Creation Science" out of its public schools. Eve and Harrold show (as of 1987) that 83 percent of California's high school students claim to have been taught both evolution and creationism. These authors also show (as of 1986) that 30 percent of Kentucky's science teachers report teaching creationism in their classes and that 29 percent of science teachers in Georgia report feeling significant pressure to teach creationism or to downplay evolution. A national sample of science teachers (as of 1986) showed that 45 percent agreed that creationism should be taught in the public schools.[43] With such data as these, it is clear that "Creation Science" will make headway even without the accreditation of its educational institutions. Accreditation would, however, help. Then the ICR, for example, could keep its students at home, as it were, where their progress in dogma could be monitored more closely than it could if students were required to leave the reservation, so to speak, transferring to other schools to gain accreditation and teacher certification.[44] The foregoing pages indicate that we Americans have a great deal of "Creation Science" in our future.[45]

American Fundagelicals in general and "Scientific Creationists" in particular mean to be good citizens on the whole. In some instances, as we all know, they are even superpatriots. On other occasions they are neither but are, in point of fact, subversives. All of this is true of everyone who tries to live in two realms simultaneously and whose dual citizenship involves conflicts of interest. True believers in the Bible-god are theocratic religiously even while trying to be democratic politically. Such folk may break the law of their land in the name of a higher law and do so with perfectly clear consciences. On those occasions when the theological price is too high for the pious to pay, they will set aside a human instrument such as the Constitution in favor of the "Sovereign" of their faith. Although the "Scientific Creationists" are potent politically, they should not be viewed as just another interest group such as the Nature Conservancy or the National Rifle Association. Even less are they a political party, and the extent to which they are a movement, such as the civil rights movement or the antiwar movement during the late 1960s and early 1970s, is very dubious. Theologically (i.e., in faith), they are not an interest group, not a party, and not a movement, but, rather, in their view, the *people of the Bible-god*. As such they feel themselves to be as much above mere human laws as they presume their deity to be. Theologically, *their* interest is the Bible-god's interest, and *their* interest is the *true* interest of their country or so their faith would have it.

In the United States in our day and time, the "Scientific Creationists" have had the peace promised by their soteriology (which passeth all understanding) shattered by discordancies emanating from scientific circles. Furthermore, they have been aggrieved by public school systems that have become far too secular for their religion to tolerate. Finally, they have found themselves alienated from their federal government, which they find altogether too humanistic. All of this has caused them to fear for the "souls" of their children, to fear for the "souls" of the "unsaved," and to fear for their country.

Since the faithful always yearn to be supported or reinforced in their faith rather than troubled because of it, they seek to set things straight when unduly disturbed. This is precisely the condition in which biblical inerrantists in America find themselves today. In the interest of their soteriology and in the service of the "Sovereign" of their "heavenly kingdom," they are rising up to set things straight. In so doing, they have, perforce, embroiled the rest of us and will do so for the rest of our lives. The big question is this: What should we who are not biblical inerrantists do about it or, better, perhaps, try to do about it?[46]

Notes

1. See the review given the caption "Put Your Money on Evolution." The book being reviewed was *Blueprints*, subtitled *Solving the Mysteries of Evolution* by Maitland A. Edey and Donald C. Johanson, *The New York Times Book Review* 94 (April 9, 1989), p. 35.

2. Ibid.

3. Professor Eugene C. Bjorklun divides the creation/evolution controversy into two phases, the first of which ended with Scopes's conviction in 1925, the second of which began with the *Epperson* decision in 1968. See "Evolution and Creationism in the Public School Curriculum: The Academic Freedom Issue," *Education Law Reporter* 70 (December 19, 1991): 277-78. He did not, however, comment on religious developments between the end of the first phase and the beginning of the second (i.e., between the late 1930s and the late 1960s), nor did he note the attempts of biology textbooks to retain evolution but to soft peddle it during this time. See Professor Lawrence S. Lerner, "Killing Darwin for Christ," *Freethought Today* 9, no. 3 (April 1992): 8.

4. The author knows personally a professor of homiletics at Lexington Theological Seminary in Kentucky (Protestant) who exchanged teaching duties with his opposite number at St. Meinrad Seminary (Catholic) in Indiana. This would have been unthinkable in any earlier generation.

5. See Dean M. Kelley, *Why Conservative Churches Are Growing: A Study in the Sociology of Religion* (New York: Harper and Row, 1977). Also, "New Fundamentalist Alliance Challenges Church-State Separation," *Voice of Reason* (Newsletter of Americans for Religious Liberty) 27 (Fall 1988): 1. Over the years *Religion Watch* (a monthly digest of trends and ideas in religion) has carried articles on the relative decline of the mainline churches and the rise of more conservative churches. See, for example, "Can the Liberal-Conservative Rift Be Healed?" 1, no. 10 (September 1986): 1-2; "Younger Clergy More Conservative Today?" 2, no. 8 (June 1987): 5; "Prophetic Ministries Growing," 4, no. 10 (September 1989): 3-4; "Mainline Structures Crumbling?" 4, no. 4 (February 1989): 1-2; "Evangelicals Edging Out Catholics in Schooling," 3, no. 4 (April 1988): 6; "Envisioning American Religion in the Nineties," 5, no. 4 (February 1990): 1; "Mainline Protestantism Declining in Inner-Cities, Reviving Downtown," 5, no. 9 (July/August 1990): 3-4; "Presbyterian, Adventist and Jewish Conventional Trends," 5, no. 10 (September 1990): 1-2; "Ecumenical Slump Reaching Younger Generation," 6, no. 2 (December 1990): 5; "WCC [World Council of Churches] Experiencing New Divisions With Indigenous Theologies," 6, no. 6 (April 1991): 1-2.

6. Bjorklun, "Education and Creationism," p. 278.

7. John Peloza, a biology teacher in the Capistrano Unified School District in California, was proselytizing students and teaching "Creation Science" when, in 1991, he was told to cease and desist. His lawsuit charging that "the school district had wrongfully reprimanded him" came to naught. See *Voice of Reason*, no. 40 (Winter 1992): 10.

8. 463 U.S. at 792.

9. 465 U.S. at 673.

10. Ibid., at 683.

11. 472 U.S. at 107.

12. Ibid., at 113.

13. Ibid., at 114.

14. These good friends at Court are busy attacking the *Lemon* test, but not as I did in chapter 7, which also see. Professor David Schimmel in his "Education, Religion & the Rehnquist Court: Demolishing the Wall of Separation," *Education Law Reporter* 56 (9), 1990, p. 10, n. 3, especially mentions with alarm Justices Kennedy, Scalia, and White as joining the Chief Justice in attacking *Lemon*. If Justices Souter and Thomas also join in, the *Lemon* test will be dismantled, but not for the reasons why it should be dismantled.

15. 482 U.S. at 612, 622.

16. Ibid., at 612.

17. Ibid,, at 622.

18. Ibid., at 623.

19. Dawkins, *Blueprints*, p. 35.

20. Ibid.
21. *Aguillard*, at 623.
22. Dawkins, *Blueprints*, p. 35.
23. *Aguillard*, at 623.
24. Ibid., at 624. The statement that the Court has held secular humanism to be a religion is misleading. This contention occured in an obiter dictum in *Torcaso v. Watkins, Clerk*, 367 U.S. 488, 495, n. 11 (1961). Obiter dicta are not binding.
25. *Aguillard*, at 627-28.
26. Ibid, at 612 for Scalia's view; at 625 for Senator Keith's vehement denial.
27. Ibid., at 622.
28. Bruce Watson, " 'Thou Shalt Not Suffer a Witch to Live,'" *Smithsonian* 23, no. 1 (April 1992): 117.
29. *The Secular Humanist Bulletin* (of *Free Inquiry*) 7, no. 1 (March 1991): 1, says, "More exorcists have been appointed worldwide under papal authority in modern times than ever before. As for Karol Wojtyla himself [Pope John Paul II], he has not only given thirteen addresses on the devil since beocming pope, he has personally conducted two exorcisms in the Vatican...." The same source, 7, no. 2 (September 1991): 2, reports the findings of a recent Gallup Poll as follows: "A startling 55 percent of [American] poll respondents reported belief in the devil; 49 percent accepted the reality of satanic possession."
30. In the 1992 session of the Alabama House, a bill was introduced that would require all school board members to be high school graduates.
31. National Center for Science Education *Reports* 10, no. 6 (November-December 1990): 6.
32. NCSE *Reports* 11, no. 3 (Fall 1991): 4.
33. Ibid. It is very convenient for the ICR that TRACS is headed by its own president, Dr. Henry M. Morris. TRACS's accreditation of the ICR is much like baptizing one's own self. See NCSE *Reports* 11, no. 4 (Winter 1991): 21.
34. *Reports* 11, no. 3: 4.
35. Ibid.
36. Ibid.
37. NCSE *Reports* 11, no. 4: 1. Also see the following issues for details on the lawsuit against Bill Honig and the accreditation controversy involving the ICR: 9, no. 1 (January-February 1989): 21; 10, no. 1 (January-February 1990): 1, 14; 10, no. 2 (March-April 1990): 15; 10, no. 4 (July-August 1990): 8; 10, no. 5 (September-October 1990): 6; 10, no. 6 (November-December 1990): 6; and "California Evolution Defender Indicted," *Science* 256 (April 10, 1992): 173.
38. NCSE *Reports* 11, no. 3: 4.
39. "Creationist Victory," *Nature* 355 (February 27, 1992): 757.
40. NCSE *Reports* 11, no. 4: 21.
41. Raymond A. Eve and Francis B. Harrold, *The Creationist Movement in Modern America* (Boston: Twayne Publishers, 1991): 124-25. This is an extremely informative book, highly recommended. Its attempts at explaining the "Scientific Creationists" fail, however, because they do not focus sufficiently on the importance of soteriology in fundagelical religion.
42. NCSE *Reports* 11, no. 3: 4.
43. Eve and Harrold, *Creationist Movement in Modern America*, pp. 163-66. See also NCSE *Reports* 11, no. 4: 19, which quotes an article in the *Houston Chronicle* (of November 6, 1991) to the effect that 67 percent of Texas teachers "believe in the literal Biblical account of man's origin, compared with 25 percent who believe man evolved from lower life forms."
44. There is, for example, a lingering dispute between members of the American Scientific Affiliation (ASA) and the members of the Creation Research Society with its Institute for Creation Research (ICR). ASA members, for example, are able to harmonize their fundagelical faith with the possibility that the earth may be very old, whereas the "Scientific Creationists"

associated with the ICR have traditionally insisted that it must be young. This has led to a dispute between old-earthers and young-earthers, not primarily on scientific grounds, but on theological grounds. See "ASA to Endorse Teaching Evolution as Science," NCSE *Reports* 10, no. 5 (September–October 1990): 5. Whatever of science dogmatists may impart to students, they must, first of all, be sure to keep the doctrines of their faith pure. Hence the importance of keeping ICR students at the ICR for accredited work rather than running the risk that they might learn false doctrines elsewhere while trying to get a legitimate degree with easy access to teacher certification. See Eve and Harrold, *The Creationist Movement in Modern America*, pp. 46–48, 52.

45. See, for example, NCSE *Reports,* "Attacks on the Freedom to Learn Evolution," 9, no. 2 (March–April 1989): 17, carries reports from seven states; "Creationism Bill Filed in Missouri," 9, no. 3 (May–June 1989): 6; "Evolution in Geology Books Challenged in Texas," 9, no. 4 (July–August 1989): 1, also same issue, "Teacher Harassed Over Evolution [in Ohio]": 3; "Creation Science Still Plays Well in Peoria," 10, no. 3 (May–June 1990): 1, same issue, "Creationist Course in Colorado": 7; "Minister Preaches Creationism in Weed, California Public School Science Class," 10, no. 4 (July–August 1990): 1; "Illinois Schools Teach Creationism as Science," 10, no. 6 (November–December 1990): 1; "Florida Poll Supports Biblical Creationism in Schools," 11, no. 6 (November–December 1990): 11; "School District Institutes Creationism Unit [Morton, Ill.]," 11, no. 1 (1991): 1; "Florida Creationism Battle," 11, no. 2 (Summer 1991): 1.

46. Many of the preceding chapters touch on what we who are not scriptural inerrantists might do. See especially the last paragraph of chapter 6.

Index

The reader is reminded that the following entries merely indicate where certain names, terms, titles, etc. can be found in the text. These entries do not necessarily presuppose nor imply the existence of anything. 'Vickie Frost,' for example, names an existing person; 'Jack Frost' does not, if by that one means to refer to an elfin creature who paints tree leaves each year in the autumn.

Abington v. *Schempp.* See *School District of Abington* v.
Abiogenesis, 78, 108
Abrupt appearance, 161
Academic, 119, 120, 128
   freedom, 51–53, 113, 152–53, 156
   integrity, 120–22
Acausal(ly). *See* Noncausal
Accommodate (religion), 119
Accommodationism, 129, 153–54
Accommodationist(s), 153
Acid test, 157
Acts, book of, 21, 143
Adam (and Eve), 30, 42, 44, 48–49, 56, 60, 74, 108, 138
Advance(s) (religion), 119, 122, 128, 154
Agency, 102
Agent, 101–102
Agnosticism, 19, 110, 128, 157

Agnostic(s), 18, 19, 77, 90, 95
Aguillard. See *Edwards* v.
Air bubble, 146–47
Alabama, 93, 94, 108, 109, 126, 137–38, 154, 161
   textbook committee of, 93
Alpher, Ralph, 102–103
Analogy, 99
   reasoning by, 94, 98, 100
Animal(s), 43–45, 48–49, 64, 77, 95, 99–100, 107–108, 138
Animist tradition, 22
Annihilate(d), 50, 145
Annihilation, 50
Anthropologist(s), 78
Anthropology, 108
Ape(s), 49, 155
Apoleto. See Annihilate(d)
Apostate(s), 16, 97–98

Ararat, 47, 63
Archaeology, 76, 108
Arkansas, 69, 137
Article(s) of faith, 37, 40, 98, 121, 124, 135
Artifact, 12, 38–39, 42, 56, 94–96, 99, 157
Artifice, 99
Artificer, 12, 38, 39, 42, 56–57, 94–96, 157
Asimov, Isaac, 61, 136–37
Astrologer(s), 54
Astrology, 53
Astronomer(s), 38, 108
Astronomy, 46, 53–54, 108, 156, 161
Astrophysicist(s), 53, 78
Astrophysics, 108
Atheism, 18–19, 25, 110, 128, 157
Atheistic(ally), 72, 77, 118, 151–52
Atheist(s), 18–19, 90, 95
Axiom(s), 67–68, 71–77

Balance (in education), 51, 95
Balanced treatment, 109, 111, 137, 152, 154, 156
Balanced Treatment for Flat-Earth Science and Spherical Science Act, 137
Balanced Treatment for Scientific Creationism and Evolution Act, 137, 154–55, 157
Baptist, 26, 117
Barclay, William, 143
Barth, Karl, 28, 89, 151
Begs the question. *See* Question begging
Bible, 12–15, 29, 30, 40–51, 54–55, 57, 60, 62–64, 71–73, 76, 81–84, 86, 88–91, 97, 119–21, 125, 128, 145–48, 158–59
Bible-devil, 14, 16, 55, 58, 75, 90, 136, 138, 159–60
Bible-god, 13–14, 18, 27–29, 45–46, 48–50, 55, 58, 60, 63, 70–77, 83–90, 94, 97, 100, 107–108, 133, 135, 149–51, 157, 160, 163–64
Bible (or biblical) scholar(s), 15

Bible science, 64, 158–59
Biblical(ly), 14–15, 17, 25, 41–43, 45, 50–51, 54, 57, 67, 89–91, 97–99, 106–108, 113, 121–24, 134–37, 141–42, 150, 157, 161
 creationism, 68, 70, 78, 124, 152, 163
 interpretation, 16, 61
 literalism, 45, 161
 literalist(s), 49, 73–74, 124
 scholars, 151
 scholarship, 152
 text(s), 16, 71, 81
Big
 Bang, 38, 46, 48, 51, 74–75, 102, 135, 160–61
 Brother, 133–34, 139
 Crunch, 75
 Drought, 48
 sea monster, 49–50
 Wash, 46, 48, 135
 Wisdom, 49
Biological(ly), 41, 44, 55, 70, 99, 101, 108, 112, 124
Biologist(s), 38, 53, 96, 155, 160
Biology, 49, 53, 94, 98, 120, 125, 156, 161–62
Bird(s), 46, 146–47
Bird, Wendell R., 30, 69–70, 111
Bliss. *See* Everlasting life
Board of Education v. *Allen,* 119
Boltzmann, Ludwig, 76
Boylan, David, 137
Brande, Scott, 93
Bronowski, Jacob, 23
Brown, John Wick, 145
Buddhist(s), 122, 127
Burger, Warren, 129, 153
Burstyn. See Joseph Burstyn, Inc. v.

California, 94, 127, 161–63
Canon (of Hebrew Bible), 84
Carbon-14 (dating by), 76
Catastrophe, 47, 71
Catastrophism, 47
Catholic(s), 12, 29, 58, 117, 122, 142, 151

Catholic Church. *See* Roman Catholic Church
Causal, 101
Causality, 26, 39, 101
Cause, 94, 102
Chance, 94, 101
Chemist(s), 38
Chemistry, 108
Christ. *See* Jesus
Christian(s), 13, 24, 28-31, 42, 62, 88-89, 91, 96-98, 100, 106, 112, 117, 122, 128, 133, 139, 144-45, 147
Christian
  doctrines, 59
  evolutionist(s), 77
  Fundagelicals, 73
  schools, 36, 78, 148
Christianity, 24, 30, 37, 42, 54, 56-57, 73, 77, 83, 85-88, 106-107, 124, 126, 128, 133, 150-51
Church(es), 28, 120
Church/State, 118, 128-29
  relations, 112
  separation of, 37, 69, 153
Clark, Gordon, 143
Clark, Tom, 129
Clausius, Rudolf J. E., 76
Cleanses, 27
Cleansing, 23-24
Colossians, letter to, 142
Communism, 110, 151-52
Communists, 16
Confirm, 159
Confirmable, 77
Confirmation, 16, 77
Conscience, 23-24
Constitution (of the United States), 70, 105-107, 112, 118, 128-29, 152-53, 163
Constitutionally, 78, 107, 120, 129, 150, 155
Contradiction(s), 81, 89
Copernican(ism), 112, 158
Copernicus, 29, 40, 158
Corinthians
  first letter to, 27, 62, 75
  second letter to, 159
Corollary(ies), 67-68, 70, 72, 77-78
Corrupt communication(s), 120
Cosmic, 45, 55, 57, 69, 112
Cosmogonic, 50
Cosmogony(ies), 26, 30, 49, 50, 135
Cosmologist(s), 38, 160-61
Cosmology(ies), 26, 30-31, 48-49, 53, 74-75, 134, 161
Cosmos, 39, 49, 124
Council for Private Postsecondary and Vocational Education, 162
Court. *See* Supreme Court
Creation, 25, 30, 36-38, 41, 50, 54, 63, 70, 76, 78, 98, 107, 111, 135, 142-44, 146
Creation-Life Publishers, 68
Creation model, 68, 124, 142, 159, 160, 162
Creation Research Society (CRS), 41-42, 68, 134
Creation Research Society Quarterly, 41-42, 137
"Creation Science" (or "Creation-science"), 15-16, 30, 36, 51-55, 76, 105, 109, 111, 133-34, 136-39, 149, 152-59, 162-63
Creation-Science Research Center, 68, 134
Creation stories, 152
Creation Week, 41
Creationism, 37-38, 40, 45, 105, 133, 138, 163
Creation(ist)
  institutes, 162
  religions, 111, 158
  textbook(s), 36
Creationist(s), 37, 39, 68, 78, 105, 109, 111-13, 147
Creator, 12, 69
Creedal affirmation, 41

Damning knowledge, 71, 75
Darwin, Charles, 19, 29-30, 35, 53, 97, 121

172 INDEX

Darwinian, 43, 55, 120
Darwinism, 107, 112, 158
Davies, Percival, 93
Dawkins, Richard, 150, 155–56
Declaration of Independence, 118
Deism, 25, 107, 119, 124, 128–29
Deist(s), 56, 118, 128
Deistic(ally), 96, 118–19, 128–29
Deity, 12, 14, 19, 24–25, 27, 31, 57–58, 73, 96–97, 100, 106–108, 164
Demonic possession, 159
Demonic(ally), 71, 97
Denominational, 128, 162
Denomination(s), 118, 128, 142, 152, 155
Design, 95
Devil. *See* Satan
Dewey, John, 18
Dinosaur(s), 47, 59, 160
Disconfirm, 159–60
Disconfirmation, 16, 78, 110
Disconfirmatory, 78
Disconfirmed, 76
Divine
    autographs, 41–42, 58, 71, 90
    creation, 70
    fiat, 109
Divine(ly), 14, 38–39, 42, 45, 50, 54, 71, 77, 89, 94–95, 97, 103, 106–108, 153
Divinity, 31
DNA, 100–101
Doctrine(s), religious, 18, 24, 41, 45, 56, 59, 86, 91, 97, 107, 118, 123, 129, 133, 142, 155, 157
Dogma(s), 31, 41–43, 57, 70, 97, 129, 152, 163
Dogmatic(ally), 15, 56, 58–59, 119–21, 123–24, 128, 162–63
Dogmatism, 58
Dogmatists, 55, 58, 141

Earth, 41–42, 46–50, 55–56, 61, 63–64, 69–70, 72–73, 76, 78, 87, 107–108, 124, 135–36, 144–45, 158
Eastern Orthodox Churches, 151
Ecclesiastes, book of, 86

Ecumenical Movement, 151–52
Eddy, Mary Baker, 125
Education, 119
Educators, 37, 40
Edwards v. *Aguillard,* 36–37, 79, 110, 124, 153–54
Einstein, Albert, 51, 95, 142
Eisegesis, 67
Emanation(ism), 45
Entanglement(s) of government and religion, 119, 128–29
Entelechy, 96
Entropy, 44, 60, 71–72, 76, 136–37
Ephesians, letter to the, 120, 143
Epimetheus, 43–45, 77, 155
Epperson v. *Arkansas,* 152
Equal time, 43–45, 53, 70, 156
Ergot
    hypothesis, 159
    model, 159
Establishment Clause, 69, 154, 156
Establishment of religion, 153
Esther, book of, 86
Evangelicals, 11
Eve, Raymond A., 162–63
Everlasting life (or bliss), 14, 24, 30, 56, 71–72, 81, 83, 149–50
Evolution, 18, 21–22, 30, 35–36, 41–42, 51, 53, 55, 63–64, 69–71, 75–76, 78, 96–98, 108–12, 121, 124, 126, 133, 135–38, 150–53, 155–57, 159
Evolution model(s), 70, 158, 162–63
Evolutionary, 43, 53, 70, 72, 95, 101, 160
    descent, 94, 96–98, 136, 159
Evolutionist(s), 56, 70, 77–78, 96, 98
Excessive entanglement. *See* Entanglement
Exegesis, 16, 67, 72
Exodus, book of, 41, 61, 89, 107
Explanatory fiction, 54
Ezekiel, book of, 85, 89–90

Faith, 13–15, 17, 23–24, 26, 28, 39, 41–43, 54–55, 58, 61, 64, 74, 84, 94–97, 99, 110, 121, 123, 129, 134–35,

143, 149–50, 152, 160, 163–64
Falsifiability criterion, 160
Falsifiable, 159
Falsification, 96
Falsify(ied), 30, 160
Falwell, Jerry, 15, 162
Fire, 145
Firmament, 50, 63, 135, 146–47
First Amendment, 52, 54, 69–70, 106, 109, 113, 119, 129, 154
First Earth, 142, 145–47
First Heaven, 142, 145–47
First World, 145–46
Fish, 73–74, 107
Flat-earth(ers), 64
  theory of, 156
Flat Earth Society, 64, 137
Flood. *See* Noachian flood
Fool, 75
Foolishness, 28, 30, 35, 45, 75
Forgiven, 24, 57, 82–83
Forgiveness, 24, 57, 150
Fortas, Abe, 129
Fossil record, 72
Fossil(s), 77–78
Founding Fathers, 106, 112, 117
Fraud, 103
Free exercise, of religion, 69, 109, 111–12, 123
Free speech, 51
Free will, 31, 109
Freud, Sigmund, 29
Frost, Jack, 53
Frost, Vicki, 126
Fundagelical(s), 11–13, 15–19, 21, 54, 81–84, 87, 90, 105–106, 112, 120–23, 125, 128, 133–34, 149, 152, 157, 162–63
Fundamentalist(s), 11, 25, 36, 103

Galatians, letter to, 63
Galaxy(ies), 49, 63
Gallup Poll, 108
Gastaldo, Robert A., 105
Genealogical, 72

Genealogy(ies), 41, 87
Genesis, book of, 27, 41, 44–50, 60, 63, 70–71, 73–74, 76, 97, 107–109, 124, 135, 138, 142, 144–45, 152
Genetics, 108
Gentile(s), 77, 88
Geocentric, 29, 40, 124
Geocentrism, 137
Geocentrist(s), 124
Geologist(s), 38, 78, 108, 159
Geology, 53, 76, 98, 105, 108, 161
Georgia, 69, 137, 163
Gish, Duane T., 19, 25, 36
Gnosticism, 27
God, 13, 25–26, 28, 30–31, 37–38, 43–44, 62, 85, 89, 102, 142–47
God-breathed, 86
Godless, 42, 144
Godless religion, 69, 70, 111
Godless secular humanism. *See* Secular humanism
God's Word. *See* Word of God
Gospel, 24, 30, 88
Gould, Stephen J., 25, 107, 112
Government, 153–54
Grand Rapids School District v. Ball, 156
Graves, Robert, 14
Gravitation(al), 156–57
Greek(s), 28, 84, 86, 88, 96, 144–45
Green, Jay, 144
Green, Michael, 145
Guilt, 24, 82–83

Hand, W. Brevard, 110, 126
Harrold, Francis B. *See* Eve, Raymond A.
Hazelwood School District v. Kuhlmeier, 153
Heaven(s), 14, 46, 49–50, 55–57, 63, 69, 107, 135, 144–46
Hebrew(s), 14, 48, 55, 57, 64, 84
  book of, 50, 143
Hechinger, Fred, 125
Heliocentric(ity), 40, 112, 158

174 INDEX

Hell, 14, 57, 59, 72
Heresy, 59
Heretic(al), 73, 75, 152
High Court. *See* Supreme Court
Holy, 17–18
Holy Book, 73
Holy Ghost, 84, 86
Honig, Bill, 162
Hostile (toward religion), 113, 118–19, 122, 129
Human origins, 30
Humanism, 17, 138
Humanistic, 164
Humanist(s), 17, 18
Humanities, 17
Humanitists (sic), 17–18
Humanity, 17
Humankind, 58, 73, 77–78, 124
Human(s), 27, 29, 31, 38–39, 42–45, 53, 56–58, 60, 64, 69, 71–73, 77, 79, 83, 98–99, 108–109, 112, 137, 151, 160–61, 163–64
Hume, David, 99–101
Huxley, Julian, 18
Hypothesis, 16, 77, 103, 110

I Claudius, 14
Idaho, 93
Ideological(ly), 31, 55, 125, 138–39
Ideologue(s), 31
Ideology(ies), 30, 39, 106
Illinois, 52
Immortal, 82
Immortality, 31
Inconsistency(ies), 89, 96
Indoctrination, 156
Inerrancy, 12, 36, 41, 55, 71, 76, 81–86, 88–91, 97, 107, 110, 113, 123, 136, 150, 157
Inerrant, 12, 58, 63, 74, 85, 87, 89, 90
Inerrantist(s), 25, 42, 55, 60, 64, 81–82, 86, 88, 90–91, 97–98, 107, 150, 164
Inhibit(s), religion, 119, 123–25, 129
Inhibited religion, 122, 125, 128
Inhibiting religion, 118, 123–24, 127

Inhibition(s) of, 122–23, 125, 127, 129
Institute for Creation Research (ICR), 68, 161–63
Intelligence, human, 95, 100
Intelligent cause, 95, 100–101
Intelligent design(er), 53, 94–99, 101
Intelligibility, 95
Intelligible order, 95–96
Inward parts, 23–24, 27
Iowa, 69
Iowa Committee of Correspondence, 21
Irreligion, 18, 154
Isaiah, book of, 31, 50, 61, 75, 97, 107, 124, 145–46
Islam, 56, 124, 128

Jaffree, Ishmael, 154
James, brother of Jesus, 87–88
Jamnia, Council of, 84
Jehovah's Witnesses, 125
Jeremiah, book of, 61, 146
Jerome, 84
Jerusalem Church, 88
Jesus, 21, 27–28, 30–31, 42, 56, 61–63, 75, 81, 86–89, 97, 107, 126
Jew(s), 12, 28, 31, 56, 77, 88, 97, 117, 147
Jewish, 21, 26, 36, 42, 46, 61, 84, 87, 112, 122
Jewish Christians, 28
Job, book of, 27, 50, 61, 146
Joel, book of, 145
John, gospel of, 27, 86, 142–43
John Burstyn Inc. v. *Wilson*, 129
Joshua, book of, 46, 89, 124
Judaism, 24, 124, 128
Judeo-Christian, 19, 72
Justice(s) of the Supreme Court, 110, 118–19, 128–29, 155, 157
Justification, 23–24

Keith, Bill, 154–57
Kentucky, 163
Kenyon, Dean H., 93
Khomeini, Ayatollah, 19, 54–55

Kind(s), 97
King James, translation of the Bible, 15–16, 144
Kings
   first book of, 57–58, 61, 85
   second book of, 61, 146
Knapp, Ronald, 36
Knowledge, 27–29, 31, 39, 71, 81, 112
Koran, 55, 57, 73
Kuhn, Thomas, 137

La Haye, Tim, 138
Language, 44, 48, 137–38
Larue, Gerald, 48
Law, 117, 119, 163–64
Law of Nature, 39
Law of Parsimony, 39
Leany, A. R. C., 145
Legal(ly), 79, 108, 111, 129
Lemon test, 118–19, 129, 158
Lemon v. *Kurtzman*, 118, 120, 122–23, 125, 128–29
Leviathan. *See* Rahab
Leviticus, book of, 61
Liberal Christians, 56, 73, 151
Liberalism, 113, 150
Liberty University, 15, 162–63
Linguistics, 108
Literalist(s), 30, 55, 108
Literalistic, 16
Lord, the, 14, 27, 41, 85, 89–90, 144, 146, 148
Lord and Saviour. *See* Savior
Louisiana, 36, 69, 137, 154, 156
Louisiana law, 37
Louisiana ruling. See *Edwards* v. *Aguillard*
Luke, gospel of, 86–87, 143, 159
Luther, 28
Lutherans, 12
Lynch v. *Donnelly*, 153

Make-believe, 41
Malachi, book of, 145–46
Man, 43–45, 48–49, 74, 76, 87, 138, 143

Mann, Newton, 35–36
Mark, gospel of, 62, 121, 143, 159
Marsh v. *Chambers* 153
Materialism, 110
Matter, 96
Matter/Energy, 94, 96
Matters of fact, 40, 121
Matthew, gospel of, 62, 81, 86–88, 95, 121, 143, 159
McKown's Maxim, 39
MacLean, Paul, 109
McLean v. *Arkansas*. *See* Rev. Bill McLean
Metaphysical(ly), 13, 97
Metaphysics, 96
Miracle(s), 14, 107, 146
Miraculous, 79
Mobile. *See* Alabama
Models of origins, 45, 70
Monkey(s), 49
Monod, Jacques, 22
Moon, 46–48, 63, 72–74, 78, 107, 146–47
Moore, John N., 137
Morality, 17–18, 26, 31
Mormon, Book of, 90
Mormons, 12, 90
Mormonism, 90
Moronic, 28, 75
Morris, Henry M., 19, 136
Mosaic law, 61–62, 81, 87–88
Moses, 30–31, 88, 142
Moslem. *See* Muslim
Mother Goose, 53
Mozert, Robert B., 126
Muhammad, 31
Muslim(s), 12, 31, 106, 112, 122, 127
Myth, 43–44, 146
Mythology(ies), 26

Nahum, book of, 145
Naked ape, 45
National Center for Science Education (NCSE), 21, 162
National Council of Churches of Christ

in the United States, 151
Natural, 39, 94–95, 100–101
Natural knowledge. *See* Neutral knowledge
Natural selection, 53
Naturalism, 70, 110
Naturalistic, 42, 95, 110
  assumptions, 152
  methods, 95
Naturalist(s), 17–18
Nature, 25, 39–41, 43, 45, 59, 95–96, 98–99, 109
Nebraska, 153
Neutral knowledge, 71, 73, 75
New Covenant, 87–88, 147
New earth, 76, 145, 147
New heaven(s), 76, 145, 147
New Testament, 14–15, 27, 50, 61, 63, 83–89, 121–22, 142–43
Newspeak, 133–136, 138–139
Noachian flood, 14, 30, 41–42, 46–47, 50, 70–71, 76, 78, 107–108, 135–36, 145–47, 160
Noah, 14, 46–47, 147
Noah's ark, 145–47
Nonbiblical, 108
Noncausal(ly), 101, 135
Nonnaturalistic, 95
Nonsupernaturalistic, 42
North Carolina, 125

Of Pandas and People, 93–97, 99, 101–103
Old Covenant, 22, 87, 147
Old Testament, 14–15, 27–28, 41, 61–63, 83–85, 87–89, 121–22, 142–43
Origin(s), 41–45, 49–51, 54, 69–70, 77, 97, 111–12, 137, 152, 156, 158–59
Origin of Species, the, 19, 35, 96
Original autographs. *See* Divine autographs
Original sin, 44, 56, 60
Orthodox(y), 12, 24, 58, 121
Orwell, George, 133, 138
Overton, William, 109, 111

Padia, Kevin, 162
Paleontologist(s), 53, 78, 108, 159
Paleontology, 98
Pandas. *See Of Pandas and People*
Panspermia, 77–78
Paradigm(s), 70, 72, 78
Paul, 21, 27–28, 31, 62–63, 75, 87–88, 142. *See also* Pauline
Pauline, 28
Peloza, John, 153
Peter
  first letter of, 84, 88, 143, 159
  second letter of, 50, 63, 85, 97, 143–45
Peter, the apostle, 84, 142, 147
Philosopher(s), 17, 28, 75, 82, 96, 101, 137, 154
Philosophical(ly), 13, 17–18, 43, 110
Philosophy, 26, 35, 42–43, 158
Physicist(s), 38, 61
Physics, 159
Pi, 58, 63
Picket fence, 153
Pious(ly), 31, 71, 138, 163
Planet(s), 53
Planetary catastrophe, 71, 136
Plato, 43, 45, 77, 155
Platonic, 43, 45
Platonism, 45
Plotinus, 45
Pope, the, 59, 159
Popper, Karl, 137
Postmortem, 30, 72
Powerful Parson, 134–39
Presbyterian Church, 25, 151
Primary effect, 119, 122
Primary intent, 118, 123
Primate(s), 49
Probability(ies), 101–102
Profane, 17, 110
Prometheus, 43–44, 77, 155
Propaganda, 42–43, 121, 154, 158
Propagandist, 96
Prophecy(ies), 30, 84–85, 143, 145
Prophetic, 84–85

Protagoras, 43, 77
Protestant(s), 28–29, 117, 122, 142, 151–52
Proverbs, book of, 27, 49, 97, 126, 146
Provine, William, 25
Psalms, book of, 27, 46, 50, 97, 135, 145–46
Pseudoscience, 16, 21, 24, 29–30, 54, 64, 93, 163
Pseudoscientific, 59
Pseudoscientists, 22
Ptolemy, 112
Public education, 21, 30, 43, 64, 69, 112–13, 118, 123
   curriculum(a) of, 37, 70, 91, 112–13, 123–24, 129
   instruction, 69, 152
   school(s), 11, 18, 36, 40, 52–54, 64, 67, 69–70, 78, 82, 91, 95, 108–12, 117–25, 127–29, 134, 136, 138–39, 142, 152, 154–58, 160, 163
   school system(s), 69, 107, 164
   teachers, 52, 121, 160
   texts, 91, 126, 133

Question begging, 13–14, 38, 94–96, 98, 123

Radioactive decay, 47
Radiometric data, 47
Radiometric dating, 40, 47, 108, 136
Rahab, 50
Randomness, 101
Ratzinger, Cardinal, 58
Redemption. *See* Salvation
Referent(s), 13–15, 134
Referring term, 13
Rehnquist, William, 119, 153–54, 158
Relative, 77
Relativism, 70
Religion of secular humanism, 110, 126
Religion of secularism, 119, 123–25, 128
Religion(s), 18–19, 23–27, 29–31, 36, 41–42, 52, 54–58, 70, 77, 83, 97–98, 102, 106–107, 110, 112–13, 117, 119, 120–29, 138–39, 152–54, 156–57, 164
   comparative, 119–120, 128
   evils of, 117
Religious(ly), 13–15, 17–19, 23, 25–26, 30–31, 41–45, 57–59, 64, 70, 77–78, 83, 86, 91, 95–96, 98, 106, 108–12, 117–18, 120, 122, 125–27, 129, 133–34, 136, 141, 150–51, 155–56, 162–63
Religious humanist(s), 17
Religious liberals, 16, 57, 107, 121, 133
Religious rightist(s), 12, 109
Rev. Bill McLean v. The Arkansas Board of Education, 109
Revelation, book of, 85, 124, 143, 145
Revelation(s), 18, 26, 71, 79, 89, 144
Roman Catholic Church, 121
Romans, letter to the, 143
Rushdie, Salman, 19

Sacred(ness), 17–18, 26, 84, 110, 123
Sagan, Carl, 137
Salvation, 14, 24, 27–31, 42, 56, 59, 76, 81, 83, 88, 91, 97, 151
Samuel, first book of, 146
Sarich, Vincent, 155
Satan, 159
Satanic(ally), 55, 75, 77, 120, 136
Satanism, 159
Saved, 30, 82–83, 91, 149
Saving knowledge, 59, 73
Savior(iour), 24, 42, 56, 83
Scalia, Antonin, 110, 154–58
Schadenwald, Robert J., 137
Schempp. See Sch ⁷ District of Abington v.
School(s), 55. *See also* Public school(s)
   board(s), 11, 37, 55, 68, 148, 160–61
School children, 64, 75, 103, 112, 118, 122, 156–60
School District of Abington Township, Pennsylvania v. Schempp, 119–20
Science
   classes, 82, 95

education, 40, 54–55, 64, 95, 107–108, 112–13, 138, 158, 161, 163
educator(s), 11, 16, 22, 30, 68, 109, 152
teachers, 163
Science(s), 22–31, 37–45, 51–56, 59–60, 64, 70, 76–77, 79, 94–95, 97–98, 100, 102–103, 105–13, 117–18, 123–24, 133–39, 149, 151–52, 156–59, 161–63
Scientific
cosmology, 45–46, 51
creation model, 109
hypothesis(es), 40
knowledge, 39, 59
method, 95
model, 152
noncreationist(s), 38–39
paradigm. *See* Paradigm
theory, 39
"Scientific Creationism," 11, 15–16, 19, 21, 26, 29–30, 36–37, 39–40, 45–46, 53, 67–72, 77–78, 111, 117, 141, 148, 155
"Scientific Creationist(s)," 12–16, 18–19, 21–22, 29–31, 35–38, 40–45, 47–58, 60–61, 63–64, 67–69, 72, 75–79, 81, 83, 90–91, 93–98, 100, 103, 106, 108, 110–12, 118, 120–21, 123–24, 128–29, 135–36, 139, 141–42, 146–47, 149–50, 152–58, 160–64
Scientific(ally), 16, 22, 25–27, 29–30, 37–43, 50–51, 54–55, 57, 59–60, 70–73, 76, 78, 108–109, 112–13, 124, 135–37, 139, 149–50, 152, 155, 160, 164
Scientist(s), 11, 16, 22, 26, 28, 30, 38–40, 42, 54, 59, 68, 70, 74–76, 96–97, 100, 113, 135, 139, 152, 154–55, 159–61
Scopes, John T., 151
Scott, Eugenia C., 162
Scriptural, 55, 67, 86, 124, 135, 141–42, 150
Scripture(s), 14, 30, 46, 55, 58, 74, 76, 86, 88, 142–43, 145, 147

Second earth, 50, 142, 145
Second heaven(s), 50, 142, 145
Second law of thermodynamics, 45, 60, 135–36
Second world, 145–147
Sect(s), 118, 129, 141
Sectarian, 154
Secular(ism), 17–18, 118–20, 123, 154–55, 164
Secular curriculum, 124, 127
Secular educators, 21
Secular humanism, 16–17, 42, 69, 70, 110–11, 125, 134, 138, 156
Secular humanist(s), 17–18, 43, 56, 152
Secular religion. *See* Secular humanism
Separation of Church/state. *See* Church/state
Seventh Day Adventists, 127, 151
Shi'ite(s), 19, 54, 77
Sin(s), 24, 42
Singularity(ies), 45, 107
Smith, Joseph, 90
Socialism. *See* Communism
Sociobiological, 17
Son of God, 143
Song of Solomon, 86
Soter, 24
Soteria, 24
Soteriological, 27, 29, 59, 121, 150
Soteriology, 21–22, 24–25, 28–31, 56, 139, 164
Soul(s), 14, 71–73, 75, 89, 109, 112–13, 160, 164
South Carolina, 69, 137
Southern Baptists, 12, 151
Special creation, 30, 41, 56
Special pleading, 58, 94
Species, 22, 43, 70, 72, 77
Species pride, 57
Spirit, 14, 94
Spiritual(ly), 86, 94, 125, 143–44
Spontaneity, 94
Spontaneous(ly), 101–102, 135
Star(s), 42, 46, 48, 53, 63, 72–74, 78, 87, 107, 146–47

State Boards of Public Education, 148, 160
Stork, 53, 156
Strict separationism, 129
Strict separationists, 153
Sultan, Talat, 127
Sun, 42, 46, 48, 63, 72–74, 78, 107, 136, 146–147, 158
Sunday school(s), 40, 148
Supernatural, 17, 24, 38–39, 94, 98
Supernatural being, 17
Supernatural savior, 83
Supernaturalism, 95
Supernaturalistic, 95
Supernaturalist(s), 17
Supreme Court, 19, 36–37, 52, 79, 106, 110–11, 118–24, 128–29, 149, 153–58

Tautology(ies), 82–83
Teague, Wayne, 93
Teleologist(s), 96
Teleology, 69, 96, 107
Tennessee, 78, 126, 152
Tertullian, 28, 91
Texas, 93–94, 112
Textbook publishers, 112, 152
Textbook selection committees, 37, 55
Textual transmission, 58, 71
Thaxton, Charles B., 93
Theism, 12–13, 18–19, 95
Theistic evolutionist, 70, 75
Theistic(ally), 12, 69, 72, 95–97, 126, 128
Theist(s), 56, 95–96, 98, 100, 129
Theocratic, 163
Theologian(s), 28–29, 94, 99, 123, 154
Theological(ly), 15, 21, 24–25, 28, 38–39, 62, 89, 106, 123, 139, 151–52, 163–64
Theology(ies), 12–13, 17, 24–26, 47, 57, 72, 89, 94, 99, 100, 102, 123, 164
Theopneustos. *See* God-breathed
Theoretical(ly), 94
Theorizing, 51, 53, 59, 75, 159–60
Theory(ies), 42–43, 45, 47, 49–51, 53–54, 59, 69, 71, 77, 94, 155, 157, 160
Theory of evolution. *See* Evolution
Thessalonians
  first book of, 124
  second book of, 85
Third earth, 145
Third heaven(s), 145
Third world, 144–45
Threefold creation. *See* Triune creation
Three-World Creation Society, 143, 146–48
Three-World Creationism, 142, 144, 148
Timothy
  first letter to, 87
  second letter to, 86, 143
Titus, letter to, 187
Transcendent, 38
Transitional form(s), 72, 77
Transnational Association of Christian Schools (TRACS), 161
Triune creation, 142–43
True believer(s), 74, 77, 163
True religion, 77, 107, 110, 120, 147
Two model approach, 109

Unbiblical, 30, 55
Unconscionable declaration(s), of belief, 69, 111
Uniformitarian, 71, 136
United States, 55, 68, 106, 112, 120, 137–39, 156, 161, 164
United States Department of Education (DOE), 161
Universe, 12–13, 25, 29, 38, 40–43, 45, 56–57, 60–61, 70, 76, 94–99, 101–102, 107, 111, 124, 136–37, 142, 149, 155, 157–58, 160
Unknowable, 39
Unknown, 39
Unpredictability, 101
Unpredictable, 102
Unscientific, 44–45, 51

Valid, 98
Validation, 26

Vapor canopy, 135, 146
Virginia, 117, 162
    Board of Education, 162
Vitz, Paul, 125–26
Vulgate, 84

Wall of separation, 153
Wallace, Alfred Russell, 31
Wallace, Governor of Alabama v. *Jaffree,* 153
Wallace, Jodi, 125–26
Water(s), 46–47, 49–50, 74, 135, 144, 146
Webster v. *New Lenox School District,* 153
Western Association of Schools and Colleges (WASC), 161–62
Whitehead, Alfred North, 23
Wilson, Allan, 155
Windows of Heaven, 146–47
Wisdom. *See* Big Wisdom
Woman, 48–49, 74
Word of God, 41, 89, 142
World Council of Churches, 151
World view, 124, 145–47
World(s), 50–51, 71–72, 118, 129, 142–44

Yahweh, 14
YHWY. *See* Yahweh

www.ingramcontent.com/pod-product-compliance
Lightning Source LLC
Chambersburg PA
CBHW021825090426
42811CB00032B/2029/J